Reading Metaphysics

Reading Philosophy

Reading Philosophy is a series of textbooks offering interactive commentaries on selected readings, and covering the major sub-disciplines of the field. Each volume contains a number of topical chapters each containing primary readings, accompanied by an introduction to the topic, introductions to the readings as well as the commentary. Edited by leading scholars, the aim of the books is to encourage the practice of philosophy in the process of engagement with philosophical texts.

Reading Philosophy
Samuel Guttenplan, Jennifer Hornsby and Christopher Janaway

Reading Philosophy of Language
Jennifer Hornsby and Guy Longworth

Reading Aesthetics and Philosophy of Art
Christopher Janaway

Reading Epistemology
Sven Bernecker

Reading Metaphysics
Helen Beebee and Julian Dodd

Reading Metaphysics

Selected Texts with
Interactive Commentary

Helen Beebee
and
Julian Dodd

Blackwell Publishing

BLACKWELL PUBLISHING
350 Main Street, Malden, MA 02148-5020, USA
9600 Garsington Road, Oxford OX4 2DQ, UK
550 Swanston Street, Carlton, Victoria 3053, Australia

First published 2007 by Blackwell Publishing Ltd

1   2007

Library of Congress Cataloging-in-Publication Data

Reading metaphysics : selected texts with interactive commentary / [edited by] Helen Beebee and Julian Dodd.
       p. cm. — (Reading philosophy)
    Includes bibliographical references and index.
    ISBN-13: 978-1-4051-2366-2 (hardback : alk. paper)
    ISBN-10: 1-4051-2366-4 (hardback : alk. paper)
    ISBN-13: 978-1-4051-2367-9 (pbk. : alk. paper)
    ISBN-10: 1-4051-2367-2 (pbk. : alk. paper) 1. Metaphysics. I. Beebee, Helen. II. Dodd, Julian.
    BD95.R43 2006
    110—dc22

                                                                        2006020548

A catalogue record for this title is available from the British Library.

Set in 10.5/12.5pt Dante
by SPi Publisher Services, Pondicherry, India

For further information on
Blackwell Publishing, visit our website:
www.blackwellpublishing.com

Contents

Sources and Acknowledgements

Many thanks to those Philosophy students at Manchester and Birmingham who have acted as guinea pigs for the material in this book, and to Daniel Hill, Jennifer Hornsby and Simon Langford for helpful comments.

We gratefully acknowledge the following for permission to reproduce copyright material:

Derek Parfit, 'Personal Identity', *The Philosophical Review* 80 (1971), 3–27.

Marya Schechtman, 'Personhood and Personal Identity', *The Journal of Philosophy* 87 (1990), 71–92: Copyright © 1990 by The Journal of Philosophy, Inc. Reprinted by permission of the author and The Journal of Philosophy.

Peter van Inwagen, 'The Incompatibility of Free Will and Determinism', *Philosophical Studies* 27 (1975), 189–95: Copyright © 1975 by D. Reidel Publishing Company, Dordrecht-Holland. Reprinted by permission of Springer Science and Business Media and Peter van Inwagen.

Daniel Dennett, *Elbow Room* (Cambridge, MA: Bradford Books, 1984), chapter 6 ('Could Have Done Otherwise'): Copyright © 1984 by Daniel C. Dennett. Reprinted by permission of The MIT Press.

Thomas Nagel, *The View from Nowhere*, chapter 6 ('Thought and Reality'): Copyright © 1986 by Thomas Nagel. Reprinted by permission of Oxford University Press, Inc.

Donald Davidson, 'On the Very Idea of a Conceptual Scheme', *Proceedings and Addresses of the American Philosophical Association* XLVII (1973–4), 5–20: Copyright © 1973 by the American Philosophical Association. This is an edited version of the full Presidential Address published in the *Proceedings and Addresses of the American Philosophical Association*, volume XLVII. Reprinted by permission of the American Philosophical Association.

Michael Devitt, ' "Ostrich Nominalism" or "Mirage Realism"?', *Pacific Philosophical Quarterly* 61 (1980), 433–9: Copyright © 1980 by University of Southern California. Reprinted by permission of Blackwell Publishing.

D. M. Armstrong, 'Against "Ostrich" Nominalism: A Reply to Michael Devitt', *Pacific Philosophical Quarterly* 61 (1980), 440–9: Copyright © 1980 by University of Southern California. Reprinted by permission of Blackwell Publishing.

D. K. Lewis, extract from *Counterfactuals* (Cambridge, MA: Harvard University Press, 1973): Copyright © 1973 by David Lewis. Reprinted by permission of Blackwell Publishing.

Saul Kripke, extract from *Naming and Necessity* (Cambridge, MA: Harvard University Press, 1980): Copyright © 1972, 1980 by Saul A. Kripke. Reprinted by permission of Blackwell Publishing and Harvard University Press.

D. K. Lewis, extract from *On The Plurality of Worlds* (Oxford: Blackwell, 1986): Copyright © 1986 by David Lewis. Reprinted by permission of Blackwell Publishing.

Sally Haslanger, 'Endurance and Temporary Intrinsics', *Analysis* 49 (1989), 119–25: Copyright © 1989 by Analysis. Reprinted by permission of Blackwell Publishing.

D. K. Lewis, 'Tensing the Copula', *Mind* 111 (2002), 1–13: Copyright © 2002 by Oxford University Press. Reprinted by permission of Oxford University Press and Stephanie R. Lewis.

Every effort has been made to trace copyright holders and to obtain their permission for the use of copyright material. The publisher apologizes for any errors or omissions in the above list and would be grateful if notified of any corrections that should be incorporated in future reprints or editions of this book.

Introduction

Reading Philosophy

This book is a member of the *Reading Philosophy* series: a series that aims not simply to introduce you to philosophical questions, but to teach you a technique for reading and analysing philosophical texts. It was this latter aim that struck a chord with us, because we have found that philosophy students often fail to realize how much time and effort it takes to read a philosophical text properly. Anyone who has taught philosophy seminars is probably familiar with the following situation: the tutor asks the class whether everyone has read the set text. 'Yes', everyone replies. The tutor then tries to get a discussion going by asking what she regards as a straightforward question about the text: 'What position is the author defending in this paper?', say. And the response is a deafening silence.

Of course, there can be many different reasons for this. But one common reason, we think, is that the students have not read the text in the way the text demands – not because they are lazy, but because they have not understood the extent to which reading a philosophy text is different, say, to reading a newspaper. Reading a philosophy text properly requires you to be thinking rigorously all the while; you cannot simply let the text wash over you.

A typical approach to reading philosophy is to read the text once, from beginning to end, in the space of (say) an hour, and, if you haven't really understood what's going on in that time, to conclude that this is because the text is just too advanced for you. This approach is misguided. Your tutor would not have set the text as reading if she thought it was genuinely too advanced for you to be able to make much sense of it. What she *was* expecting, however, was that you would not simply read the text once through; she was expecting you to try and work out what the argumentative structure of the text is, and to think about why the author is saying what she is saying, whether her claims are plausible, whether the arguments are any good, and so on. If you have done all of that, you are all set for an interesting seminar discussion.

We generally provide students with a 'study budget': a rough indication of how long they should be spending on the various aspects of a particular course. Normally we say that students should be spending around six hours on reading the set seminar text each week. We suspect that many students think we aren't serious, or that we must be assuming that they are extremely slow readers or that they will also read a lot of secondary material during this time as well. Not a bit of it. We really do expect (or at least hope) that students will spend that long reading and thinking about the text. If you find this puzzling – 'How could I possibly spend that long reading a 20-page article?' – then this book is definitely for you. By the time you reach the end, you should have no difficulty answering that question.

The benefits of reading philosophy in a way that equips one to engage in genuine philosophical discussion are not, of course, restricted to what goes on in the seminar room. Every philosopher gets her ideas largely by thinking long and hard about the views of others – because she agrees with those views but thinks they can be applied to other areas, or need to be modified in one way or another, or are subject to *prima facie* objections that can, in fact, be met; or because she disagrees with the views and wants to explain why she is right to disagree, or to articulate a rival position, or whatever.

That this is so may not always be clear to the uninitiated reader, because philosophers do not always explicitly say, for example, whose views they are attempting to refute or why they are doing it. For example, there is not, in the whole of Descartes's famous *Meditations on First Philosophy*, a single reference to any other philosopher: Descartes presents the work as though he simply sat down in his dressing-gown one afternoon and worked everything out from first principles, purely by thinking things through for himself. But the *Meditations* could not have been written by someone who had not read and thought a great deal about the works of others. Descartes has distinctively philosophical reasons for not presenting the *Meditations* in a way that makes this explicit, but his philosophical debt to others is there none the less, hidden just below the surface.

The point here is that reading philosophy is best seen as an activity that is part of *doing* philosophy. Philosophy students sometimes have difficulty believing that they should think of themselves as doing philosophy rather than simply learning *about* it. But learning *about* philosophy, just by itself – learning who said what and when, being able to remember four objections to Russell's Theory of Descriptions, and so on – is not actually very interesting. Or, at any rate, it is a lot less interesting than *doing* philosophy. Trying to work out whether the nature of the world is independent of our beliefs or concepts or sensory experience, or whether moral responsibility requires the falsity of determinism, or what (if anything) it means to say that some object has an essential nature is, we think, much more interesting. And the only sensible starting-point for thinking about such things is reading and thinking carefully about what other philosophers have thought.

None of the texts in this book are easy. Some of them are really quite demanding, and not just for undergraduate students. But we think that by the time you have finished working through this book, you will realize that demanding philosophical texts, written not for students but for professional philosophers, are in general within your intellectual grasp. You might not always be able to understand absolutely everything the author says, or have a clear idea of what alternative views one might adopt, or be able to think of any decisive objections to the author's view. That's perfectly natural; it happens to philosophers all the time. But you will have understood a lot more than you thought you could: enough, we hope, both to stimulate your interest in metaphysical questions and to encourage you to think philosophically about them.

The Nature of Metaphysics

So far, so good; but this is a book about a metaphysics. 'So what exactly *is* metaphysics?', you might ask. This in itself is a controversial issue, and you don't need to be armed with a fully worked-out answer before you start working through this book. After all, physicists generally don't worry too much about what physics is – they just get on with it – and such an attitude doesn't seem to hold *them* back: physicists don't need to have a worked out view about the nature of physics before they start to get their hands dirty. None the less, a provisional answer may be helpful, not least because it may help you to understand why we have chosen the topics we have.

So what, in our view, does metaphysics amount to? In the most general terms, metaphysics is the philosophical (that is, the *conceptual* rather than the scientific) engagement with questions concerning the nature of reality: how things are. For example, supposing – as most of us ordinarily do – that we have free will, how must the world be constituted? Is freedom of the will compatible with the universe being completely deterministic? Or supposing – again, as most of us ordinarily do – that there are facts about how the world might have been (you might have had toast for breakfast this morning, rather than the cereal you actually had), does this mean that there exists a 'possible world' in which you *did* have toast for breakfast? And if so, what sort of thing *is* a possible world?

What you'll notice about the latter question is that it concerns the existence and nature of a disputed type of entity. (Some philosophers think that there is only one possible world, namely the actual world. Other philosophers think that other possible worlds exist, but disagree amongst themselves about what sorts of thing those other possible worlds are.) Such questions are *ontological*: they concern what there is. Other metaphysical questions are not obviously ontological. For example, what makes it the case that Bill Clinton, today, is the same person as the person who won the 1992 US presidential election? Some philosophers think that the answer lies in the fact that today's Bill has the same body as the winner of the 1992 election; others think that the question should be answered by appealing to psychological facts: it lies in the fact that today's Bill can remember the actions and experiences of the 1992 election winner. In the case of this debate, what there *is* is not in dispute. Both sides agree about which bodies and psychological states exist; they just disagree about which of these are relevant to the identity of Bill, now, with the 1992 election winner.

Having said this, many introductory books construe metaphysics as narrowly ontological. In our view, however, metaphysics is not exhausted by pure ontology. There are questions of a broadly metaphysical nature that are not straightforwardly ontological questions; and we think that such questions should be represented in an introduction to metaphysics. Indeed, especially so, because beginners are more likely to have intuitions about less narrowly ontological matters, and, hence will find it easier to get started by focussing on these. This, then, is why the book starts by considering personal identity, free will, and realism and anti-realism, before moving on to the thoroughly ontological terrain of universals, possible worlds and persistence through time.[1]

Naturally, what we are offering you is a taster of the subdiscipline of metaphysics, not an exhaustive survey. Inevitably, we have had to leave out topics that fascinate us: topics such as the nature of facts, states of affairs and events; the reality of time; causation; substance; and the distinction between primary qualities (such as square-ness) and secondary qualities (for example, redness). But don't be downhearted! Once you have worked through this book, you will have the knowledge, understanding and, above all, the analytical techniques to approach further metaphysical questions with confidence.

How to Use This Book

Each philosophical text reproduced in the book is followed by a commentary, which includes questions in shaded boxes: you will be asked to state a claim made at a particular point in the text in your own words, or whether you can think of any objections to it, and so on. The chapters, each of which contains two or three sets of text + commentary together with a brief introduction, can be taken in any order. There are occasional references in later chapters to earlier ones, but they can be ignored if you have taken the chapters in a different order.

The book's format is determined by our objectives in writing it, objectives common to those of the series it belongs in. As befits a book in the *Reading Philosophy* series, its purpose is that of encouraging you to regard reading a philosophical text as a matter of engaging philosophically with the views and arguments it expresses – to think of *reading* philosophy as a part of *doing* philosophy – and to show you how to regard philosophical texts in that way. Like most human activities, however, you cannot improve at it just by reading about how to do it; you need to practise. Treat this

---

[1]   Personal identity and free will are also both treated in the first book in the series, *Reading Philosophy: Selected Texts with a Method for Beginners*. However, there is no overlap in the texts used in the two books, and, if you have worked through *Reading Philosophy* already, we hope that returning to these issues will enable you to achieve greater depth in your thinking.

book a bit like an instruction manual on how to swim or play the violin: it will not actually make you a better philosopher unless you practise doing what it says. And so we shall start by saying some very general things about how to go about reading a philosophical text in general, and using this book (and others in the series) in particular.

Before you start on the first text in a particular chapter, read through the introduction. It will provide you with some basic information about the topic addressed by the texts, so that you don't start reading the texts without knowing anything about what to expect. Then follow the first three steps listed below *before* turning to the commentary (step 4). The purpose of the commentaries, and the tasks in the shaded boxes, is to *help* you through steps 2 (figuring out the argumentative structure) and 3 (thinking philosophically about the text). You will get most out of the book if you, first of all, try to get as much out of the texts themselves as you can, and then use the commentaries to help you get still more out of them. The first few times you attempt to follow the first three steps without the aid of the commentaries, you might find that you don't get very far, and so will need to rely heavily on the commentaries and tasks. However, we hope that as you work through the book, you will get better at working through the texts for yourself, and will correspondingly need to rely less and less on the commentaries and tasks. If this happens, we will have achieved our aim: to help you learn how to understand, engage with, and think critically about a variety of philosophical texts for yourself. And, of course, you will have learned quite a lot about metaphysics along the way.

1.   Read the Text Through

A good beginning strategy (but note: this is just a prelude to the main event) is to read the whole text through quite quickly. This will give you at least some sense of the size of the task ahead of you: you might get the gist of what the author is doing, find yourself having sceptical thoughts, and so on at this stage; or you might find the whole paper confusing and hard to follow. Make a note of any words you don't understand, and look them up in a dictionary or a philosophy encyclopaedia (there are some good online encyclopaedias) afterwards. If you have any philosophical thoughts, worries or objections at this stage, make a note of these too.

2.   Work Out the Structure of the Text

The most important things you need to work out are what position the author is arguing for or defending, and roughly how she does it: what the structure of the argument is. So now you need to start again from the beginning of the text and go through it slowly and carefully, armed with a pen and paper.

There are of course many different argumentative structures a paper might exemplify. The author might, for example, be attempting to show that philosophical view X is false, by arguing that X is subject to three counter-examples. Or she might do all that, and then proceed to diagnose why X is subject to those counter-examples and suggest a way to modify X, or sketch an alternative view. Or she might be advancing an argument, or several different arguments, for her own view Y, without saying explicitly which views Y is a rival to. And so on.

If the text is divided into sections, a good way to start is to try to write down, for each section, what the author is doing in that section. If the text is not divided into sections, or if the author appears to be doing several things in each section, you will have to figure out for yourself where the natural breaks are: at which points the author stops discussing one issue and moves on to the next. You might like to pencil in these natural breaks as you go along.

Next, try to work out what the relationship is *between* the sections or parts of the paper: does section 2 establish a claim on which the argument of section 3 depends? Do sections 4 and 5 independently establish two separate claims to which the author appeals later on? And so on. You might also try representing the structure of the author's argument in a diagram or flow chart: something that shows what the central claims made in the text are and how they are related to others: that is, which claims depend on which other claims. This part of the process will become useful later on, when you start thinking of objections to things the author says: you will be able to tell whether a particular objection undermines the author's whole argument, or whether it shows merely that she has failed to refute a rival position but in a way that does not directly undermine her own view; and so on.

Of course, this part of the job – working out the overall structure of the argument – can be relatively straightforward or extremely difficult. This depends partly on the extent to which the author makes your job easy by being clear about what he or she is doing. If you are very lucky, she might state clearly, right at the beginning, which view she is defending or attacking and how exactly she is going to defend or attack it; and then, as the text unfolds, she might be very clear about which stage she has reached. ('In the previous section I argued that X; in the current section I show that Y is a consequence of X', and so on.) However, when confronted with this kind of well-signposted text, don't be fooled into thinking that the job of *understanding* the argumentative structure is completely straightforward. For example, you might be able to tell that the author is presenting a dilemma in a particular paragraph, because this is what the author says she is doing. But it's one thing to know *that* a dilemma is being presented, and quite another to understand what the dilemma really *is*. A good test is always this: close the book and then try to write down the argument or objection or dilemma, or whatever, in your own words.

3.   Thinking Philosophically about the Text

Once you've figured out as much about the argumentative structure of the text as you can, you're in a position to start thinking critically about the views and arguments the author puts forward. Think about the major claims the author makes: her overall conclusion, and other claims she makes along the way that she uses to support that conclusion. Any philosophy text will contain some unargued assumptions somewhere along the way – otherwise the text would never end. Are those assumptions intuitively plausible? If not, why not? What alternative view might one have instead? Think about the author's arguments too: are they good arguments? Do they really establish what the author claims they establish, or do they only establish some weaker claim? Can you think of any unstated consequences of the author's view? Are they plausible or implausible consequences?

4. Approaching the Commentaries

Once you've followed the first three steps as far as you think you can, read through the commentary slowly and carefully, stopping to complete the tasks in the shaded boxes as you go along. The more successful you have been in carrying out steps 2 and 3, the easier you will find this.

While you are reading the commentary and doing the tasks, keep asking yourself questions like: 'Did I really need to be told this, or could I have worked it out for myself?', 'Could I have asked myself that question, or set myself that task, without being told to do it?', and so on. Ideally, by the time you reach the end of the book, you will hardly need the commentaries at all.

5. What Next?

A philosopher's job is never done. Every topic in this book has a vast literature associated with it, and the texts reproduced in each chapter are the tip of a very large iceberg. Generally the texts launch you into the middle of a debate that has been going on for a very long time, and which has continued to develop in the years since the texts were written. We hope that you will have found the topics sufficiently interesting to want to pursue some issues in more detail; and a good way to start doing this is, of course, to find out what other philosophers have said about those issues and to apply your critical skills to those texts as well. You might want to pursue these issues by going, as it were, either forwards or backwards in time from the text that aroused your interest. For example, you might want to read the views the author is criticizing for yourself, to see whether they have represented those views accurately, or whether there are other directions in which to take the views, which avoid the author's criticisms. Or you might have formulated some worries or objections about the views expressed in the text, and want to find out whether other philosophers have had similar worries or objections and whether there has been any attempt in the literature to respond to them.

At the end of each chapter we have provided a brief list of other texts on the same topic that you might like to read. However, if you want to pursue a specific issue raised by a particular text rather than simply find out more about the general topic, you might want to locate texts that address that specific issue in detail, and ploughing through a lot of texts on the same general topic might be an inefficient way of finding them. An obvious way to start is to track down any books or articles mentioned in the part of the text that has got you interested – although of course this will only take you backwards in time, to the author's sources, and not forwards to responses to their view. So try, for example, searching the *Philosopher's Index* database (available through most university library websites), or entering some fairly specific search terms into Google (www.google.com).

6.   And Finally...

We have also provided, at the end of each chapter, a list of essay questions based on issues discussed in or raised by the preceding texts. The purpose of these is not to give you an indication of what sorts of exam questions (say) you might be set for a metaphysics course dealing with the relevant topic. It is rather to give you some ideas about the sorts of issue you might reasonably be able to tackle on your own, if you have worked through the texts and read some of the suggested additional texts.

Speaking of essay questions, it's worth pointing out one more virtue of reading carefully, and thinking hard about, the texts reproduced in this book. When you are reading and thinking about the texts – in particular when you are trying to discern their argumentative structure – think about why it is that you are finding it easy or difficult. What strategies has the author adopted in order to make the text easy to follow? What might she have done differently to make your job easier? Are there points at which she changes topic without being clear that she is doing so? If you find a particular philosophical position or objection raised in the text especially hard to understand, how might the author have helped you out? Would an example have helped, or perhaps a few more sentences of explanation?

Thinking carefully about this sort of question should help you to improve your own philosophical writing. The texts in this volume are, of course, more philosophically sophisticated and better-informed than a student essay: the authors of the texts have been doing philosophy a lot longer than you have. But the basic principles of good, clear philosophical writing are the same for students of philosophy as they are for professional philosophers.

It's also worth noticing, as you work your way through the texts, that even though every text in this book constitutes, in essence, an argument for or against a particular philosophical thesis, the methods and styles employed by the different authors vary dramatically. For example, the core of van Inwagen's paper (chapter 2) is a single, explicitly-stated argument whose validity can be ascertained by deploying some fairly basic logical principles. Parfit (chapter 1) deploys some extremely far-fetched science-fiction scenarios, while the central counter-example in Schechtman's paper (chapter 1) is a perfectly everyday experience, which she describes in great detail. Taken together, the papers in this book demonstrate that even when one is required to abide by the principles of good, clear philosophical writing, there is still a lot of room for creativity and individuality: for finding one's own, distinctive philosophical voice.

1

Personal Identity

Introduction

It seems to be an obvious truth that we are directly morally responsible only for actions that *we* perform ourselves. If Eric robs a bank single-handed, then it is Eric who is responsible for the robbery and nobody else. If Eric has an identical twin brother, Ernie, who is physically indistinguishable from him and who has similar beliefs, mannerisms, personality and so on, it is still Eric who is responsible – no matter how similar to him Ernie is.

But what *makes* it the case that, after the robbery, one of the twins and not the other is the *same person as* the person who committed the crime? One possible answer is that sameness of person goes along with sameness of body. While Eric and Ernie are physically very similar, their bodies are numerically distinct: Eric's and Ernie's bodies are different bodies. If we had somehow inserted a tracking device under Eric's skin prior to the robbery, we would later know which of Eric and Ernie had committed the crime by discovering which one of them housed the device (assuming, of course, that Eric hasn't discovered it and surreptitiously transferred it to Ernie).

One might wonder, however, whether sameness of body – bodily identity – really is either necessary or sufficient for *personal* identity. As it happens, people cannot swap bodies with one another. But one might regard this as merely a contingent truth, so that while *in fact* judgements of personal identity and judgements of bodily identity go together, it doesn't follow that personal identity *consists* in bodily identity. Imagine that it is somehow possible to 'swap bodies', in a way that leaves all one's psychological features intact, by transplanting, say, *A*'s brain into *B*'s body and *B*'s brain into *A*'s body. (Of course, the brain is part of the body. But think of the 'body', for current purposes, as the body minus the brain. Or, alternatively, you might imagine that we could 'rewire' *A*'s and *B*'s brains, so that no brain transplant is necessary.)

Before the operation, then, we have two persons, A and B, and two bodies: call these 'the A-body' and 'the B-body' respectively. Imagine that A had an unhappy childhood and now works as an English teacher. She regrets never having been to the Bahamas and intends to go there next year. B had a happy childhood, has a boring job in a supermarket, and (to spice up her dull life) recently robbed a bank and took an extended holiday in the Bahamas on the proceeds – but she feels rather guilty about the robbery.

Now imagine that, after waking up, the person now 'inhabiting' the A-body – call her 'the A-body person' – is psychologically exactly like B was before the operation. She has all the same beliefs and personality traits as B used to have. Moreover, she can vividly remember everything about B's past: events in B's happy childhood, her boring job, the excitement of robbing the bank, and the holiday in the Bahamas. She feels remorse for the robbery, just as B did. Similarly, the person now inhabiting the B-body ('the B-body person') is psychologically just like A used to be. She remembers A's unhappy childhood, is well-acquainted with the works of Shakespeare, regrets never having been to the Bahamas, and intends to go next year, just as A did before the operation.

Now, which of these two persons – the A-body person and the B-body person – is B? Or, to make the question more vivid, which of them do you regard as morally responsible for the robbery? Most people would say that it is the A-body person. After all, it is she who remembers the robbery and feels guilty about it. The B-body person, by contrast, has no memory whatever of robbing any bank, and if asked whether she did it, she would sincerely deny it.

If it is right to say that the A-body person is B – the bank-robber – then personal identity cannot consist in bodily identity, since a 'bodily criterion' of personal identity delivers the result that it is the B-body person who is B. So perhaps what makes someone the same person over time is whatever it is that leads us to judge that the A-body person is B – and that seems to be a matter of psychological rather than physical criteria.

As an introduction to the two texts reproduced here, we shall describe three problems that a theory of personal identity based on psychological rather than physical criteria has to solve. The first two are very old problems, first raised against John Locke's account of personal identity (1690). Locke's theory is often characterized as follows (though it is debatable whether this is exactly what he had in mind):

(M)   X (at a later time) is the same person as Y (at an earlier time) if and only if X can remember Y's experiences.

Because it appeals just to memory, (M) is often known as the 'memory theory' of personal identity.

Problem 1: The transitivity of identity

The first problem faced by the memory theory was originally raised by Thomas Reid (1785). Suppose a young boy (A), at time t_1, steals apples from an orchard. Some years later, at time t_2, an officer (B) remembers stealing the apples. So, by (M), B is the same person as *A*. Many years after that, a general (*C*) can remember the officer's experiences. So, by (M), *C* is the same person as *B*. But *C* cannot remember stealing the apples. So, again by (M), *C* is not the same person as *A*.

Now, identity is what is known as a *transitive relation*. A transitive relation is a relation *R* such that if *X* bears *R* to *Y* and *Y* bears *R* to *Z*, it follows that *X* bears *R* to *Z*. So, for example, *is an ancestor of* is a transitive relation: if George is an ancestor of Mary, and Mary is an ancestor of John, it follows that George is an ancestor of John. Similarly for identity: if Bruce Wayne is Batman, and Batman is the Caped Crusader, it follows that Bruce Wayne is the Caped Crusader. *Is a cousin of*, by contrast, is not transitive: if Sue is a cousin of Sam and Sam is a cousin of Dr. Jones, it doesn't follow that Sue is a cousin of Dr Jones. (Sue might be Dr. Jones's sister, or Sue might *be* Dr. Jones.)

The problem for the memory theory is that *remembers the experiences of* is not a transitive relation: in the example given above, *C* remembers *B*'s experiences and *B* remembers *A*'s experiences, but *C* does not remember *A*'s experiences. So personal identity cannot *be* the *remembers the experiences of* relation. (M) delivers the result that *A* = *B* and *B* = *C*, but *A* ≠ *C*, and this cannot be true, because it violates the transitivity requirement: if *A* = *B* and *B* = *C*, then *A* *must* be identical with *C*. The challenge for someone who wants to hold that personal identity consists in the holding of psychological relations is thus to come up with *transitive* psychological relations which might reasonably be thought to be what personal identity consists in. Parfit addresses this issue in the first text reproduced below.

Problem 2: The circularity objection

This problem, first raised against Locke by Joseph Butler (1736), is that it seems to be a *precondition* of *X*'s remembering *Y*'s actions that *X* and *Y* are the same person. It is a conceptual truth – a truth about the concept of memory – that if *X* is not the same person as *Y*, then *X* cannot genuinely remember *Y*'s experiences. If *X* and *Y* are different people, then, while *X* can have memory-*like* experiences and mistakenly *think* that they are memories of *Y*'s experiences – a madman can mistakenly think that he can remember leading the French troops at the battle of Waterloo – those memory-like experiences cannot be genuine memories. Only Napoleon could genuinely *remember* leading the French troops into battle.

Now, the point of this objection is not that it renders (M) *false*; it doesn't. Rather, the problem is that according to the memory theory, memory is supposed to provide a *criterion* or *definition* or *analysis* of personal identity: it is supposed to *explain* what makes it the case that *X* is the same person as *Y*. But it cannot do this if facts about memory themselves depend upon facts about personal identity; and the circularity objection allegedly shows that facts about memory *do* depend on facts about personal identity. If someone sincerely claims to remember winning the 2004 Best Director Oscar for *The Return of the King*, we cannot infer with certainty that he is Peter Jackson; he might be someone completely different and just be suffering from a delusion. In order to be able to infer with certainty that he really is Peter Jackson, we have to ascertain that he really does *remember* winning the Oscar. But we can only do *that* by *first* ascertaining that he is Peter Jackson. So whether or not the person remembers winning the Oscar cannot *determine* whether or not he is Peter Jackson. In the first text reproduced below, Parfit attempts (*inter alia*) to meet the circularity objection; in the second text, Schechtman argues that Parfit's attempt fails.

Problem 3: Divided brains

The recent literature on personal identity is full of outlandish thought-experiments. We are asked to imagine a very odd science-fiction scenario, and then asked whether our intuitive judgements about personal identity in that scenario are the same as those delivered by a particular theory of personal identity. One such thought-experiment is what we'll call 'the divided-brain case'. Imagine that A's brain is cut in half and each half is transplanted into a new body: one half into the B-body and the other into the C-body. (A's body is destroyed.) Imagine that having half of A's brain results in no psychological loss, so that *each* of the people who wake up after the operation (B and C) is psychologically continuous with A: each of them can remember A's childhood, has the same hopes and fears and intentions as A did, feels remorse about some of A's past actions, and so on.

If we hold that psychological continuity is sufficient for personal identity, it seems that we have to conclude that B is the same person as A, but also that C is the same person as A. But this is surely impossible. B and C are, it seems, numerically distinct persons. Ten years later, B might rob a bank; and, intuitively, C would not bear any moral responsibility for the robbery. But in that case, it cannot be the case both that $B = A$ *and* that $C = A$, because they together entail that $B = C$. (This is just the transitivity of identity again: if $B = A$ and $A = C$ then $B = C$.) Identity is, as Parfit puts it, 'logically one–one': one person cannot be identical to two distinct people.

One way to respond to the divided-brain case would be to give up on psychological continuity altogether, and hold that personal identity must after all be analysed in terms of bodily identity. (One might be especially inclined to draw this conclusion if one thinks that at least one of problem 1 and problem 2 cannot be solved satisfactorily.) However, Parfit argues instead that it is not personal *identity* that matters after all. What matters – for example, for the purposes of allocating moral responsibility – is the fact that B is psychologically continuous with A, and also that C is psychologically continuous with A. For example, if A committed a terrible crime just before undergoing the operation, we should hold *both* B and C responsible for it, and it would be appropriate for both of them to feel remorse. But what matters cannot therefore be *identity*, because there is no good answer to the question, 'which of B and C is the same person as A?' Parfit calls what matters 'survival': A 'survives' both as B and as C, but is identical with neither of them.

The texts

Parfit's overall aim in the ground-breaking paper 'Personal Identity' (1973), reproduced below, is to provide an account of 'survival', in terms of what he calls 'psychological connectedness', and to argue that we should think of our own lives in terms of survival rather than identity. Psychological connectedness comes in degrees: you can be more or less psychologically connected to a 'past self', depending on the extent to which you can remember the experiences of that past self, you still intend to realize your past self's intentions, you hold the same beliefs and desires, and so on. So, for example, rather than the general in problem 1 above thinking of himself as *identical* to both the apple-stealing boy and the officer, he should think of one of his past selves – the boy – as surviving as his present self to a very small degree (or perhaps not at all), while another, more recent past self – the captain – has survived to a much greater degree.

Because Parfit's account of survival appeals to psychological relations, including the *remembers-the-experiences-of* relation, he needs to find a way of meeting the circularity problem (problem 2 above), which is just as much a problem for Parfit's view as it is for the memory theory of personal identity. This he attempts to do; however, in her paper 'Personhood and Personal Identity' (1990), Marya Schechtman argues that Parfit's attempt fails. She concludes that we should abandon the search for a non-circular psychological criterion of personal identity (and, by extension, survival) altogether, but attempts to diagnose why we are inclined to find the mistaken thought that there is such a criterion so seductive.

Derek Parfit, 'Personal Identity'[1]

We can, I think, describe cases in which, though we know the answer to every other question, we have no idea how to answer a question about personal identity. These cases are not covered by the criteria of personal identity that we actually use.

Do they present a problem?

It might be thought that they do not, because they could never occur. I suspect that some of them could. (Some, for instance, might become scientifically possible.) But I shall claim that even if they did they would present no problem.

My targets are two beliefs: one about the nature of personal identity, the other about its importance.

The first is that in these cases the question about identity must have an answer.

 No one thinks this about, say, nations or machines. Our criteria for the identity of these do not cover certain cases. No one thinks that in these cases the questions "Is it the same nation?" or "Is it the same machine?" must have answers.

---

[1]   I have been helped in writing this by D. Wiggins, D. F. Pears, P. F. Strawson, A. J. Ayer, M. Woods, N. Newman, and (through his publications) S. Shoemaker.

Some people believe that in this respect they are different. They agree that our criteria of personal identity do not cover certain cases, but they believe that the nature of their own identity through time is, somehow, such as to guarantee that in these cases questions about their identity must have answers. This belief might be expressed as follows: "Whatever happens between now and any future time, either I shall still exist, or I shall not. Any future experience will either be *my* experience, or it will not."

This first belief – in the special nature of personal identity – has, I think, certain effects. It makes people assume that the principle of self-interest is more rationally compelling than any moral principle. And it makes them more depressed by the thought of aging and of death.

I cannot see how to disprove this first belief. I shall describe a problem case. But this can only make it seem implausible.

Another approach might be this. We might suggest that one cause of the belief is the projection of our emotions. When we imagine ourselves in a problem case, we do feel that the question "Would it be me?" must have an answer. But what we take to be a bafflement about a further fact may be only the bafflement of our concern.

I shall not pursue this suggestion here. But one cause of our concern is the belief which is my second target. This is that unless the question about identity has an answer, we cannot answer certain important questions (questions about such matters as survival, memory, and responsibility).

Against this second belief my claim will be this. Certain important questions do presuppose a question about personal identity. But they can be freed of this presupposition. And when they are, the question about identity has no importance.

I

We can start by considering the much-discussed case of the man who, like an amoeba, divides.[2]

 Wiggins has recently dramatized this case.[3] He first referred to the operation imagined by Shoemaker.[4] We suppose that my brain is transplanted into someone else's (brainless) body, and that the resulting person

---

[2] Implicit in John Locke, *Essay Concerning Human Understanding*, ed. by John W. Yolton (London, 1961), vol. II, Ch. XXVII, sec. 18, and discussed by (among others) A. N. Prior in "Opposite Number," *Review of Metaphysics*, 11 (1957–1958), and "Time, Existence and Identity," *Proceedings of the Aristotelian Society*, LVII (1965–1966); J. Bennett in "The Simplicity of the Soul," *Journal of Philosophy*, LXIV (1967); and R. Chisholm and S. Shoemaker in "The Loose and Popular and the Strict and the Philosophical Senses of Identity," in *Perception and Personal Identity: Proceedings of the 1967 Oberlin Colloquium in Philosophy*, ed. by Norman Care and Robert H. Grimm (Cleveland, 1967).

[3] In *Identity and Spatio-Temporal Continuity* (Oxford, 1967), p. 50.

[4] In *Self-Knowledge and Self-Identity* (Ithaca, NY, 1963), p. 22.

has my character and apparent memories of my life. Most of us would agree, after thought, that the resulting person is me. I shall here assume such agreement.[5]

Wiggins then imagined his own operation. My brain is divided, and each half is housed in a new body. Both resulting people have my character and apparent memories of my life.

What happens to me? There seem only three possibilities: (1) I do not survive; (2) I survive as one of the two people; (3) I survive as both.

The trouble with (1) is this. We agreed that I could survive if my brain were successfully transplanted. And people have in fact survived with half their brains destroyed. It seems to follow that I could survive if half my brain were successfully transplanted and the other half were destroyed. But if this is so, how could I *not* survive if the other half were also successfully transplanted? How could a double success be a failure?

We can move to the second description. Perhaps one success is the maximum score. Perhaps I shall be one of the resulting people.

The trouble here is that in Wiggins' case each half of my brain is exactly similar, and so, to start with, is each resulting person. So how can I survive as only one of the two people? What can make me one of them rather than the other?

It seems clear that both of these descriptions – that I do not survive, and that I survive as one of the people – are highly implausible. Those who have accepted them must have assumed that they were the only possible descriptions.

What about our third description: that I survive as both people?

It might be said, "If 'survive' implies identity, this description makes no sense – you cannot be two people. If it does not, the description is irrelevant to a problem about identity."

I shall later deny the second of these remarks. But there are ways of denying the first. We might say, "What we have called 'the two resulting people' are not two people. They are one person. I do survive Wiggins' operation. Its effect is to give me two bodies and a divided mind."

It would shorten my argument if this were absurd. But I do not think it is. It is worth showing why.

We can, I suggest, imagine a divided mind. We can imagine a man having two simultaneous experiences, in having each of which he is unaware of having the other.

We may not even need to imagine this. Certain actual cases, to which Wiggins referred, seem to be best described in these terms. These involve

---

[5] Those who would disagree are not making a mistake. For them my argument would need a different case. There must be some multiple transplant, faced with which these people would both find it hard to believe that there must be an answer to the question about personal identity, and be able to be shown that nothing of importance turns upon this question.

the cutting of the bridge between the hemispheres of the brain. The aim was to cure epilepsy. But the result appears to be, in the surgeon's words, the creation of "two separate spheres of consciousness,"[6] each of which controls one half of the patient's body. What is experienced in each is, presumably, experienced by the patient.

There are certain complications in these actual cases. So let us imagine a simpler case.

Suppose that the bridge between my hemispheres is brought under my voluntary control. This would enable me to disconnect my hemispheres as easily as if I were blinking. By doing this I would divide my mind. And we can suppose that when my mind is divided I can, in each half, bring about reunion.

This ability would have obvious uses. To give an example: I am near the end of a maths exam, and see two ways of tackling the last problem. I decide to divide my mind, to work, with each half, at one of two calculations, and then to reunite my mind and write a fair copy of the best result.

What shall I experience?

When I disconnect my hemispheres, my consciousness divides into two streams. But this division is not something that I experience. Each of my two streams of consciousness seems to have been straightforwardly continuous with my one stream of consciousness up to the moment of division. The only changes in each stream are the disappearance of half my visual field and the loss of sensation in, and control over, half my body.

Consider my experiences in what we can call my "right-handed" stream. I remember that I assigned my right hand to the longer calculation. This I now begin. In working at this calculation I can see, from the movements of my left hand, that I am also working at the other. But I am not aware of working at the other. So I might, in my right-handed stream, wonder how, in my left-handed stream, I am getting on.

My work is now over. I am about to reunite my mind. What should I, in each stream, expect? Simply that I shall suddenly seem to remember just having thought out two calculations, in thinking out each of which I was not aware of thinking out the other. This, I submit, we can imagine. And if my mind was divided, these memories are correct.

In describing this episode, I assumed that there were two series of thoughts, and that they were both mine. If my two hands visibly wrote out two calculations, and if I claimed to remember two corresponding series of thoughts, this is surely what we should want to say.

If it is, then a person's mental history need not be like a canal, with only one channel. It could be like a river, with islands, and with separate streams.

To apply this to Wiggins' operation: we mentioned the view that it gives me two bodies and a divided mind. We cannot now call this absurd. But it is, I think, unsatisfactory.

---

[6] R. W. Sperry, in *Brain and Conscious Experience*, ed. by J. C. Eccles (New York, 1966), p. 299.

There were two features of the case of the exam that made us want to say that only one person was involved. The mind was soon reunited, and there was only one body. If a mind was permanently divided and its halves developed in different ways, the point of speaking of one person would start to disappear. Wiggins' case, where there are also two bodies, seems to be over the borderline. After I have had his operation, the two "products" each have all the attributes of a person. They could live at opposite ends of the earth. (If they later met, they might even fail to recognize each other.) It would become intolerable to deny that they were different people.

Suppose we admit that they are different people. Could we still claim that I survived as both, using "survive" to imply identity?

We could. For we might suggest that two people could compose a third. We might say, "I do survive Wiggins' operation as two people. They can be different people, and yet be me, in just the way in which the Pope's three crowns are one crown."[7]

This is a possible way of giving sense to the claim that I survive as two different people, using "survive" to imply identity. But it keeps the language of identity only by changing the concept of a person. And there are obvious objections to this change.[8]

The alternative, for which I shall argue, is to give up the language of identity. We can suggest that I survive as two different people without implying that I am these people.

When I first mentioned this alternative, I mentioned this objection: "If your new way of talking does not imply identity, it cannot solve our problem. For that is about identity. The problem is that all the possible answers to the question about identity are highly implausible."

We can now answer this objection.

We can start by reminding ourselves that this is an objection only if we have one or both of the beliefs which I mentioned at the start of this paper.

The first was the belief that to any question about personal identity, in any describable case, there must be a true answer. For those with this belief, Wiggins' case is doubly perplexing. If all the possible answers are implausible, it is hard to decide which of them is true, and hard even to keep the belief that one of them must be true. If we give up this belief, as I think we should, these problems disappear. We shall then regard the case as like many others in which, for quite unpuzzling reasons, there *is* no answer

---

[7] Cf. Wiggins, p. 40.

[8] Suppose the resulting people fight a duel. Are there three people fighting, one on each side, and one on both? And suppose one of the bullets kills. Are there two acts, one murder and one suicide? How many people are left alive? One? Two? (We could hardly say, "One and a half.") We could talk in this way. But instead of saying that the resulting people *are* the original person – so that the pair is a trio – it would be far simpler to treat them as a pair, and describe their relation to the original person in some new way. (I owe this suggested way of talking, and the objections to it, to Michael Woods.)

to a question about identity. (Consider "Was England the same nation after 1066?")

Wiggins' case makes the first belief implausible. It also makes it trivial. For it undermines the second belief. This was the belief that important questions turn upon the question about identity. (It is worth pointing out that those who have only this second belief do not think that there must *be* an answer to this question, but rather that we must decide upon an answer.)

Against this second belief my claim is this. Certain questions do presuppose a question about personal identity. And because these questions *are* important, Wiggins' case does present a problem. But we cannot solve this problem by answering the question about identity. We can solve this problem only by taking these important questions and prizing them apart from the question about identity. After we have done this, the question about identity (though we might for the sake of neatness decide it) has no further interest.

Because there are several questions which presuppose identity, this claim will take some time to fill out.

We can first return to the question of survival. This is a special case, for survival does not so much presuppose the retaining of identity as seem equivalent to it. It is thus the general relation which we need to prize apart from identity. We can then consider particular relations, such as those involved in memory and intention.

"Will I survive?" seems, I said, equivalent to "Will there be some person alive who is the same person as me?"

If we treat these questions as equivalent, then the least unsatisfactory description of Wiggins' case is, I think, that I survive with two bodies and a divided mind.

Several writers have chosen to say that I am neither of the resulting people. Given our equivalence, this implies that I do not survive, and hence, presumably, that even if Wiggins' operation is not literally death, I ought, since I will not survive it, to regard it *as* death. But this seemed absurd.

It is worth repeating why. An emotion or attitude can be criticized for resting on a false belief, or for being inconsistent. A man who regarded Wiggins' operation as death must, I suggest, be open to one of these criticisms.

He might believe that his relation to each of the resulting people fails to contain some element which is contained in survival. But how can this be true? We agreed that he *would* survive if he stood in this very same relation to only *one* of the resulting people. So it cannot be the nature of this relation which makes it fail, in Wiggins' case, to be survival. It can only be its duplication.

Suppose that our man accepts this, but still regards division as death. His reaction would now seem wildly inconsistent. He would be like a man who, when told of a drug that could double his years of life, regarded the taking of this drug as death. The only difference in the case of division is that the extra years are to run concurrently. This is an interesting difference. But it cannot mean that there are *no* years to run.

I have argued this for those who think that there must, in Wiggins' case, be a true answer to the question about identity. For them, we might add, "Perhaps the original person does lose his identity. But there may be other ways to do this than to die. One other way might be to multiply. To regard these as the same is to confuse nought with two."

For those who think that the question of identity is up for decision, it would be clearly absurd to regard Wiggins' operation as death. These people would have to think, "We could have chosen to say that I should be one of the resulting people. If we had, I should not have regarded it as death. But since we have chosen to say that I am neither person, I *do*." This is hard even to understand.[9]

My first conclusion, then, is this. The relation of the original person to each of the resulting people contains all that interests us – all that matters – in any ordinary case of survival. This is why we need a sense in which one person can survive as two.[10]

One of my aims in the rest of this paper will be to suggest such a sense. But we can first make some general remarks.

II

Identity is a one–one relation. Wiggins' case serves to show that what matters in survival need not be one–one.

Wiggins' case is of course unlikely to occur. The relations which matter are, in fact, one–one. It is because they are that we can imply the holding of these relations by using the language of identity.

This use of language is convenient. But it can lead us astray. We may assume that what matters *is* identity and, hence, has the properties of identity.

In the case of the property of being one–one, this mistake is not serious. For what matters is in fact one–one. But in the case of another property, the mistake *is* serious. Identity is all-or-nothing. Most of the relations which matter in survival are, in fact, relations of degree. If we ignore this, we shall be led into quite ill-grounded attitudes and beliefs.

The claim that I have just made – that most of what matters are relations of degree – I have yet to support. Wiggins' case shows only that these relations need not be one–one. The merit of the case is not that it shows this in particular, but that it makes the first break between what matters and identity. The belief that identity *is* what matters is hard to overcome. This is shown in most discussions of the problem cases which actually occur: cases,

[9] Cf. Sydney Shoemaker, in *Perception and Personal Identity: Proceedings of the 1967 Oberlin Colloquium in Philosophy, loc. cit.*
[10] Cf. Wiggins, p.54.

say, of amnesia or of brain damage. Once Wiggins' case has made one breach in this belief, the rest should be easier to remove.[11]

f → To turn to a recent debate: most of the relations which matter can be provisionally referred to under the heading "psychological continuity" (which includes causal continuity). My claim is thus that we use the language of personal identity in order to imply such continuity. This is close to the view that psychological continuity provides a criterion of identity.

Williams has attacked this view with the following argument. Identity is a one–one relation. So any criterion of identity must appeal to a relation which is logically one–one. Psychological continuity is not logically one–one. So it cannot provide a criterion.[12]

Some writers have replied that it is enough if the relation appealed to is always in fact one–one.[13]

I suggest a slightly different reply. Psychological continuity is a ground for speaking of identity when it is one–one.

If psychological continuity took a one-many or branching form, we should need, I have argued, to abandon the language of identity. So this possibility would not count against this view.

We can make a stronger claim. This possibility would count in its favor.

The view might be defended as follows. Judgments of personal identity have great importance. What gives them their importance is the fact that they imply psychological continuity. This is why, whenever there is such continuity, we ought, if we can, to imply it by making a judgment of identity.

If psychological continuity took a branching form, no coherent set of judgments of identity could correspond to, and thus be used to imply, the branching form of this relation. But what we ought to do, in such a case, is take the importance which would attach to a judgment of identity and attach this importance directly to each limb of the branching relations. So this case helps to show that judgments of personal identity do derive their importance from the fact that they imply psychological continuity. It helps to show that when we can, usefully, speak of identity, this relation is our ground.

[11]   Bernard Williams' "The Self and the Future," *Philosophical Review*, LXXIX (1970), 161–180, is relevant here. He asks the question "Shall I survive?" in a range of problem cases, and he shows how natural it is to believe (1) that this question must have an answer, (2) that the answer must be all-or-nothing, and (3) that there is a "risk" of our reaching the *wrong* answer. Because these beliefs are so natural, we should need in undermining them to discuss their causes. These, I think, can be found in the ways in which we misinterpret what it is to remember (cf. Sec. III below) and to anticipate (cf. Williams' "Imagination and the Self," *Proceedings of the British Academy*, LII [1966], 105–124); and also in the way in which certain features of our egoistic concern – e.g., that it is simple, and applies to all imaginable cases – are "projected" onto its object. (For another relevant discussion, see Terence Penelhum's *Survival and Disembodied Existence* [London, 1970], final chapters.)

[12]   "Personal Identity and Individuation," *Proceedings of the Aristotelian Society*, LVII (1956–1957), 229–253; also *Analysis*, 21 (1960–1961), 43–48.

[13]   J. M. Shorter, "More about Bodily Continuity and Personal Identity," *Analysis*, 22 (1961–1962), 79–85; and Mrs. J. M. R. Jack (unpublished), who requires that this truth be embedded in a causal theory.

g→   This argument appeals to a principle which Williams put forward.[14] The principle is that an important judgment should be asserted and denied only on importantly different grounds.

Williams applied this principle to a case in which one man is psychologically continuous with the dead Guy Fawkes, and a case in which two men are. His argument was this. If we treat psychological continuity as a sufficient ground for speaking of identity, we shall say that the one men is Guy Fawkes. But we could not say that the two men are, although we should have the same ground. This disobeys the principle. The remedy is to deny that the one man is Guy Fawkes, to insist that sameness of the body is necessary for identity.

Williams' principle can yield a different answer. Suppose we regard psychological continuity as more important than sameness of the body.[15] And suppose that the one man really is psychologically (and causally) continuous with Guy Fawkes. If he is, it would disobey the principle to deny that he is Guy Fawkes, for we have the same important ground as in a normal case of identity. In the case of the two men, we again have the same important ground. So we ought to take the importance from the judgment of identity and attach it directly to this ground. We ought to say, as in Wiggins' case, that each limb of the branching relation is as good as survival. This obeys the principle.

To sum up these remarks: even if psychological continuity is neither logically, nor always in fact, one–one, it can provide a criterion of identity. For this can appeal to the relation of *non-branching* psychological continuity, which is logically one–one.[16]

The criterion might be sketched as follows. "*X* and *Y* are the same person if they are psychologically continuous and there is no person who is contemporary with either and psychologically continuous with the other." We should need to explain what we mean by "psychologically continuous" and say how much continuity the criterion requires. We should then, I think, have described a sufficient condition for speaking of identity.[17]

We need to say something more. If we admit that psychological continuity might not be one–one, we need to say what we ought to do if it were not one–one. Otherwise our account would be open to the objections that it is incomplete and arbitrary.[18]

[14]   *Analysis*, 21 (1960–1961), 44.
[15]   For the reasons given by A. M. Quinton in "The Soul," *Journal of Philosophy*, LIX (1962), 393–409.
[16]   Cf. S. Shoemaker, "Persons and Their Pasts," to appear in the *American Philosophical Quarterly*, and "Wiggins on Identity," *Philosophical Review*, LXXIX (1970), 542.
[17]   But not a necessary condition, for in the absence of psychological continuity bodily identity might be sufficient.
[18]   Cf. Bernard Williams, "Personal Identity and Individuation," *Proceedings of the Aristotelian Society*, LVII (1956–1957), 240–241, and *Analysis*, 21 (1960–1961), 44; and also Wiggins, *op. cit.*, p. 38: "if coincidence under [the concept] *f* is to be *genuinely* sufficient we must not withhold identity...simply because transitivity is threatened."

I have suggested that if psychological continuity took a branching form, we ought to speak in a new way, regarding what we describe as having the same significance as identity. This answers these objections.[19]

We can now return to our discussion. We have three remaining aims. One is to suggest a sense of "survive" which does not imply identity. Another is to show that most of what matters in survival are relations of degree. A third is to show that none of these relations needs to be described in a way that presupposes identity.

We can take these aims in the reverse order.

III

The most important particular relation is that involved in memory. This is because it is so easy to believe that its description must refer to identity.[20] This belief about memory is an important cause of the view that personal identity has a special nature. But it has been well discussed by Shoemaker[21] and by Wiggins[22] So we can be brief.

It may be a logical truth that we can only remember our own experiences. But we can frame a new concept for which this is not a logical truth. Let us call this "q-memory."

To sketch a definition[23] I am q-remembering an experience if (1) I have a belief about a past experience which seems in itself like a memory belief, (2) someone did have such an experience, and (3) my belief is dependent upon this experience in the same way (whatever that is) in which a memory of an experience is dependent upon it.

According to (1) q-memories seem like memories. So I q-remember *having* experiences.

This may seem to make q-memory presuppose identity. One might say, "My apparent memory of *having* an experience is an apparent memory of *my* having an experience. So how could I q-remember my having other people's experiences?"

This objection rests on a mistake. When I seem to remember an experience, I do indeed seem to remember *having* it.[24] But it cannot be a part of

---

[19]   Williams produced another objection to the "psychological criterion," that it makes it hard to explain the difference between the concepts of identity and exact similarity (*Analysis*, 21 [1960–1961], 48). But if we include the requirement of causal continuity we avoid this objection (and one of those produced by Wiggins in his note 47).

[20]   Those philosophers who have held this belief, from Butler onward, are too numerous to cite.

[21]   *Op. cit.*

[22]   In a paper on Butler's objection to Locke (not yet published).

[23]   I here follow Shoemaker's "quasi-memory." Cf. also Penelhum's "retrocognition," in his article on "Personal Identity," in the *Encyclopedia of Philosophy*, ed. by Paul Edwards.

[24]   As Shoemaker put it, I seem to remember the experience "from the inside" (*op. cit.*).

what I seem to remember about this experience that I, the person who now seems to remember it, am the person who had this experience.[25] That I am is something that I automatically assume. (My apparent memories sometimes come to me simply as the belief that *I* had a certain experience.) But it is something that I am justified in assuming only because I do not in fact have *q*-memories of other people's experiences.

Suppose that I did start to have such *q*-memories. If I did, I should cease to assume that my apparent memories must be about my own experiences. I should come to assess an apparent memory by asking two questions: (1) Does it tell me about a past experience? (2) If so, whose?

[h] → Moreover (and this is a crucial point) my apparent memories would now come to me *as q*-memories. Consider those of my apparent memories which do come to me simply as beliefs about my past: for example, "I did that." If I knew that I could *q*-remember other people's experiences, these beliefs would come to me in a more guarded form: for example, "Someone – probably I – did that." I might have to work out who it was.

I have suggested that the concept of *q*-memory is coherent. Wiggins' case provides an illustration. The resulting people, in his case, both have apparent memories of living the life of the original person. If they agree that they are not this person, they will have to regard these as only *q*-memories. And when they are asked a question like "Have you heard this music before?" they might have to answer "I am sure that I *q*-remember hearing it. But I am not sure whether I remember hearing it. I am not sure whether it was I who heard it, or the original person."

We can next point out that on our definition every memory is also a *q*-memory. Memories are, simply, *q*-memories of one's own experiences. Since this is so, we could afford now to drop the concept of memory and use in its place the wider concept *q*-memory. If we did, we should describe the relation between an experience and what we now call a "memory" of this experience in a way which does not presuppose that they are had by the same person.[26]

---

[25] This is what so many writers have overlooked. Cf. Thomas Reid: "My memory testifies not only that this was done, but that it was done by me who now remember it" ("Of Identity," in *Essays on the Intellectual Powers of Man*, ed. by A. D. Woozley [London, 1941], p. 203). This mistake is discussed by A. B. Palma in "Memory and Personal Identity," *Australasian Journal of Philosophy*, 42 (1964), 57.

[26] It is not logically necessary that we only *q*-remember our own experiences. But it might be necessary on other grounds. This possibility is intriguingly explored by Shoemaker in his "Persons and Their Pasts" (*op. cit.*). He shows that *q*-memories can provide a knowledge of the world only if the observations which are *q*-remembered trace out fairly continuous spatiotemporal paths. If the observations which are *q*-remembered traced out a network of frequently interlocking paths, they could not, I think, be usefully ascribed to persisting observers, but would have to be referred to in some more complex way. But in fact the observations which are *q*-remembered trace out single and separate paths; so we can ascribe them to ourselves. In other words, it is epistemologically necessary that the observations which are *q*-remembered should satisfy a certain general condition, one particular form of which allows them to be usefully self-ascribed.

This way of describing this relation has certain merits. It vindicates the "memory criterion" of personal identity against the charge of circularity.[27] And it might, I think, help with the problem of other minds.

But we must move on. We can next take the relation between an intention and a later action. It may be a logical truth that we can intend to perform only our own actions. But intentions can be redescribed as q-intentions. And one person could q-intend to perform another person's actions.

Wiggins' case again provides the illustration. We are supposing that neither of the resulting people is the original person. If so, we shall have to agree that the original person can, before the operation, q-intend to perform their actions. He might, for example, q-intend, as one of them, to continue his present career, and, as the other, to try something new.[28] (I say "q-intend as one of them" because the phrase "q-intend that one of them" would not convey the directness of the relation which is involved. If I intend that someone else should do something, I cannot get him to do it simply by forming this intention. But if I am the original person, and he is one of the resulting people, I can.)

The phrase "q-intend as one of them" reminds us that we need a sense in which one person can survive as two. But we can first point out that the concepts of q-memory and q-intention give us our model for the others that we need: thus, a man who can q-remember could q-recognize, and be a q-witness of, what he has never seen; and a man who can q-intend could have q-ambitions, make q-promises, and be q-responsible for.

To put this claim in general terms: many different relations are included within, or are a consequence of, psychological continuity. We describe these relations in ways which presuppose the continued existence of one person. But we could describe them in new ways which do not.

This suggests a bolder claim. It might be possible to think of experiences in a wholly "impersonal" way. I shall not develop this claim here. What I shall try to describe is a way of thinking of our own identity through time which is more flexible, and less misleading, than the way in which we now think.

This way of thinking will allow for a sense in which one person can survive as two. A more important feature is that it treats survival as a matter of degree.

---

[27]   Cf. Wiggins' paper on Butler's objection to Locke.

[28]   There are complications here. He could form *divergent* q-intentions only if he could distinguish, in advance, between the resulting people (e.g., as "the left-hander" and "the right-hander"). And he could be confident that such divergent q-intentions would be carried out only if he had reason to believe that neither of the resulting people would change their (inherited) mind. Suppose he was torn between duty and desire. He could not solve this dilemma by q-intending, as one of the resulting people, to do his duty, and, as the other, to do what he desires. For the one he q-intended to do his duty would face the same dilemma.

IV

We must first show the need for this second feature. I shall use two imaginary examples. [...] [Parfit next briefly describes a case of 'fusion', where two beings with different psychological characteristics (memories, beliefs, character traits, etc.) are amalgamated into a single being.]

We can now turn to a second example. This is provided by certain imaginary beings. These beings are just like ourselves except that they reproduce by a process of natural division.

We can illustrate the histories of these imagined beings with the aid of a diagram. (Figure 1.) The lines on the diagram represent the spatiotemporal paths which would be traced out by the bodies of these beings. We can call each single line (like the double line) a "branch"; and we can call the whole structure a "tree." And let us suppose that each "branch" corresponds to what is thought of as the life of one individual. These individuals are referred to as "A," "B + 1," and so forth.

Now, each single division is an instance of Wiggins' case. So A's relation to both B + 1 and B + 2 is just as good as survival. But what of A's relation to B + 30?

I said earlier that what matters in survival could be provisionally referred to as "psychological continuity." I must now distinguish this relation from another, which I shall call "psychological connectedness."

Let us say that the relation between a q-memory and the experience q-remembered is a "direct" relation. Another "direct" relation is that which holds between a q-intention and the q-intended action. A third is that which holds between different expressions of some lasting q-characteristic.

"Psychological connectedness," as I define it, requires the holding of these direct psychological relations. "Connectedness" is not transitive, since these

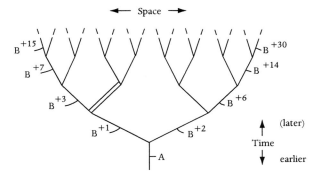

Figure 1

relations are not transitive. Thus, if X q-remembers most of Y's life, and Y q-remembers most of Z's life, it does not follow that X q-remembers most of Z's life. And if X carries out the q-intentions of Y, and Y carries out the q-intentions of Z, it does not follow that X carries out the q-intentions of Z.

"Psychological continuity," in contrast, only requires overlapping chains of direct psychological relations. So "continuity" *is* transitive.

To return to our diagram. A *is* psychologically continuous with B + 30. There are between the two continuous chains of overlapping relations. Thus, A has q-intentional control over B + 2, B + 2 has q-intentional control over B + 6, and so on up to B + 30. Or B + 30 can q-remember the life of B + 14, B + 14 can q-remember the life of B + 6, and so on back to A.[29]

A, however, need *not* be psychologically connected to B + 30. Connectedness requires direct relations. And if these beings are like us, A cannot stand in such relations to every individual in his indefinitely long "tree." Q-memories will weaken with the passage of time, and then fade away. Q-ambitions, once fulfilled, will be replaced by others. Q-characteristics will gradually change. In general, A stands in fewer and fewer direct psychological relations to an individual in his "tree" the more remote that individual is. And if the individual is (like B + 30) sufficiently remote, there may be between the two *no* direct psychological relations.

Now that we have distinguished the general relations of psychological continuity and psychological connectedness, I suggest that connectedness is a more important element in survival. As a claim about our own survival, this would need more arguments than I have space to give. But it seems clearly true for my imagined beings. A is as close psychologically to B + 1 as I today am to myself tomorrow. A is as distant from B + 30 as I am from my great-great-grandson.

Even if connectedness is not more important than continuity, the fact that one of these is a relation of degree is enough to show that what matters in survival can have degrees. And in any case the two relations are quite different. So our imagined beings would need a way of thinking in which this difference is recognized.

V

What I propose is this.

First, A can think of any individual, anywhere in his "tree," as "a descendant self." This phrase implies psychological continuity. Similarly, any later individual can think of any earlier individual on the single path[30] which connects him to A as "an ancestral self."

---

[29]   The chain of continuity must run in one direction of time. B + 2 is not, in the sense I intend, psychologically continuous with B + 1.
[30]   Cf. Wiggins, *op. cit.*

Since psychological continuity is transitive, "being an ancestral self of" and "being a descendant self of" are also transitive.

To imply psychological connectedness I suggest the phrases "one of my future selves" and "one of my past selves."

These are the phrases with which we can describe Wiggins' case. For having past and future selves is, what we needed, a way of continuing to exist which does not imply identity through time. The original person does, in this sense, survive Wiggins' operation: the two resulting people are his later selves. And they can each refer to him as "my past self." (They can share a past self without being the same self as each other.)

Since psychological connectedness is not transitive, and is a matter of degree, the relations "being a past self of" and "being a future self of" should themselves be treated as relations of degree. We allow for this series of descriptions: "my most recent self," "one of my earlier selves," "one of my distant selves," "hardly one of *my* past selves (I can only *q*-remember a few of his experiences)," and, finally, "not in any way one of *my* past selves – just an ancestral self." [...] [Parfit next briefly describes a second kind of being, which alternately divides into two beings (as in the divided brain case) and then fuses with another beings (as in the case of 'fusion') every six months.]

m⟩→ But let us look, finally, at a third kind of being.

In this world there is neither division nor union. There are a number of everlasting bodies, which gradually change in appearance. And direct psychological relations, as before, hold only over limited periods of time. This can be illustrated with a third diagram (figure 2). In this diagram the two shadings represent the degrees of psychological connectedness to their two central points.

These beings could not use the way of thinking that we have proposed. Since there is no branching of psychological continuity, they would have to

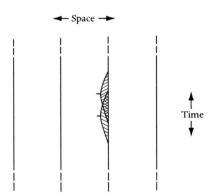

Figure 2

regard themselves as immortal. It might be said that this is what they are. But there is, I suggest, a better description.

Our beings would have one reason for thinking of themselves as immortal. The parts of each "line" are all psychologically continuous. But the parts of each "line" are not all psychologically connected. Direct psychological relations hold only between those parts which are close to each other in time. This gives our beings a reason for *not* thinking of each "line" as corresponding to one single life. For if they did, they would have no way of implying these direct relations. When a speaker says, for example, "I spent a period doing such and such," his hearers would not be entitled to assume that the speaker has any memories of this period, that his character then and now are in any way similar, that he is now carrying out any of the plans or intentions which he then had, and so forth. Because the word "I" would carry none of these implications, it would not have for these "immortal" beings the usefulness which it has for us.[31]

To gain a better way of thinking, we must revise the way of thinking that we proposed above. The revision is this. The distinction between successive selves can be made by reference, not to the branching of psychological continuity, but to the degrees of psychological connectedness. Since this connectedness is a matter of degree, the drawing of these distinctions can be left to the choice of the speaker and be allowed to vary from context to context.

On this way of thinking, the word "I" can be used to imply the greatest degree of psychological connectedness. When the connections are reduced, when there has been any marked change of character or style of life, or any marked loss of memory, our imagined beings would say, "It was not I who did that, but an earlier self." They could then describe in what ways, and to what degree, they are related to this earlier self.

This revised way of thinking would suit not only our "immortal" beings. It is also the way in which we ourselves could think about our lives. And it is, I suggest, surprisingly natural.

One of its features, the distinction between successive selves, has already been used by several writers. To give an example, from Proust: "we are incapable, while we are in love, of acting as fit predecessors of the next persons who, when we are in love no longer, we shall presently have become...."[32]

Although Proust distinguished between successive selves, he still thought of one person as being these different selves. This we would not do on the way of thinking that I propose. If I say, "It will not be me, but one of my future selves," I do not imply that I will be that future self. He is one of

---

[31]   Cf. Austin Duncan Jones, "Man's Mortality," *Analysis*, 28 (1967–1968), 65–70.

[32]   *Within a Budding Grove* (London, 1949), I, 226 (my own translation).

my later selves, and I am one of his earlier selves. There is no underlying person who we both are.

To point out another feature of this way of thinking. When I say, "There is no person who we both are," I am only giving my decision. Another person could say, "It will be you," thus deciding differently. There is no question of either of these decisions being a mistake. Whether to say "I," or "one of my future selves," or "a descendant self" is entirely a matter of choice. The matter of fact, which must be agreed, is only whether the disjunction applies. (The question "Are X and Y the same person?" thus becomes "Is X *at least* an ancestral [or descendant] self of Y?")

VI

I have tried to show that what matters in the continued existence of a person are, for the most part, relations of degree. And I have proposed a way of thinking in which this would be recognized.

I shall end by suggesting two consequences and asking one question.

It is sometimes thought to be especially rational to act in our own best interests. But I suggest that the principle of self-interest has no force. There are only two genuine competitors in this particular field. One is the principle of biased rationality: do what will best achieve what you actually want. The other is the principle of impartiality: do what is in the best interests of everyone concerned.

The apparent force of the principle of self-interest derives, I think, from these two other principles.

The principle of self-interest is normally supported by the principle of biased rationality. This is because most people care about their own future interests.

Suppose that this prop is lacking. Suppose that a man does not care what happens to him in, say, the more distant future. To such a man, the principle of self-interest can only be propped up by an appeal to the principle of impartiality. We must say, "Even if you don't care, you ought to take what happens to you then equally into account." But for this, as a special claim, there seem to me no good arguments. It can only be supported as part of the general claim, "You ought to take what happens to everyone equally into account."[33]

The special claim tells a man to grant an *equal* weight to all the parts of his future. The argument for this can only be that all the parts of his future are *equally* parts of *his* future. This is true. But it is a truth too superficial to bear the weight of the argument. (To give an analogy: The unity of a nation is, in its nature, a matter of degree. It is therefore only a superficial truth that all of

---

[33] Cf. Thomas Nagel's *The Possibility of Altruism* (Oxford, 1970), in which the special claim is in effect defended as part of the general claim.

a man's compatriots are *equally* his compatriots. This truth cannot support a good argument for nationalism.)[34]

I have suggested that the principle of self-interest has no strength of its own. If this is so, there is no special problem in the fact that what we ought to do can be against our interests. There is only the general problem that it may not be what we want to do.

The second consequence which I shall mention is implied in the first. Egoism, the fear not of near but of distant death, the regret that so much of one's *only* life should have gone by – these are not, I think, wholly natural or instinctive. They are all strengthened by the beliefs about personal identity which I have been attacking. If we give up these beliefs, they should be weakened.

My final question is this. These emotions are bad, and if we weaken them we gain. But can we achieve this gain without, say, also weakening loyalty to, or love of, other particular selves? As Hume warned, the "refined reflections which philosophy suggests . . . cannot diminish . . . our vicious passions . . . without diminishing . . . such as are virtuous. They are . . . applicable to all our affections. In vain do we hope to direct their influence only to one side."[35]

That hope *is* vain. But Hume had another: that more of what is bad depends upon false belief. This is also my hope.

Commentary on Parfit

On first reading Parfit's paper, you might wonder why we should care about the increasingly bizarre thought-experiments he presents. Stories about brains being split in half and housed in two different bodies are pretty far-fetched as it is; but we also have imaginary beings who divide routinely, and even 'immortal' beings. What light can all this possibly shed on the nature of actual, mortal, non-dividing beings like us?

The answer implicit in Parfit's discussion is that it is precisely by examining our intuitions about such cases that we come to a better understanding of issues that really matter to us: whether it is more rational to be concerned with what happens to oneself in the future than to be concerned with what happens to other people, and whether we should find the fact that we will eventually die depressing. Of course,

---

[34] The unity of a nation we seldom take for more than what it is. This is partly because we often think of nations, not as units, but in a more complex way. If we thought of ourselves in the way that I proposed, we might be less likely to take our own identity for more than what it is. We are, for example, sometimes told, "It is irrational to act against your own interests. After all, it will be *you* who will regret it." To this we could reply, "No, not me. Not even one of my future selves. Just a descendant self."

[35] "The Sceptic," in "Essays Moral, Political and Literary," *Hume's Moral and Political Philosophy* (New York, 1959), p. 349.

whether or not Parfit really does succeed in shedding any light on these issues is up for dispute; none the less, the fact that Parfit himself thinks he does succeed should make you think again if your first reaction to the text was, 'how can all this science fiction possibly tell us anything interesting about how things *actually* are?'

Introduction

In the short introductory section, Parfit identifies two very widely-held beliefs which are going to be the targets of his paper. The first is that every question of the form, 'is X, at time 1, the same person as Y at time 2?' must have an answer. The second is that there are 'important questions' that cannot be answered in the absence of an answer to a question of the first kind.

> 1. Parfit says at $\boxed{a}\!\!\to$: 'Our criteria for the identity of [nations and machines] do not cover certain cases'. Say in your own words what he means by this, and illustrate the claim with as realistic and convincing an example as you can. (It doesn't have to involve a nation or a machine; a house, say, would do just as well.)

Section I

Parfit starts by claiming, at $\boxed{b}\!\!\to$, that if my brain were transplanted into someone else's body, the 'resulting person' would be *me*, on the grounds that they would have 'my character and apparent memories of my life'. He is thus clearly presupposing that our criteria for identity across time for persons are *psychological* criteria.

Parfit next considers the divided-brain case (problem 3 in the introduction to this chapter). His argument runs roughly as follows. Suppose that the question, 'which, out of B and C (each of whom wakes up after the operation with half of A's brain) is the same person as A?', has an answer. Then the answer must be one of these:

1) Neither: A ceases to exist, and two new persons (B and C) come into existence, neither of whom is A.
2) Exactly one of B and C. (Either B is the same person as A, and C is not; or C is the same person as A, and B is not.)
3) The 'sum' of B and C. After the operation there is really one person (A) with two bodies. So B and C are not in fact two distinct *people* at all.

Parfit spends most of section I arguing that none of the three possible answers is plausible.

> 2. How exactly does Parfit's discussion at $\boxed{c}\!\!\to$ of the maths exam fit into this argument?
> 3. At $\boxed{d}\!\!\to$, Parfit says that 'we need to prize apart' survival and identity. Explain in your own words what he means and why he thinks this is the moral that ought to be drawn from the divided-brain case.

Section II

The central thesis which Parfit wants us to agree with so far is the claim that person *A* at time 1 can in principle 'survive as' two *different* people – *B* and *C* – at time 2. Clearly, Parfit thinks that 'survival' is an important notion; and, equally clearly, survival has something to do with *psychological continuity.*

The central distinction you need to grasp in order to make sense of this section is the distinction between a relation that is 'logically one–one' and a relation that is 'in fact one–one'. As we have already seen, identity is logically one–one. If person *A* at time 1 is the same person as *B* at time 2, and is also the same person as *C* at time 2, it follows that *B* and *C* are the same person: we have one person at time 2, and not two. We have also seen, from the divided-brain case, that Parfit thinks that *survival is not* logically one–one: *A* can 'survive as' two *different* people, *B* and *C*. While *B* and *C* are different people, it would be very odd to say that *A* has ceased to exist, since *B* and *C* each have *A*'s character traits and apparent memories; hence *A* survives as, but is not identical with, each of *B* and *C*.

However, as Parfit says at $\boxed{e} \mapsto$, Wiggins' case is 'unlikely to occur. The relations which matter are, in fact, one–one'. The relations which matter, for Parfit, are evidently psychological relations: what matters is *psychological continuity.* Since *in fact* nobody ever gets their brain split in half and housed in two new bodies, we are never actually faced with a situation where one person at an earlier time gets to be psychologically continuous with two different people at a later time; they only ever get to bear the relevant psychological relations to *one* person at a later time. So the relations that matter are *in fact* one–one, but not (as Parfit thinks the divided-brain case demonstrates) *logically* one–one.

One of Parfit's main claims in this section is, in effect, that 'we use the language of personal identity in order to imply [psychological] continuity' ($\boxed{f} \mapsto$). When we say that person *A* at time 1 is identical with person *B* at time 2, we imply (*inter alia*) that *B* is psychologically continuous with *B*. Because *in fact* we are never confronted with cases of 'branching' psychological continuity, as with the split-brain case, the language of identity serves us pretty well; we are not forced into absurd consequences, as we would be if split-brain operations were freely available on the National Health Service. But we should not be misled by this into thinking that it is really *identity,* as opposed to psychological continuity, that is what is important.

The other central claim of this section is that the split-brain case should not drive us towards the view that actually it is sameness of body, rather than psychological continuity, that is what is really important.

5. At $\boxed{g} \mapsto$, Parfit describes a principle put forward by Williams. (i) Describe in your own words exactly how the principle applies in the divided-brain case (see the paragraph immediately following the statement of the principle). (ii) Describe the two different conclusions that Williams and Parfit draw from its application. (iii) Which conclusion seems most plausible to you? Why?

Section III

In this section, Parfit aims to establish that 'psychological relations' can be understood in a way that does not appeal to facts about personal identity. The objection he is aiming to meet is the 'circularity objection': problem 2 in the introduction to this chapter. Let's first get clear on what he means by 'psychological relations'. Imagine that, last weekend, you formed the intention to go to Paris this weekend; and imagine that you did, in fact, go to Paris this weekend. You thereby *realized* your intention to go to Paris: there is a relation between your intending to go and your actually going. Or imagine that you are now remembering going shopping last Saturday. Then there is a relation between your current state of mind – what we might call your 'memory-experience' – and your previous experience of going shopping.

We have already seen what the circularity objection amounts to in the case of memory: it seems to be a conceptual truth that you can only remember your own experiences, and so we cannot appeal to memory to fix facts about personal identity. The same point applies to other psychological relations – intentions, for example. If *you* intend to go to Paris, then it is a conceptual truth that only you can realize that intention: nobody else's going to Paris could possibly count as realizing or carrying out *your* intention to go.

Parfit attempts to meet the circularity objection by defining psychological relations whose obtaining does not conceptually require that the persons standing, as it were, on each end of the relation are the same person, and by claiming that it is the obtaining of *these* relations that one can appeal to in one's account of personal identity – or (more importantly for Parfit) in one's account of survival.

Parfit's response to the circularity objection is the focus of Schechtman's paper, so we shall return to it in the next commentary; for now, we'll just give an illustration of the kind of thing Parfit has in mind.

Imagine that, far in the future, a company, Rekall, offers 'memory implants' to its customers. (We have borrowed this from the Philip K. Dick short story, 'We Can Remember It for You Wholesale', later made into the film *Total Recall*.) It can be pleasant, on a cold, rainy night, to reminisce about that wonderful beach holiday you had in the Bahamas, when you snorkelled in the warm sea, sunbathed, drank cocktails under tropical palm trees while the sun set, and so on. But what if you could somehow enjoy just the same 'memories' without having gone to the expense of actually taking the holiday? This is the service Rekall offers: 'memories' of holidays and other happy events that you never actually experienced are implanted into your brain.

Now imagine an extra twist. Imagine that it is prohibitively expensive – or perhaps just impossible – to actually *invent* all these apparent memories from scratch. It's much cheaper for the company to take someone else's *actual* memories – someone who actually had a very nice holiday in the Bahamas – and transfer them from their mind into the customers' minds. So when you 'remember' the holiday, what is going on in your mind – your memory-experience – is exactly like what is going on in the mind of the person who actually had the holiday when she remembers the holiday. But of course you do not genuinely *remember* the holiday, because the experiences you are 'remembering' were not yours but somebody else's.

Imagine that you become hooked on memory-implants: you keep going back for more and more of them, so that eventually you start losing track of which of your apparent memories are really memories and which aren't. By 'apparent memories' we here mean just what Parfit (following Sydney Shoemaker) means by a 'q-memory' ('q' for 'quasi'). An apparent memory *might* be a real memory – you might be recalling an experience that *you* originally had. Or it might not be: it might have been implanted, and somebody else originally had the experience. If you did start to lose track, Parfit thinks you would be in the position described at $\boxed{h}\!\!\mapsto$. You might have to work out – by consulting an old diary, say – whether or not a particular q-memory is a q-memory of your own experience, or of somebody else's.

To sum up: Parfit thinks that psychological relations – q-remembering, q-intending, and so on – can be used to characterize, non-circularly, a notion of psychological continuity. And we can then use that notion of psychological continuity to characterize survival (or, if we wanted to, personal identity – though Parfit takes himself to have given good reasons already not to want to do that.)

> 6. Do you think that the story about 'memory'-implants (or rather, q-memory implants) is coherent? If not, why not? If you do think it's coherent, do you think *any* memory whatsoever could in principle be implanted into someone else, or could only certain kinds of memory be implanted?

Section IV

In this section, we finally get to understand what Parfit's talk about 'relations of degree' is all about. In this section, his aim – as stated at $\boxed{i}\!\!\mapsto$ – is to show that we *need* to be able to think of survival as a matter of degree, and he demonstrates this by using an imaginary example involving 'branching' beings.

> 7. Explain how the 'branching beings' example is supposed to show that survival can be a matter of degree.

At $\boxed{j}\!\!\mapsto$, Parfit draws an important distinction between 'psychological continuity' and 'psychological connectedness'.

> 8. (i) Explain, in the light of problem 1 described in the introduction to this chapter, why Parfit needs to draw this distinction. (ii) Parfit says at $\boxed{k}\!\!\mapsto$ that, for the branching beings, 'connectedness is a more important element in survival' than is continuity. Do you agree? Why or why not?

Section V

Parfit describes a different kind of imaginary being in this section: the immortal beings. (In the original version of the paper, there are also two other examples: 'fusing' beings in section IV, fusing-and-dividing beings in section V.) By this stage, you might be wondering what the point of all this is. Parfit is no longer arguing, or at least not obviously, for or against a particular identifiable philosophical position. So what *is* he doing?

Well, what he is interested in, in these admittedly bizarre cases, is what kinds of ways of thinking and talking the imagined beings might need to adopt in order to express things that are important to them. For example, the dividing beings cannot use the language of identity (recall the moral of section I); Parfit suggests at $\boxed{l}\mapsto$ that they might instead use expressions like 'an ancestral self of mine' to denote continuity, and 'a past self of mine' to denote connectedness. Parfit's overall purpose (we think) is to wean us off our addiction to thinking that there is something inherently special about *identity*. Unlike dividing beings, personal identity talk is *coherent* for us, over long periods of time – indeed over a whole human lifetime – because we do not divide. But it doesn't follow that thinking in terms of personal identity is the *best* way for us to think about our own case.

The case of the 'immortal' beings (at $\boxed{m}\mapsto$) illustrates this point. Such a being (call him 'S') *can* think of himself as immortal (just as *we* can think of him as immortal). He can coherently use the word 'I' to refer to someone (call him 'T') who existed hundreds of years ago but who is psychologically continuous with S. But Parfit thinks this would not be a very 'useful' way in which to think. (This is why 'immortal' is in scare quotes: Parfit thinks the beings would *not* think of themselves as immortal.) S cannot q-remember any of T's experiences, for example. S's attitude to T would presumably be one of detached interest – much like our attitude to the past actions of our own great-grandparents, say. We are especially interested in what they (as opposed to other people's great-grandparents) got up to because they are *our* ancestors, but we do not attempt to carry out their intentions, we do not feel remorse for their actions, and so on.

At $\boxed{n}\mapsto$, Parfit suggests that we could think of our own lives in much the same way as (he claims) the 'immortal' beings would think about *their* lives – indeed, it would be 'surprisingly natural'.

---

9. Imagine that human beings only had a memory-span of five years. (i) What kinds of differences (for example, practical, emotional, moral differences), if any, would that make to us? (ii) Do you think we would then regard connectedness (which comes in degrees) as more important than continuity (which is all-or-nothing)? (iii) Do you think we would regard the language of personal identity as just as important as most of us actually regard it? (iv) Now thinking about how we *actually* are, do you think Parfit is right to say that it is 'surprisingly natural' for us to think about our lives in the way that he claims the 'immortal' beings would think about their lives?

Section VI

Parfit finally returns to a claim made at the beginning of the paper: that belief in the special nature of personal identity has bad effects. We would be better off if we thought of 'what matters in the continued existence of a person' as 'relations of degree' $\boxed{\text{O}}\mapsto$.

10. (i) Describe in your own words the two consequences which Parfit thinks this new way of thinking would have. (ii) Do you think there would be any consequences of this way of thinking that might be bad for us? (iii) Parfit ends the paper with a question. What is he worried about? What do you think is the answer to the question?

Marya Schechtman, 'Personhood and Personal Identity'*

The question 'Who am I?' might be asked either by an amnesia victim or by a confused adolescent, and requires a different answer in each of these contexts. In the former case, the questioner is asking which history her life is a continuation of, and, in the latter, the questioner presumably knows her history but is asking which of the beliefs, values, and desires that she seems to have are truly her own, expressive of who she is. These can be called, respectively, the *question of reidentification* and the *question of self-knowledge*. Contemporary philosophical discussion of what has been called the problem of personal identity is generally considered to be concerned with the question of reidentification. Those involved in this discussion say virtually nothing about the self-knowledge question. Instead, they attempt to spell out the necessary and sufficient conditions for saying that a person at time t_1 is the same person as a person at time t_2 – to give criteria of personal identity over time which would enable us to answer the amnesiac's question.

The primary contenders for a criterion of personal identity have been the bodily criterion and the psychological criterion, which are based, respectively, on the intuitions that it is sameness of body and sameness of personality which are responsible for sameness of person. Of these two, the psychological criterion has been by far the more widely accepted, and

*At all stages of this paper, I was greatly helped by discussion with friends and colleagues. I would like especially to thank Stanley Cavell, Juliet Floyd, Hannah Ginsborg, Dorothy Grover, Anil Gupta, Nick Pappas, Tim Scanlon, Miriam Solomon, Paul Teller, Jennifer Whiting, and the editors of the Journal.

current philosophical discussion of personal identity has focused almost exclusively on attempts to refine and defend this criterion.

In what follows, I shall argue that psychological continuity does not and cannot provide the sort of criterion of personal identity which identity theorists wish to provide. My claim will be that such criteria are inherently circular – that they cannot answer the circularity objection that is standardly raised against them in the literature, and hence cannot provide an analysis of our concept of the persistence of a person.

I shall start, in section I, by giving an exposition of the central features of these psychological-continuity theories. To do this, I shall look in detail at Derek Parfit's[1] version of this theory, and shall use Parfit as a representative of psychological-continuity theorists throughout the paper. I choose Parfit for three reasons. First, his view is, for my purposes, perfectly representative. There is no argument I make against Parfit which could not be applied to any other standard psychological-continuity theory without significant alteration. Second, Parfit's view is one of the strongest versions of this theory, and, finally, it is the version of the psychological-continuity theory which has been most discussed in the recent literature.

After laying out Parfit's view in section I, I proceed, in section II, to describe the circularity objection that has standardly been raised against such views, and the standard response as offered by Parfit. In section II, I shall argue that this response relies implicitly on a highly implausible view of human experience, and that when this view is made explicit it becomes clear that not only does the standard response fail to overcome the circularity objection, but that this objection cannot be overcome, that psychological accounts of identity, to be accurate, must be circular. Finally, in section IV, I shall suggest that the dead end that psychological-continuity theorists have encountered is a result of their conflating the two questions of personal identity outlined above – the reidentification and self-knowledge questions – and suggest what I believe to be a more fruitful direction for philosophical work on personal identity to take.

I

Parfit begins the statement of his version of the psychological-continuity theory with some preliminary definitions. The first is of *direct psychological connections*, which are connections of the following sort: that between a memory and the experience of which it is a memory, that between an intention and the later act in which it is carried out, and the persistence of a belief, desire, or other psychological feature (205–6). Parfit goes on to define a second relation:

---

[1] *Reasons and Persons* (New York: Oxford, 1984); page references in the text are to this book.

[a] →   *"Psychological connectedness* is the holding of particular direct psychological connections." He then says that "we can claim that there is enough connectedness [for personal identity] if the number of connections over any day, is *at least half* the number of direct connections that hold, over every day, in the lives of nearly every actual person. When there are enough direct connections, there is what I call *strong* connectedness" (206). He thus takes as the criterion of personal identity over time,

> The Psychological Criterion: (1) There is *psychological continuity* if and only if there are overlapping chains of strong connectedness. X today is one and the same person as Y at some past time if and only if (2) X is psychologically continuous with Y, (3) this continuity has the right kind of cause, and (4) there does not exist a different person who is also psychologically continuous with Y. (5) Personal identity over time just consists in the holding of facts like (2) to (4). (207)

It is worth considering just what information this criterion is supposed to provide.

Identity theorists take it for granted that we can, in ordinary circumstances, make accurate judgments of personal identity. What they wish to determine is what it is which underlies these judgments. Parfit says that, by 'the criterion of personal identity over time', he means "*what this identity necessarily involves, or consists in*" (203). These theorists are trying to give us an analysis of our concept of personal identity, and so the criterion that they provide will not only have to capture our intuitive notion of personal identity, but it will have to do so in terms more basic. Parfit acknowledges

[b] →   this when he argues that the physical and psychological criteria as he has defined them,

> ... are both *Reductionist*. They are both Reductionist because they claim (1) that the fact of a person's identity over time just consists in the holding of certain more particular facts,
>
> and
>
> (2) that these facts can be described without either presupposing the identity of this person, or explicitly claiming that the experiences in this person's life are had by this person, or even explicitly claiming that this person exists. These facts can be described in an *impersonal* way. (210)

Parfit is attempting to give an identity criterion that does not employ facts about persons or their identities in its specification, because if such facts were included then this criterion would not provide an analysis of the appropriate sort. It is in the context of this understanding of the project of giving an identity criterion that the circularity objection that I shall discuss in the next section has its force.

II

The circularity objection as it is standardly raised is an adaptation of an objection that was originally raised against John Locke by Bishop Butler. Butler's objection is roughly as follows: memory connectedness seems like a plausible criterion of personal identity, because, properly speaking, we can remember only our own experiences. We can *seem* to remember experiences which are not ours, however, and such seeming memories are no basis for claims of personal identity. A madman may think he remembers leading the troops at Waterloo, but this does not make him Napoleon. Therefore, if memory connectedness is to be a criterion of personal identity, we must have some way of distinguishing between real and merely apparent memory. But that distinction, the argument continues, is no more than this: real memories are apparent memories in which the person remembering is the person who actually had the experience. The obvious problem with the memory criterion of personal identity, then, is that one must already have a criterion of personal identity in order to define memory. Butler argues that, since the fact of identity is prior to the distinction between real and apparent memory, personal identity cannot be defined in terms of memory connectedness.

Psychological-continuity theorists consider a version of this objection, which addresses more general psychological accounts of identity. Parfit indicates that he takes Butler's objection to apply to his psychological-continuity theory when he says:

> On one interpretation, the objection would be this: 'It is part of our concept of memory that we can remember only *our own* experiences. The continuity of memory therefore presupposes personal identity. The same is therefore true of your Relation R [non-branching psychological continuity]. You claim that personal identity just consists in the holding of Relation R. This must be false if Relation R itself presupposes personal identity'. (220)

To defend his psychological criterion, then, Parfit needs to show that none of the connections that constitute psychological continuity – memory connections, the connections between an intention and the action that carries it out, or between the temporal parts of a persistent psychological feature – presupposes facts about personal identity.

Before looking at Parfit's response to this objection, it is worth considering why these other connections might be taken to presuppose personal identity. The objection holds that delusional memories are distinguished from real memories by the nonidentity of the rememberer with the person who had the remembered experience, and thus that when we talk about a genuine memory connection we have already presupposed the persistence of a single individual. The case is similar with the connection between intentions and the actions in which they are realized.

It seems to be part of our conception of intention that I can only properly be said to intend actions that I can reasonably believe it is in my power to undertake. If I am sane and rational, I cannot, in ordinary circumstances, intend to leap tall buildings in a single bound, though I may fantasize about doing so. Similarly, I cannot intend the actions of other people, because they are not under my control. An intention, then, is necessarily an intention that *I* do something, and so it seems that an action will count as the action that carries out an intention only if the same person who forms the intention takes the action. In this way, the connection between an intention and the action in which it is realized seems to presuppose the persistence of a single person.

We do sometimes speak as if we could frame intentions for others. I may, having asked someone to bring me a book, and finding that she has brought the wrong book, say something like, 'That's not the one I intended for you to bring'. Here, I think, this phrase is an abbreviation for 'That's not the one I intended to direct you to bring', and so the intention in question is still an intention that *I* do something. Even if we do not take such phrases to be abbreviations, however, and do admit that we can form intentions for others, it is clear that the only connections between intentions and actions which are going to be relevant to identity over time are those in which I intend that *I* do something, and *I* carry the intention out, and so the connections that concern us between intentions and the actions that carry them out seem to presuppose the persistence of a single person.

The connections between the different temporal parts of a persistent belief, desire, or other psychological feature seem to presuppose identity in a slightly different way. The problem here seems to be that our saying that we have the same belief or desire at two different times requires not only that there are occurrent beliefs or desires at these two times with the same content, but also that these two occurrent beliefs or desires be had by the same person. Countless people can have beliefs and desires that could be described as having roughly the same content, but this connection does not seem relevant to questions of personal identity. The fact that I believe we should avoid an all-out nuclear war at all costs makes me, in this respect, more *like* all the other people who hold that belief, but it seems irrelevant to the question of identifying me with them. Certainly the fact that someone now holds this belief and someone in the future holds this belief does not, in the absence of any further information, give me any information as to whether or not these two people should be identified. My continuing belief that we should avoid nuclear war is not, therefore, relevant to my persistence through time only because it guarantees that my later self will hold beliefs *like* my earlier self, but because the claim that the *same* belief has persisted presupposes that I have continued to exist.

Butler's objection, then, can be expanded to an objection against psychological-continuity theories. In the case of each psychological connection, qualitative identity of the contents of consciousness is not enough to capture what is relevant to personal identity. It is not enough that the madman's memory is qualitatively like Napoleon's experience, that an action taken by someone else can be described as qualitatively like the action I intended, or that my fellow peace lover's belief that we should avoid nuclear war is qualitatively like mine. Something more must be added to this qualitative similarity to make genuine psychological connections. This something more seems to be persistence of a single individual through the two temporal parts of the connection, and this makes relation R look circular.

Parfit's response to this objection derives from a commonly used strategy in the contemporary literature. To give a noncircular identity criterion he must give an account of the distinction between genuine and merely apparent psychological connections which does not appeal to facts about personal identity. Like other psychological-continuity theorists, he attempts to make out this distinction in terms of the cause of the later state. He starts with memory, and says of Butler's objection:

> To answer this objection, we can define a wider concept, *quasi-memory*. I have an accurate quasi-memory of a past experience if
>
> (1)   I seem to remember having an experience,
> (2)   *someone* did have this experience,
>
> and
>
> (3)   my apparent memory is causally dependent, in the right kind of way, on that past experience. (220)

This notion, he says, will answer the objection by giving us a way to distinguish between the kind of apparent memory that is relevant to personal identity and the kind that is not, without appealing to facts about the persistence of persons. Parfit does not explicitly define quasi desires, quasi beliefs, or quasi intentions, but he does recognize their importance within his view, and suggests that they can be specified in the same way that quasi memory is (226).

In the next section, I shall argue that, though quasi states seem initially like a plausible solution to the circularity objection, on deeper reflection it is by no means clear exactly how we are actually to imagine such states, and that on any understanding these states cannot do the work they are supposed to without implicitly presupposing an unacceptably superficial view of the nature of experience. Before turning to my argument, though, it is necessary to consider in a little more depth just how quasi states are supposed to help defend psychological-continuity theories, and to clarify some of the terminology that will be used in what follows. Here I shall

discuss mostly memory connections, but anything I say can be extended to
the other connections that make up psychological continuity as well.

[d] → The circularity objection is based on the claim that it is part of the
definition of memory that we can only properly be said to remember our
own experiences. In acknowledging the need to respond to this objection,
identity theorists implicitly accept this definition of memory, and, in offering
quasi memory as a response to the objection, they implicitly claim that it is
not this fact about memory which makes memory connectedness a plausible
criterion of personal identity. If, as they claim, quasi-memory connectedness
will do just as well as genuine memory in specifying an identity criterion,
then it must be the case that whatever it is about memory which makes it a
central part of what constitutes personal identity is also present in quasi
memory. It follows, then, that it cannot be the fact that memory presupposes the identity of the rememberer with the person who had the experience that underlies the crucial role that memory is taken to play in the
constitution of personal identity.

Part of what is behind this conviction, I think, is a conflation of what I
take to be two separate issues: the nondelusionality of a memory, and its
relevance to the constitution of personal identity. The circularity objection
itself relies on a claim that memory, by definition, presupposes personal
identity. The examples that are given to support this claim, however, rely on
the need to use personal identity to distinguish between delusional and
nondelusional memories (e.g., between the madman's apparent memory of
Waterloo and Napoleon's), and this distinction is a slightly different one.

In defending the use of quasi memory, psychological-continuity theorists
present arguments to show that such connections can provide us with a way
of capturing the nondelusionality of a genuine memory without the presupposition of personal identity. I shall argue that this does not yet show us
that quasi memories capture what is relevant to personal identity in genuine
memory, and that this cannot be captured without the presupposition of
personal identity. Before making these arguments, though, it is important to
have a clear view of how it is that quasi memories are thought to be
nondelusional.

The idea, I believe, is this. What makes the madman's apparent memory
of Waterloo delusional is not simply the fact that an apparent memory with
this qualitative content occurs in his psyche, but rather the fact that he takes
this apparent memory to be of an experience that he had. To just have an
apparent memory with this content and remain agnostic about whose
experience is being remembered would not be to have a delusion on this
[e] → view, even if the quasi rememberer has had no experience that corresponds
in content to the quasi memory. The distinction that is being made, then,
can be described as follows: to have a *memory*, is to have an apparent memory
of an experience that one actually had, and to take it (correctly) to be one's
own experience. To have a *delusion* is to have an apparent memory of an

experience that one did not in fact have, and to take it (incorrectly) to be one's own. To have a *quasi memory* is to have an apparent memory (properly caused) and to hold no view about whose memory it is.[2] Insofar, then, as this last case describes a nondelusional apparent memory, quasi memory seems to give us a way of specifying nondelusionality without reference to sameness of person.

That this is the kind of categorization that identity theorists have in mind can be seen in the example of quasi memory that Parfit gives. After giving his definition of quasi memory he says: "We do not quasi-remember other people's past experiences. But we might begin to do so. . . . Suppose that . . . neuro-surgeons develop ways to create in one brain a copy of a memory-trace in another brain. This might enable us to quasi-remember other people's past experiences" (220). He then goes on to offer an example, the story of Jane and Paul, in order to show that it is possible for one person to have another person's memory nondelusionally. We are to imagine that Jane has copies of some of Paul's memory traces implanted in her brain, and shortly thereafter has a new vivid set of apparent memories of experiences that she knows she never had. In particular, she has an extremely vivid memory of a storm in Venice and of a bolt of lightning hitting the bell tower of San Giorgio, though she has never been to Venice. On asking Paul, she discovers that he did have exactly such an experience. Parfit concludes: "Given all of this, Jane should not dismiss her apparent memory as a delusion. She ought to conclude that she has an accurate quasi-memory of how this flash of lightning looked to Paul" (221). Jane, then, has an accurate recreation of the qualitative content of Paul's memory of seeing the flash of lightning, and it is (by Parfit's definition), appropriately caused. This qualitative similarity is to be taken quite seriously; we are really to think of Jane as having Paul's memory exactly recreated, and, in regard to this one incident, experiencing exactly the inner state Paul would in a genuine memory.

Having set up the example, Parfit immediately considers the objection that for Jane to be given Paul's memory in this way would amount to her having a delusion, and he dismisses it. He says: "It may be claimed: 'Since Jane seems to remember *seeing* the lightning, she seems to remember *herself* seeing the lightning. Her apparent memory may tell her accurately what Paul's experience was like, but it tells her, falsely, that it was *she* who had this experience' " (221). If this objection stands, then quasi memory will be no help against the circularity objection. But Parfit has a response. He says:

f → Because we do not have quasi-memories of other people's past experiences, our apparent memories do not merely come to us in the first-person mode. They come with a belief that, unless they are delusions, they are about our

2 I am extremely grateful to Paul Teller both for suggesting the necessity of laying out this distinction, and for his helpful comments in formulating it.

own experiences. But in the case of experience-memories, this is a separable belief. If like Jane we had quasi-memories of other people's past experiences, these apparent memories would cease to be automatically combined with this belief. (222)

This, then, supports my claim that quasi memory is thought to avoid the problems of the circularity objection because it can characterize a nondelusional memory without reference to personal identity.

In the remainder of this paper, I shall argue that quasi memory fails to do the work it is supposed to, avoiding the circularity objection because relations between the specification of the qualitative content of a memory, presuppositions about the identity of the rememberer, and the issue of nondelusionality are far more complex than identity theorists recognize. I shall argue that simply deleting the "nametag" from a memory is not sufficient to make it nondelusional, and that in order to make an apparent memory truly nondelusional one will either have to presuppose the identity of the rememberer with the person who had the experience, or else remove so much of the content of the memory that it is no longer plausible to say that what is relevant to personal identity in genuine memory is preserved in quasi memory. So I shall argue that not only do quasi states not fulfil the role that they are supposed to, but furthermore that they cannot – that there is no way to capture what is relevant to personal identity in memories without presupposing identity.

III

I shall start my argument with a detailed look at an example offered by Edward Casey in his book, *Remembering: A Phenomenological Study,*[3] where he describes one of his own memories. If we ask what would happen if this memory experience were given as a quasi memory, the limitations of quasi states will become clearer. Casey recalls a memory of a recent family outing:

> I recall going to the movie *Small Change* a few weeks ago – exactly when, I am not certain. After dinner nearby at Clark's, my two young children, my wife, and I had walked briskly over to the Lincoln Theater, stopping briefly at a paperback bookstore on the way. Anticipating a large crowd, we arrived early and were among the first to purchase tickets. There ensued a wait that seemed much longer than the ten or fifteen minutes it actually was. The children were especially restive and had difficulty staying in the line that had formed – Erin attempting some gymnastic tricks on the guardrail by the entrance, Eric looking at the posted list of coming attractions. Finally the doors were flung open, and we entered at the head of what was, by then, a considerable line. Once inside, we

---

[3]   Bloomington: Indiana UP, 1987.

sought seats approximately in the middle of the theater, settled there, and interchanged positions a couple of times to adjust to the height of those sitting in front of us. The lights dimmed, and *Small Change* began directly. (Or was there not a short feature first? – I cannot say for sure.) The film was in French, with English subtitles. I have only a vague recollection of the spoken words; in fact, I cannot remember any single word or phrase, though I certainly remember the characters *as speaking*. The same indefiniteness applies to the subtitles, at which I furtively glanced when unable to follow the French. Of the music in the film I have no memory at all – indeed, not just of *what* it was but *whether* there was any music at all. In contrast with this, I retain a very vivid visual image of the opening scene, in which a stream of school children are viewed rushing home, seemingly in a downhill direction all the way. Two other scenes also stand out in my present recollection: an infant's fall from the window of a high-rise apartment (the twenty-ninth floor?) and the male teacher (whose name, along with all others in the film, I have forgotten) lecturing passionately to his class about child-abuse. Interspersed between these scenes is a medley of less vividly recalled episodes, ranging from fairly distinct (the actions of a child-abusing mother) to quite indistinct (e.g., children's recitations in the classroom). While I am recollecting this uneven and incomplete sequence of filmic incidents, I find myself at the same time remembering my own children's ongoing reactions to the film. I do not remember their behavior in detail but only as a kind of generalized response consisting of laughing, whispered questions, outright comments, and the like. These reactions are as intrinsic to the memory as is the unfolding of the film itself; so too is the mixture of pleasure and exasperation which I felt in being located, as it were, *between* children and film. Suddenly my memory of *Small Change* comes to an end: the lights go up, and we leave through a side exit near us, overhearing expressions of amusement and satisfaction from those around us as we walk out into the night. (ibid., pp. 25–6)

Parfit's claim is that our relation to the experiences we remember (taking them to be our own) is separable from their content, and that, if this relation is changed, we can be given someone else's memory nondelusionally. There are a number of features of Casey's memory which show this view to be problematic.

One striking difference between this example of an actual memory and the fictitious example that Parfit gives us is the detail and richness of the former as opposed to the latter. Casey's memory of the trip to see *Small Change* includes memories of his family, the restaurant where he has eaten more than once, the theater at which he has seen more than one movie, and so on. Certainly memories that consist of a striking visual image, like the memory of Venice that Parfit describes, are one sort of experience memory, but more of our memories are like the one Casey describes; they are memories of family vacations, or writing a paper, or turning thirty. These memories are much more complex due to the number of personal associations and details about the individual's life which are involved in them. Intuitively, it seems that these memories are more likely to be the sort that lend plausibility to the idea that memory connectedness is an essential feature of personal identity than memories of the sort Parfit describes, and in any event, since quasi memory is meant to provide a defense of psychological-continuity theories, memories of this richer sort will also have to be possible quasi memories.

This fact, however, commits Parfit and other identity theorists to some quite implausible views about the inner lives of persons. To see this, let us consider what it would be like for Jane to be given Casey's memory of *Small Change* as a quasi memory. The amount of personal detail that this memory includes makes it difficult to imagine Jane receiving it as a quasi memory. Some striking visual image is an experience that could, given the appropriate circumstances (i.e., if Jane had really been in that spot in Venice at that time), be had by virtually any sighted person, regardless of the rest of her psychological makeup. Casey's memory is not like that; it contains a good many elements that make reference to other parts of his life and his personality. It includes, for instance, the familiarity with the town in which he lives, the restaurant where he eats, the theater where he has seen numerous movies, and so on. His knowledge or lack of knowledge of French also plays a role. More important, perhaps, is the fact that his relationship to his children is central in what he remembers; his response to the gymnastics on the guardrail, and his mixture of pleasure and exasperation at their responses to the movie are, he says, essential parts of this memory.

These features of the memory are going to be very alien to Jane, who presumably does not have a wife, and, we may assume to make our point, does not have children. Not only will the physical locations seem unfamiliar, but so much else about the memory will seem anomalous. If Jane speaks fluent French, then the experience of reading the subtitles will be puzzling. And if she happens to have acted in this movie, or to be a musician, then her failure to recognize herself, or to remember whether there was music will be very disturbing. Furthermore, the idea of having a wife and children, as well as the interest/pride/embarrassment/concern relating to the behavior of these particular children, remembered as Erin and Eric, will be out of place in Jane's psyche.

Once we have noticed that this memory contains so many elements personal to Casey and anomalous to Jane, it is no longer easy to imagine what her quasi memory will be like. It seems to me that there are only two possibilities. The first is that Jane will reproduce all of the visual content of the memory without interpreting it as Casey does. That is, upon awakening from the quasi-memory implant surgery, Jane will have images of being in a strange restaurant, then a bookstore, then a theater, with a woman and two children whom she does not recognize, and she will also have images of seeing a movie with these people. The second alternative is that she will reproduce the memory exactly as it occurs in Casey, with all of the same personal elements and associations. Neither of these alternatives will allow quasi memory to do the work it is supposed to.

Consider the first alternative. It is, first of all, not entirely clear that this alternative is even actually possible. Our memories may not be strictly visual in the way that this alternative suggests. We should not take it for granted that Casey's remembering his family, for instance, is his having visual images of some people whom he is able to recognize. Instead he may remember them nonvisually as his wife and children, and this would be impossible to reproduce neutrally in Jane. Even if there were a way to reproduce this memory in some neutral way in Jane's consciousness, though, this alternative would fail because quasi memory of this sort would not capture what is relevant to personal identity in genuine memory connections. If so much of what this memory is to Casey is missing, if instead of a memory of a family evening out there is only a series of images, then we have little basis to say that Jane's quasi memory is qualitatively the same as Casey's memory, even though it does contain many of the same elements. Since memory is serving as a possible basis for personal identity, it seems that the personal elements, the ones that will be missing in Jane, are likely to be the most crucial.

There is good reason to question whether Jane's experience, so understood, is qualitatively like a memory at all. Phenomenologically, it will be drastically different from Casey's experience, appearing not as a coherent memory of a family outing, but as a blur of unidentifiable sights and sounds, which will make it not only unlike Casey's memory, but unlike any memory. If this quasi memory is different from Casey's experience in such a fundamental way, then we seem to have no good reason to call it a quasi memory of Casey's experience. This in turn makes it seem quite unreasonable to say that this quasi memory captures what is relevant in the connection between a genuine memory and the experience remembered.

The second possible way to imagine this case is to imagine Casey's memory reproduced in Jane exactly, with all of its personal elements. In this quasi memory, then, it will seem to Jane that these people are her wife and children; Clark's, the bookstore, and the Lincoln Theater will seem familiar, and the emotional responses to the movie and to Casey's family will seem like her own. If this is what happens, though, then it is difficult to make out Parfit's claim that the belief that an experience I remember is my experience is separable from the memory itself. If the memory must be such that I think of it as *my* family and *my* hometown, then the mineness of the experience seems to be part of the content of the memory. Parfit might respond that, whereas that is true to a point, the belief is separable at a later stage; whereas the apparent memory itself may carry the semblance of the experience being hers, on reflection Jane would be able to separate this out. This would involve her having a memory qualitatively just like Casey's, but reflecting on it and saying to herself something like, 'These people seem to be my family, so they must be the family of whoever's memory I've been given, for they certainly aren't mine'.

There are problems with this solution, too, however. The first is that it is again not clear that we are entitled to say that Jane's quasi memory is qualitatively the same as Casey's memory. Although it contains all of the same elements, there are additional elements that will be added by Jane's psyche. If Jane has no children, no spouse, never goes to movies, and has never been in Casey's hometown, then surprise and confusion are likely to accompany this quasi memory in Jane. It will seem extremely foreign, anomalous, and as if it cannot be right but must be some sort of delusion or fantasy. This is not just a memory that Jane cannot quite place; it is one that cannot, in principle, be a part of a coherent life history for her, since it contradicts what she knows about herself. A memory that is familiar and nostalgic to Casey seems foreign and fantastic to Jane. It seems quite plausible, therefore, to say that this memory, with its dimension of strangeness, is a qualitatively different experience for Jane than for Casey. If, therefore, we really wanted to reproduce the qualitative content of Casey's memory in Jane, we would not only have to recreate a great many of Casey's states in Jane, but suppress a great many of Jane's as well, and this begins to look suspiciously like replacing Jane's psychology with Casey's.

Even if we took this route, though, Parfit would still be in trouble because Jane's memory would no longer be nondelusional. We have seen that giving Jane the full content of Casey's memory requires the inclusion of facts about who has the memory. These facts, however, are false in relation to Jane, so their inclusion will make her quasi memory delusional. For Jane to experience something like Casey's memory, she will have to take his family to be her family, his town to be her town, his emotional reactions to be her emotional reactions, and so on. But these are not her family, town, and emotional reactions any more than Napoleon's troops are the madman's, and as long as Jane has to take these components of Casey's memory to be her own, there is no way to make this memory nondelusional.

This discussion has shown that quasi memory cannot do what it was devised to do, because presuppositions about who has a psychological state come in at a level deeper than the level of the connections between states; they are necessary to defining those states as well. The original circularity objection charged that specifying the connections between psychological states required appeal to facts about the identity of the person who had the states. Parfit's original response, therefore, was that he needed to find an impersonal way of differentiating between two qualitatively identical apparent states (say, the madman's memory of Waterloo and Napoleon's), one of which was genuinely connected to an earlier state and one of which was not. It was presumed that the content of the memory could be defined independently of facts about whose memory it was, and that all that was needed to avoid circularity was to show that the relevant connection of this impersonally defined memory to an impersonally defined earlier experience could also be defined impersonally. This is what Jane's case was supposed to show.

What I have argued, though, is that facts about whose memory a given memory is are an integral part of its qualitative content. Without the associations to facts about the rememberer's life and psychology which a memory ordinarily has, an experience loses so much of its content that it seems arbitrary to call it even the same apparent memory, and so to take it to be in any way relevant to questions about personal identity. If, on the other hand, the entire content of the apparent memory is reproduced, then the inclusion of the facts that allow this will guarantee that the memory is delusional. The fact, then, that presuppositions about who has a memory are inseparable from its content means that one cannot, as Parfit claims, specify nondelusionality impersonally by keeping the content of a memory and simply deleting presuppositions about whose memory it is. . . . [Schechtman next argues briefly that other quasi states – in particular, beliefs and desires – are subject to the same difficulties.]

What this discussion has shown is that, on either of the two possible pictures of what it is to have a quasi state, quasi states fail to do the work they are supposed to because they include either too little or too much of the state they reproduce. If they include too little, they do not capture what is relevant to personal identity, and if they include too much, then, unless sameness of person is assumed, they are delusional.

IV

My objection is not just an objection against quasi states, but also against the project that includes them. The attempt to give a noncircular analysis of identity over time requires that the distinction between genuine and apparent continuity be made without presuppositions about the identity or existence of the person having the states which constitute such continuity. This turns out to be impossible. My argument that quasi states cannot serve this function has not relied on any particular facts about such states as Parfit defines them; it has relied only on the fact that we cannot imagine a state qualitatively like Paul's occurring in Jane without that state being delusional. The mineness of a psychological state cannot be separated from its content, and so, to define a state that can be properly called one of the states constitutive of personal identity, we will have to presuppose the existence of a persistent person who is the subject of that state. This means that the strong noncircularity condition cannot be met, and so an analysis of personal identity of the type identity theorists wish to give is not possible.

It would certainly be unfortunate if this meant that we had to give up on psychological accounts of personal identity altogether, since the intuition that psychology and personality are essential to our identities is extremely strong. Luckily, the above discussion does not have this consequence. It does, however, require us to rethink what such criteria will be like, and what will be required of them. I would like to conclude, then, by offering a sketch of an alternative way of conceiving of what it is to give a psychological account of identity. This alternative promises to capture many of the intuitions that support Parfit's psychological-continuity theory without running into the problems which his view does. Such a view will not provide us with a reductionist analysis of personal identity of the sort that psychological-continuity theorists try to offer, but it can provide us with a great deal of insight into what is involved in the identities of persons by emphasizing rather than neglecting the complexities of our psyches.

In order to understand this alternative better, it is helpful to return to the issues that I raised at the beginning of this paper. There I suggested that the problems that psychological-continuity theorists encountered could be explained by their conflation of the two questions of personal identity: the question of reidentification, on the one hand, and of self-knowledge, on the other. I cannot fully argue for this claim here, but I can say something about how such an argument would proceed, and this will be helpful in developing an alternative psychological account of personal identity.

[j]→ It is a philosophical commonplace that we have a dual perspective on persons. On the one hand, we view persons as one of the types of objects in the world, but, on the other, we view them as subjects and agents, creatures with a way of experiencing the world and with affect and volition. Because we have these two views, we tend to use the word 'person' in two different ways. Viewing persons as objects of our knowledge, we tend to use the term as if it were more or less coextensive with 'live human body'. Viewing persons as subjects and agents, we tend to use 'person' as an honorific term, having to do with autonomy, moral agency, and volition. In this sense, not all human beings will necessarily be persons, and not all actions of human bodies will be actions of persons.

[k]→ It is my claim that the two questions of personal identity come from these two perspectives also. Insofar as we view persons as objects of our knowledge, it will make sense to view the question of personal identity as a subspecies of more general metaphysical questions about the identity of complex objects, and to employ the same methods that are used in this pursuit to answer questions of personal identity. These methods involve looking at time slices of persons from an atemporal third-person perspective, and attempting to give objective criteria for saying that two time-slices belong to the same person. Ultimately, I believe, these methods can only support a bodily criterion of personal identity. Viewing persons as subjects and moral agents, on the other hand, discourages such an objective approach to identity, and leads us to emphasize the subjective experience of a person and questions of responsibility in addressing questions of identity (the sorts of identity questions raised in ethics, action theory, and literature, for example).

My claim is that contemporary psychological-continuity theorists like Parfit have taken their goal of providing a noncircular identity criterion from the reidentification question, and the intuitions that support the psychological criterion over the bodily criterion from the self-knowledge question. It is this, I claim, which has pushed these theorists to hold such an implausible view of our psychological states. The arguments that support a psychological criterion all rely on hypothetical puzzle cases, in which we are asked to imagine someone changed in certain ways, and then to observe our intuitions about whether or not the original person should be concerned about the future of the resultant person, held responsible for her actions, or take her beliefs to be her own. Issues of agency and self-knowledge are emphasized, and it is on the basis of these that we are being asked to judge questions of identity. The assumption is that when we concentrate on such questions we will judge that responsibility and concern (and hence identity) go with the psychology or consciousness rather than the body.

These thought experiments, then, are taken to support the view that psychology rather than the body is the constitutive factor of identity, but the question is never raised as to what kind of thing it is the identity of which is at issue – the person taken as subject or as object. The intuitions we have in response to the thought experiments, I claim, come from our view of persons as subjects, but the methods that identity theorists use to turn these intuitions into a criterion of identity come from a view of persons as objects. Taking the fact that psychology is what turns out to be important in these cases, psychological-continuity theorists thus make the unwarranted assumption that sameness of psychology can be used to provide a noncircular criterion of identity of the sort which is given for objects. But such a criterion cannot focus on subjectivity; it is, by definition, to be objective, and must be capable of being spelled out without including the first-person perspective of a given individual. The pieces that make up a person's psychology, must, to fulfil this purpose, be viewed to be as discrete and detachable as are the planks of a ship or the grains of sand in a heap. It is because psychological-continuity theorists are trying to force the insights gained from consideration of questions of self-knowledge and responsibility into the mold of questions of the persistence of material objects that they are forced to view psychological states as atomic, isolable, and in principle independent of the subject who experiences them – a view that I have argued to be highly implausible.

The intuitions that support psychological criteria come from the considerations that are at play in the self-knowledge question, and so it seems reasonable to hope that the sort of work done to address this question will be of some help in reconceiving the notion of a psychological account of personal identity. Let us consider this question for a moment. The person interested in self-knowledge will ask herself questions of the following sort: 'Is this really what I believe?' 'Is this really what I desire?' 'Is this really what I intend?' Which is to ask, in a specific way, 'Is this my belief?' 'Is this my desire?' 'Is this my intention?' The resources involved in answering these questions would be resources that allowed a person to assign particular psychological states to herself, and so would be at the same time resources for delimiting an individual person, and for answering questions of personal identity.

What kind of information, then, can be used in answering these questions? We have seen one relevant set of considerations already in the discussion of quasi states. In each of the cases we imagined, we could identify something highly anomalous about the states given to Jane even independently of the knowledge that they had come from someone else. We saw that Casey's memory or Paul's desire to join the French Foreign Legion, put into Jane's psyche in full form, were not only delusional, but jarring. This is because they contained so many details that were in conflict with the details of Jane's own life. Jane, I claimed, would be unable to appropriate these states coherently as her own, because they would conflict so violently with what she knows to be true of herself. If Paul's desire to join the French Foreign Legion were, therefore, to occur in Jane's psyche, she would have good reason to doubt that it was really her desire, even if she had no prior knowledge of its origins.

Part of what is involved in a psychological state's being mine in the sense which is at issue in the self-knowledge question, then, is its coherence with my total psychology – my ability to view it as a comprehensible part of my life, and to take it to be my own. Clearly the sort of coherence required here cannot be strict logical consistency – few of us are fortunate enough to have psyches without conflict, ambivalence, or discrepancies in our memories – but there is some way in which we are able comfortably to appropriate the various aspects of these ordinary conflicts, and view them as part of a single, comprehensible life. When the conflict is too severe, however, and the states in question are incomprehensible to us within the context of our self conception – as Casey's memory or Paul's desire might be to Jane – then these states have the character of external impositions, and a question is raised as to whether they are a genuine part of the person in whom they occur.

It is precisely when someone runs into an anomaly of this sort that we say that she is having an "identity-crisis," and the resolution of this crisis generally involves the forming of a well-grounded self-conception, and the ability to reject as not one's own beliefs, desires, and character traits that are not comprehensible as part of that self-conception.[4] As an alternative approach to offering a psychological account of personal identity, I propose

---

[4] I cannot emphasize enough that this is the sketch of the view, and that many distinctions and definitions are required to fill it out. What I want to make clear here is that what I have just said does not mean, for instance, that, if I conceive of myself as a patient person, and find suddenly that I have murderous impulses concerning the person driving five miles an hour in front of me on a one-lane road, I

that we take this talk of "identity crises" literally and not metaphorically – that we take persons (viewed as subjects and agents) to be constituted by their own self-conceptions. This view makes sense both in light of the discussion of quasi memory – which shows that the inability of someone to appropriate an experience coherently is sufficient reason to say that it is not hers – and in light of the intuitions that support the psychological criterion in the first place. These intuitions, I argued, are based on a notion of persons as self-conscious agents who are capable of moral responsibility, and such a conception seems to require as an essential feature of persons that they have a coherent self-conception. It is, after all, precisely when we find that persons do not have a coherent conception of themselves as agents that we feel we cannot legally hold them responsible for crimes they have committed – that there is a relevant sense in which these crimes are not their actions.

Furthermore, there is much philosophical precedent for viewing persons as self-constituting, the fact of their identities created by their self-conceptions. This view is central in the work of the existentialists, but it can also be found closer to home in the work, for instance, of Harry Frankfurt,[5] or Herbert Fingarette.[6] It is also very much present in the work of Locke[7] himself, who tells us that a person is "a thinking intelligent being, that has reason and reflection, and can consider itself as itself, the same thinking thing, in different times and places" (ibid., p. 39), and that "Wherever a man finds what he calls himself there, I think, another may say is the same person" (ibid., p. 50). Since contemporary psychological-continuity theorists take themselves to be addressing the question that Locke raises, it does not seem too far-fetched to believe that a view of persons as created by their self-conceptions, which Locke himself proposed, could provide a means of answering this question.

Of course, this view needs a great deal more development. I have already mentioned the need to spell out in more detail both what a self-conception is and what coherence is. The madman with Napoleonic delusions takes himself to have led the troops at Waterloo, but this does not count toward making that his action. And my refusal to accept my competitive impulses as my own does not have the consequence that I am not a competitive person. Also, it seems clear that I cannot use just *any* material to form my

---

can simply reject these murderous impulses and thereby make them not mine. I understand exactly where these impulses come from, and am forced, in the face of them, to revise my view of myself as a patient person. The type of incomprehensibility that I have in mind here is stronger and of a different sort. I shall say more about this later in the paper.

[5]   See, for instance, his "Identification and Externality," in *The Identities of Persons*, Amelie Oksenberg Rorty, ed. (Los Angeles: California UP, 1975).

[6]   See, for instance, his *Self-Deception* (London: Routledge & Kegan Paul, 1969).

[7]   "Of Identity and Diversity," from *An Essay Concerning Human Understanding*, reprinted in *Personal Identity*, John Perry, ed. (Los Angeles: California UP, 1975).

self-conception. Certain things I must view as part of my life if I am ever to have such a conception, and other things I cannot: there is no coherent way for me to appropriate Napoleon's actions at Waterloo. More must be said, then, about what it is which determines what can be involved in my self-conception, and about what a self-conception is.

Fortunately, we already have many resources available to help in filling in the gaps which we find in this view. There are, first of all, the philosophical sources that I mentioned above. We can also learn a great deal from work in psychology. Developmental psychology tells us how an infant progresses from a creature who does not distinguish between itself and the external world, to a person who distinguishes clearly between what is himself and what is other. And abnormal psychology provides us with analyses of cases where the attempt to form an identity goes awry. There are also many rich suggestions in literary treatment of identity, metamorphosis, and the double, which can be of tremendous assistance in trying to spell out this view. There is good reason to hope, then, that an alternative psychological account of persons of the sort I propose could be developed.

A view of persons as self-constituting would, when developed, provide an identity criterion of sorts. If we wanted to know, for instance, whether Jane is the person who had some particular experience, then we would need to discover whether this experience is a part of her coherent self-conception, because it is this which is the necessary and sufficient condition for assigning an experience to a particular person. This criterion, it is clear, would not fulfil the strong noncircularity condition to which psychological-continuity theorists hold themselves. It is not a reductionist analysis of persons, because it requires that in each instance we settle questions of identity with reference to the subjectivity and psyche of the person in question. I hope that the sketch I gave above will be sufficient to show, however, that this circularity is nonvicious – that such a criterion can provide us with a great deal of insight into what it is which constitutes the identities of persons, and that it can do so without doing violence to the complexities of our experience.

Commentary on Schechtman

Schechtman's paper is in many ways a model philosophy paper. The structure of the overall argument is crystal-clear. The paper contains, in section III, a single objection which strikes at the heart of all psychological-continuity theories of personal identity, the objection being that appeal to 'quasi states' fails to save such theories from the circularity objection. The paper is not merely destructive, however. Schechtman offers, in section IV, a diagnosis of the failure of psychological-continuity theories, and sketches an alternative view about personal identity – a view that is explicitly aimed at preserving the intuitions which lie behind the appeal of such theories without succumbing to the objection she raises.

Notice, however, that getting on for half the paper is devoted to scene-setting. In the short introductory section, Schechtman provides some context for the paper, tells us clearly why she has focused on Parfit in particular, and sketches a plan of the paper. In section I, she briefly lays out what she takes to be Partfit's view, as expressed in his later book, *Reasons and Persons* (Parfit 1984). And in section II, she provides a very clear and thorough explanation of what the classic circularity objection to psychological continuity theories is, and how Parfit's appeal to 'quasi states' is supposed to solve it. This expository material is useful in its own right, but it also makes Schechtman's objection much easier to grasp.

Section I

The first thing to notice, at $\boxed{a} \mapsto$, is that the view of Parfit's – from *Reasons and Persons* – described here is not the same as the view expounded in his 'Personal Identity'. In the latter work, as we have seen, Parfit is using the notion of psychological connectedness in his analysis of *survival*, and arguing that we can and should abandon the language of personal identity in favour of the language of survival. The view described in *Reasons and Persons* that Schechtman is going to criticize, by contrast, is one according to which personal *identity* can be defined by appealing to the *proportion* of 'direct connections' that hold between a person on one day and a person on the next day.

Fortunately the details need not detain us here, because it doesn't actually matter for the purposes of Schechtman's argument whether one thinks of psychological connectedness as grounding personal identity or merely survival; nor do the precise details of *how* one puts the notion of psychological connectedness to work in one's account of personal identity (or survival). For Schechtman's argument is going to be an attack on the very possibility of defining psychological connectedness, and hence continuity, in a way that does not presuppose facts about personal identity.

Next, Schechtman notes that the criteria for personal identity that Parfit proposes are 'reductionist'. Reductionism is an important concept in metaphysics. Roughly, a reductionist view about a certain kind of entity is a view according to which that kind of entity is really nothing over and above some *other* kind of entity. For example, a reductionist about the mind may say that the mind is really nothing over and above the brain: the mind isn't an extra addition to our ontology. A reductionist about goodness and badness may say that the goodness or badness of an act is really just a matter of how much pleasure or pain it causes: if we already believe that certain acts cause certain levels of pain or pleasure, we do not have to believe in anything extra in order to think that they are bad or good. And so on.

1. (i) Look at Parfit's reasons for saying that physical and psychological criteria for personal identity are reductionist, at $\boxed{b} \mapsto$. Think of some other philosophical theories you have come across. Which of them do you think are reductionist? Which are not? In each case, explain your answer. (ii) Why might one think that it is a good thing to offer a reductionist theory of something? Do you agree? If so, why? If not, why not?

Section II

Schechtman starts by describing the circularity objection. She claims that the objection works in different ways for different kinds of psychological state (memories, intentions, beliefs, and so on). In the case of memory, the idea is that in order for a mental state m to be a genuine memory of some past experience e, the person in state m must be the very same person as the one who originally had the experience e. Otherwise state m is not a memory at all; it is just a delusion. In the case of intention, for me to have a genuine intention to perform some act A, it must be an intention that *I* perform act A. In general, for person Y to carry out the intention of person X, it must be the case that person X = person Y. In the case of belief, in order for person Y's belief that nuclear war should be avoided at all costs to be the *very same belief* as person X's belief that nuclear war should be avoided at all costs, again, it must be the case that $X = Y$.

> 2. Describe in your own words the distinction drawn at $\boxed{c}\!\!\rightarrow$ between (i) X and Y having a belief with the same content, and (ii) X and Y having the very same belief. Why does Schechtman say that only the second is relevant to personal identity? Do you agree? What if X, at one time, had *all* the same beliefs, in sense (i), as person Y at some later time – would *that* be irrelevant to whether X and Y are the same person?

We now come to the notion of a 'quasi memory' or q-memory. It is this notion in particular that Schechtman will be attacking in detail later on. The original circularity objection, remember, is that in order for a mental state m to be a genuine memory of some past experience e, the person in state m must be the very same person as the one who originally had the experience e. Schechtman says at $\boxed{d}\!\!\rightarrow$ that 'identity theorists' (by which she means 'those who think that personal identity can be defined in terms of psychological continuity') accept that this is true of memories, but claim that psychological continuity can be defined instead in terms of q-memories; and it is *not* the case that in order for person X's mental state m to be a q-memory of experience e, X must be identical with – must be the same person as – the person who originally had experience e.

> 3. Using your own example, state in your own words the distinction identity theorists make between memory, delusion and q-memory (see $\boxed{e}\!\!\rightarrow$).
> 4. (i) Describe in your own words the objection to which Parfit is responding at $\boxed{f}\!\!\rightarrow$, and his response. (ii) Schechtman says at $\boxed{g}\!\!\rightarrow$ that she will argue, against Parfit, that 'simply deleting the "nametag" from a memory is not sufficient to make it nondelusional'. Explain in your own words why this claim contradicts Parfit's view.

Section III

Schechtman's argument against identity theories takes the form of a dilemma, clearly stated in the paragraph at ⌐h¬→: either Jane's *q*-memory will have only the same *visual* content as Casey's memory, or it will be qualitatively *exactly* similar to Casey's. Schechtman says: 'Neither of these alternatives will allow quasi memory to do the work it is supposed to do.'

> 5. Describe in your own words why, according to Schechtman, neither alternative will 'allow quasi memory to do the work it is supposed to do'.

Schechtman's argument, then, attempts to establish the claim that 'facts about whose memory a given memory is are an integral part of its qualitative content' ⌐i¬→. We cannot, even in principle – contrary to what Parfit claims – 'separate off' the *content* of a memory from the fact about whose memory it is. If we think of Jane's *q*-memory as just a flow of purely visual images, then 'it seems arbitrary to call it even the same apparent memory' as Casey's: what Jane experiences when *q*-remembering the trip to the cinema is qualitatively very different to what Casey experiences when he remembers the trip. But if we think of Jane's *q*-memory of the trip as qualitatively the same in *every* respect as Casey's experience when he remember the trip, then Jane's experience is delusional: it will include thoughts such as 'these are *my* children', and '*I* have been to this restaurant before', and so on, all of which are, in Jane's case, false.

> 6. Does Schechtman's argument establish that *all* (quasi) memories have this feature, or only that some do? Does she need the former claim, or only the latter, in order to establish that psychological continuity cannot be non-circularly defined?

Section IV

Finally, Schechtman attempts to diagnose what has gone wrong with psychological-continuity theories of personal identity, and sketches an outline of a positive view which does not, Schechtman claims, make the same mistake.

The notion of a 'diagnosis' in a philosophical context is a useful one. If someone wakes up with a fever and blotches on his skin, he knows there is *something* wrong with him, but he might not know what it is. When the doctor diagnoses him, she makes a claim about what the underlying cause of the symptoms is, and (if the patient is lucky) will therefore be able to cure him, by prescribing antibiotics or whatever.

A counter-example to a philosophical theory can be analogous to fever and blotches on the skin: it tells us *that* there is something wrong with the theory, and hence that the theory cannot be true as it stands. But it might not, just by itself – or at least, not in an obvious way – tell us what the underlying 'cause' of the problem is, and it might therefore be unclear whether there is a fairly easy way to fix the theory, or how one might go about constructing a new theory that avoids the problem. A diagnosis of the problem explains to us what its underlying 'cause' is, and therefore helps us to see how to respond to it.

This is precisely what Schechtman does in the four paragraphs from $\boxed{j}\mapsto$. She explains not only why we cannot expect to be able to cash psychological continuity out in a non-circular way, but also why it *seems* right to think, mistakenly, that personal identity *does* depend on psychological continuity. Roughly, she distinguishes between what she calls the 'reidentification question' and the 'self-knowledge question' (this is a distinction first introduced in the opening paragraph of the paper). She argues that philosophers want to provide a non-circular criterion of personal identity because they want to answer the re-identification question; but the intuitions that support thinking of personal identity as a matter of psychological rather than bodily continuity come from thinking about the self-knowledge question. So to attempt to provide a non-circular criterion of personal identity in terms of psychological continuity is in effect to try to provide a single answer to two very different questions.

7. State in your own words what, according to Schechtman, the connection is (i) between the 'self-knowledge question' and 'our view of persons as subjects', and (ii) between the 'reidentification question' and viewing persons as 'objects'.

Let's return to the issue of reductionism. Schechtman's own view seems to be this. A *reductionist* criterion of personal identity can be given, where we think of persons as 'objects'; and that criterion will be 'bodily' rather than psychological (see $\boxed{k}\mapsto$). (Notice, however, that she does not elaborate on what she means by a 'bodily criterion'; nor does she attempt to argue that such a criterion can in fact be given.) However, were we to think of persons as 'subjects', a psychological criterion of personal identity can be given, but it will *not* provide a 'reductionist analysis of persons' (see $\boxed{l}\mapsto$).

8. (i) State in your own words the central features of the positive view of personal identity which Schechtman sketches in the last few pages of the paper. (ii) In *Reasons and Persons*, Parfit claims: 'On the Non-Reductionist View, a person is a separately existing entity, distinct from his brain and body, and his experiences' (Parfit 1984: 275). Do you think Schechtman would or needs to agree with this claim? Why or why not?

Finally, it's worth thinking about Schechtman's paper in the context of Parfit's overall point, that survival is more important than personal identity. Schechtman ignores survival – as opposed to identity – altogether. The conclusion of her negative argument is that facts about psychological continuity presuppose facts about personal *identity*, and her positive claim is, again, a claim about personal identity. So, if one is convinced by Parfit's paper that we ought to abandon the language of identity, one *might* conclude that Schechtman's paper is just irrelevant.

9. Do you think that (i) Schechtman's negative argument and (ii) her positive proposal could be recast in a way that replaces talk of identity with talk of survival? Why or why not? What consequences does your answer have, in the light of Parfit's discussion of the divided-brain case and one or more of the other thought-experiments he discusses?

Further Reading

A good place to start might be chapter 6 of Guttenplan, Hornsby and Janaway's *Reading Philosophy* (2003). This contains abridged versions of Locke's classic discussion of personal identity (1690) and Williams 1970, along with commentaries and questions for you to work through. It's well worth reading the Locke in full as well though – as are the classic responses to Locke by Thomas Reid (1785) and Joseph Butler (1736).

Parfit has a lot more to say about personal identity and survival in his *Reasons and Persons* (1984), chapters 10–15. One area which both of the texts reproduced above touch on but do not explore in any detail is the 'bodily' criterion of personal identity: a criterion that Parfit rejects but which, as applied to persons considered as 'objects', Schechtman endorses. For more on the bodily criterion, see for example Johnston 1987 and Nagel 1986, chapter 3. Schechtman's positive view connects in interesting ways with Nagel's; again, see his 1986, chapter 3 (and also chapters 1 and 2).

An excellent edited collection on personal identity is Perry 1975. It contains some of the papers mentioned here (Locke, Butler, Reid, Williams), together with several others and a useful introduction. A good textbook is Noonan 2003; you might also try Hanley 1997, chapters 4 and 5 – particularly if you are a fan of *Star Trek*.

Essay Questions

1. Is survival more important than personal identity?
2. Can the circularity objection to psychological-continuity theories of personal identity be met?
3. Would we be better off if we abandoned or restricted the use of the language of personal identity in favour of different ways of thinking?
4. Can we be morally responsible for actions we cannot remember performing? What consequences, if any, does your answer have for personal identity?
5. What form might a 'bodily continuity' or 'bodily identity' theory of personal identity take? Could bodily continuity or identity be a necessary condition of personal identity? (That is, could it be the case that personal identity *requires* bodily continuity or bodily identity?) Could it be a sufficient condition? (That is, could it be the case that bodily continuity or identity *guarantees* personal identity?)

2

Free Will

Introduction

Picture a scene: a deserted beach, miles from the nearest person or road or phone booth. A long way out to sea, a lone swimmer is in trouble: he is waving and shouting for help, and his voice just carries as far as the beach. His cries finally catch the attention of a solitary walker on the beach, who stares out towards the swimmer, looking rather concerned. He looks around to see whether there is anyone whose attention he can attract in turn, or whether there is a phone booth or a road within sight (he doesn't have a mobile phone), but without success. Eventually, the swimmer's cries cease, and he disappears from view: he has drowned.

We can suppose that if there had been some way for the walker to get help, he would have done so. But what the walker did not do is attempt to save the drowning swimmer himself. Does he bear any moral responsibility for the swimmer's death?

A natural reaction to the case as described is that we cannot answer that question in the absence of further relevant information. In particular, we might want to know whether the walker was *able* to save the swimmer's life: whether he *could* have done so. (Certainly this looks as though this is *a* relevant consideration, though of course it might not be the only one.)

Suppose, for example, that the walker on the beach cannot swim. He is not even able to swim that far out to sea – he would certainly drown if he tried, and he knows this – let alone carry the swimmer safely back to the shore. In that case, it is natural to conclude that the walker is not morally responsible for the swimmer's death. There was simply nothing he could do: he was unable to save the swimmer, and so cannot legitimately be blamed for his death.

But now suppose that the walker on the beach is an excellent swimmer; he is, in fact, an off-duty lifeguard. He could easily swim out to sea, and if he did so it is overwhelmingly likely that he would be able to make it safely back to shore with the swimmer in tow. After all, he does this kind of thing routinely as part of his job. In that case, it is natural to conclude that the walker *is* morally responsible for the swimmer's death, since he was able to save the swimmer and yet he did not do so.

It seems, then, that our intuitions about the situations under which we hold people morally responsible for what they do (or do not do) are sensitive to whether or not they *could have done otherwise* than what they in fact end up doing. In the first case, the walker on the beach could not have saved the swimmer's life, while in the second case he could have done. And this seems to explain why we are inclined to hold the walker responsible for the swimmer's death in the second case but not the first.

What does all this have to do with free will? Well, the standard view of the matter runs as follows. Moral responsibility for an act (or, in the case described above, an omission – the *failure* to save the drowning swimmer) requires that one act freely, or 'of one's own free will'. And acting freely in turn requires that one could have done otherwise than what one actually did. So inability to do otherwise renders one's act unfree, and so renders one morally unaccountable for that act.

Given the standard view, a problem arises. (It is often referred to as 'the' problem of free will, as though if only this particular problem could be solved, there would be no remaining philosophical problems associated with free will – which is certainly not the case!) The problem arises from the possibility that *determinism* is true. Determinism is (roughly) the following thesis: a proposition expressing the total state of the universe at any one time, together with a proposition expressing all the laws of nature, *entails* a proposition expressing the total state of the universe at any later (or indeed earlier) time. To make the claim of determinism rather less abstract-sounding, consider a game of snooker. The cue ball has a particular mass, and is at rest. You hit the cue ball with the cue, with a particular force and in a particular direction (towards the black, say). All the other balls on the table, of course, have particular masses and positions, and the table itself has certain properties which affect how the balls move (it matters, for example, that it is covered in felt rather than wet tar). And of course there are gravitational forces in play. Now, assuming that all the laws governing the behaviour of the relevant entities – snooker balls and so on – are deterministic, a being who knew *all* of these facts and also knew all the laws of physics would be able to infer from all that information *exactly* what would happen to the black ball after you hit it. To put it another way, all the facts about the state of the balls, table and so on, together with the laws, leave exactly one possibility open: the possibility that actually obtains. Whether or not you or anyone else happens to know what these facts about the table and the laws of nature are is not really to the point: there *are* such facts, whether we know them or not, and those facts entail that the black will be in such-and-such a state in two seconds' time (again, whether *you*, or anyone, could possibly know this or not).

The thesis of determinism in effect says that the universe as a whole is just like our deterministic snooker table, only on a mind-bogglingly vast scale. Of course, *we* cannot possibly know the complete state of even a relatively small portion of the universe at any given time. And perhaps we will never know the laws of nature. But, according to determinism, the facts about the current state of the universe 10 minutes ago – and indeed 10,000 years ago – together with the laws of nature *entail* that at this precise moment, you and I and everything else in the universe are doing exactly what we are, in fact, doing.

Just thinking about that last sentence might make you start to worry that determinism (if true) precludes the possibility of genuinely free action. If facts about the past entail that you read these words at precisely this moment, it is hard to see how you could be reading them freely. To put it another way, it looks like you couldn't *really* have done anything any differently, since you were determined to do what you're now doing by the way the universe was before you were even born, together with the laws of nature. It might *seem* to you as though you could have decided to watch television or make a cup of coffee instead, and hence that you are now freely reading these words. But, since you could not, in fact, have decided to do anything other than what you did decide to do, you are not freely reading these words at all. This is a genuinely worrying thought – and it is this that is often known as 'the problem of free will'. Specifically, the problem is that of reconciling determinism with something we all, in our everyday lives, seem to take for granted – that we often act freely. Furthermore, if genuine moral responsibility requires that our actions are free, then the problem is also the problem of reconciling determinism with the claim that we are ever morally responsible for our actions.

Compatibilists hold that free will and determinism are compatible; in other words, they think that the problem of free will is solvable (or perhaps was never really a problem in the first place). *Incompatibilists*, as you might expect, hold that free will and determinism are incompatible: that is, that there is no solution to 'the' problem of free will.

The two texts reproduced in this chapter focus on this very central issue: the issue of whether or not determinism is compatible with free will. Van Inwagen (an incompatibilist) presents what has become the classic argument for the incompatibility of free will and determinism: what has come to be known as the 'Consequence Argument'. Dennett (a compatibilist) argues, in effect, that the argument fails: determinism is no bar to our acting freely and morally responsibly.

Peter van Inwagen, 'The Incompatibility of Free Will and Determinism'*

In this paper I shall define a thesis I shall call 'determinism', and argue that it is incompatible with the thesis that we are able to act otherwise than we do

*The writing of this paper was supported by a stipend from the National Endowment for the Humanities for the summer of 1973. The paper was read at a colloquium at the University of Maryland at College Park. Earlier versions were read at the University of Rochester and Syracuse University. The audiences at

(i.e., is incompatible with 'free will'). Other theses, some of them very different from what *I* shall call 'determinism', have at least an equal right to this name, and, therefore, I do not claim to show that *every* thesis that could be called 'determinism' without historical impropriety is incompatible with free will. I shall, however, assume without argument that what I call 'determinism' is legitimately so called.

In Part I, I shall explain what I mean by 'determinism'. In part II, I shall make some remarks about 'can'. In Part III, I shall argue that free will and determinism are incompatible. In Part IV, I shall examine some possible objections to the argument of Part III. I shall not attempt to establish the truth or falsity of determinism, or the existence or non-existence of free will.

a →

I

In defining 'determinism', I shall take for granted the notion of a proposition (that is, of a non-linguistic bearer of truth-value), together with certain allied notions such as denial, conjunction, and entailment. Nothing in this paper will depend on the special features of any particular account of propositions. The reader may think of them as functions from possible worlds to truth-values or in any other way he likes, provided they have their usual features. (E.g., they are either true or false; the conjunction of a true and a false proposition is a false proposition; they obey the law of contraposition with respect to entailment.)

Our definition of 'determinism' will also involve the notion of 'the state of the entire physical world' (hereinafter, 'the state of the world') at an instant. I shall leave this notion largely unexplained, since the argument of this paper is very nearly independent of its content. Provided the following two conditions are met, the reader may flesh out 'the state of the world' in any way he likes:

(i) Our concept of 'state' must be such that, given that the world is in a certain state at a certain time, nothing follows *logically* about its states at other times. For example, we must not choose a concept of 'state' that would allow as part of a description of the momentary state of the world, the clause, '. . . and, at *t*, the world is such that Jones's left hand will be raised 10 seconds later than *t*.'

(ii) If there is some observable change in the way things are (e.g., if a white cloth becomes blue, a warm liquid cold, or if a man raises his hand), this

these colloquia are thanked for useful comments and criticism. Special thanks are due to Rolf Eberle, Keith Lehrer, Raymond Martin, and Richard Taylor. I wish to thank Carl Ginet for his acute comments on an earlier draft, and the referee for several helpful suggestions. Of course, none of these people is responsible for any mistakes that remain.

change must entail some change in the state of the world. That is, our concept of 'state' must not be so theoretical, so divorced from what is observably true, that it be possible for the world to be in the *same* state at t_1 and t_2, although (for example) Jones's hand is raised at t_1 and not at t_2.

We may now define 'determinism'. We shall apply this term to the conjunction of these two theses:

(a)   For every instant of time, there is a proposition that expresses the state of the world at that instant.

(b)   If *A* and *B* are any propositions that express the state of the world at some instants, then the conjunction of *A* with the laws of physics entails *B*.

By a proposition that expresses the state of the world at time *t*, I mean a true proposition that asserts of some state that, at *t*, the world is in that state. The reason for our first restriction on the content of 'state' should now be evident: if it were not for this restriction, 'the state of the world' could be defined in such a way that determinism was trivially true. We could, without this restriction, build sufficient information about the past and future into each proposition that expresses the state of the world at an instant, that, for every pair of such propositions, each *by itself* entails the other. And in that case, determinism would be a mere tautology, a thesis equally applicable to every conceivable state of affairs.

This amounts to saying that the 'laws of physics' clause on our definition does some work: whether determinism is true depends on the character of the laws of physics. For example, if all physical laws were vague propositions like 'In every nuclear reaction, momentum is *pretty nearly* conserved', or 'Force is *approximately* equal to mass times acceleration', then determinism would be false.

This raises the question, What is a law of physics? First, a terminological point. I do not mean the application of this term to be restricted to those laws that belong to physics in the narrowest sense of the word. I am using 'law of physics' in the way some philosophers use 'law of nature'. Thus, a law about chemical valences is a law of physics in my sense, even if chemistry is not ultimately 'reducible' to physics. I will not use the term 'law of nature', because, conceivably, *psychological* laws, including laws (if such there be) about the voluntary behavior of rational agents, might be included under this term.[1] Rational agents are, after all, in some sense part of 'Nature'. Since I do not think that everything I shall say about laws of physics is true of such 'voluntaristic laws', I should not want to use, instead

[1]   For example, 'If a human being is not made to feel ashamed of lying before his twelfth birthday, then he will lie whenever he believes it to be to his advantage.'

of 'laws of physics', some term like 'laws of nature' that might legitimately be applied to voluntaristic laws. Thus, for all that is said in this paper, it may be that some version of determinism based on voluntaristic laws is compatible with free will.[2] Let us, then, understand by 'law of physics' a law of nature that is not about the voluntary behavior of rational agents.

But this does not tell us what 'laws of nature' are. There would probably be fairly general agreement that a proposition cannot be a law of nature unless it is true and contingent, and that no proposition is a law of nature if it entails the existence of some concrete individual, such as Caesar or the earth. But the proposition that there is no solid gold sphere 20 feet in diameter (probably) satisfies these conditions, though it is certainly not a law of nature.

It is also claimed sometimes that a law of nature must 'support its counterfactuals'. There is no doubt something to this. Consider, however, the proposition, 'Dogs die if exposed to virus V'. The claim that this proposition supports its counterfactuals is, I think, equivalent to the claim that 'Every dog is such that if it were exposed to virus V, it would die' is *true*. Let us suppose that this latter proposition *is* true, the quantification being understood as being over all dogs, past, present, and future. Its truth, it seems to me, is quite consistent with its being the case that dog-breeders *could* (but will not) institute a program of selective breeding that *would* produce a sort of dog that is immune to virus V. But if dog-breeders *could* do this, then clearly 'Dogs die if exposed to virus V' is not a law of nature, since in that case the truth of the corresponding universally quantified counterfactual depends upon an accidental circumstance: if dog-breeders were to institute a certain program of selective breeding they are quite capable of instituting, then 'Every dog is such that if it were exposed to virus V, it would die' would be false. Thus a proposition may 'support its counterfactuals' and yet not be a law of nature.

I do not think that any philosopher has succeeded in giving a (non-trivial) set of individually necessary and jointly sufficient conditions for a proposition's being a law of nature or of physics. *I* certainly do not know of any such set. Fortunately, for the purposes of this paper we need not know how to analyze the concept 'law of physics'. I shall, in Part III, argue that certain statements containing 'law of physics' are analytic. But this can be done in the absence of a satisfactory analysis of 'law of physics'. In fact, it would hardly be possible for one to *provide* an analysis of some concept if one had no preanalytic convictions about what statements involving that concept are analytic.

For example, we do not have to have a satisfactory analysis of memory to know that 'No one can remember future events' is analytic. And if someone

[2] In 'The Compatibility of Free Will and Determinism', *The Philosophical Review* (1962), J. V. Canfield argues convincingly for a position that we might represent in this terminology as the thesis that a determinism based on voluntaristic laws could be compatible with free will.

devised an analysis of memory according to which it was possible to remember future events, then, however attractive the analysis was in other respects, it would have to be rejected. The analyticity of 'No one can remember future events' is one of the *data* that anyone who investigates the concept of memory must take account of. Similarly, the claims I shall make on behalf of the concept of physical law seem to me to be basic and evident enough to be data that an analysis of this concept must take account of: any analysis on which these claims did not 'come out true' would be for that very reason defective.

II

It seems to be generally agreed that the concept of free will should be understood in terms of the *power* or *ability* of agents to act otherwise than they in fact do. To deny that men have free will is to assert that what a man *does* do and what he *can* do coincide. And almost all philosophers[3] agree that a necessary condition for holding an agent responsible for an act is believing that that agent *could have* refrained from performing that act.[4]

There is, however, considerably less agreement as to how 'can' (in the relevant sense) should be analyzed. This is one of the most difficult questions in philosophy. It is certainly a question to which I do not know any non-trivial answer. But, as I said I should do in the case of 'law of physics', I shall make certain conceptual claims about 'can' (in the 'power' or 'ability' sense) in the absence of any analysis. Any suggested analysis of 'can' that does not support these claims will either be neutral with respect to them, in which case it will be incomplete, since it will not settle *all* conceptual questions about 'can', or it will be inconsistent with them, in which case the arguments I shall present in support of these claims will, in effect, be arguments that the analysis fails. In Part IV, I shall expand on this point as it applies to one particular analysis of 'can', the well-known 'conditional' analysis.

I shall say no more than this about the meaning of 'can'. I shall, however, introduce an idiom that will be useful in talking about ability and inability in complicated cases. Without this idiom, the statement of our argument would be rather unwieldy. We shall sometimes make claims about an agent's abilities by using sentences of the form:

S can render [could have rendered]...false.

---

[3]   See, however, Harry Frankfurt, 'Alternate Possibilities and Moral Responsibility', *The Journal of Philosophy* (1969).
[4]   Actually, the matter is rather more complicated than this, since we may hold a man responsible for an act we believe he could not have refrained from, provided we are prepared to hold him responsible for his being unable to refrain.

where ' . . . ' may be replaced by names of propositions.[5] Our ordinary claims about ability can easily be translated into this idiom. For example, we translate:

> He could have reached Chicago by midnight.

as

> He could have rendered the proposition that he did not reach Chicago by midnight false.

and, of course, the translation from the special idiom to the ordinary idiom is easy enough in such simple cases. If we were interested only in everyday ascriptions of ability, the new idiom would be useless. Using it, however, we may make ascriptions of ability that it would be very difficult to make in the ordinary idiom. Consider, for example, the last true proposition asserted by Plato. (Let us assume that this description is, as logicians say, 'proper'.) One claim that we might make about Aristotle is that he could have rendered this proposition false. Now, presumably, we have no way of discovering *what* proposition the last true proposition asserted by Plato was. Still, the claim about Aristotle would seem to be either true or false. To discover its truth-value, we should have to discover under what conditions the last true proposition asserted by Plato (i.e., that proposition having as one of its accidental properties, the property of being the last true proposition asserted by Plato) would be false, and then discover whether it was within Aristotle's power to produce these conditions. For example, suppose that if Aristotle had lived in Athens from the time of Plato's death till the time of his own death, then the last true proposition asserted by Plato (whatever it was) would be false. Then, if Aristotle could have lived (i.e., if he had it within his power to live) in Athens throughout this period, he could have rendered the last true proposition asserted by Plato false. On the other hand, if the last true proposition asserted by Plato is the proposition that the planets do not move in perfect circles, then Aristotle could not have rendered the last true proposition asserted by Plato false, since it was not within his power to produce any set of conditions sufficient for the falsity of this proposition.[6]

---

[5]   In all the cases we shall consider, ' . . . ' will be replaced by names of *true* propositions. For the sake of logical completeness, we may stipulate that any sentence formed by replacing ' . . . ' with the name of a *false* proposition is trivially true. Thus, 'Kant could have rendered the proposition that $7 + 5 = 13$ false' is trivially true.

[6]   Richard Taylor has argued (most explicitly in 'Time, Truth and Ability' by 'Diodorus Cronus', *Analysis* (1965)) that every true proposition is such that, necessarily, no one is able to render it false. On my view, this thesis is mistaken, and Taylor's arguments for it can be shown to be unsound. I shall not, however, argue for it here. I shall argue in Part III that we are unable to render *certain sorts of* true proposition false, but my arguments will depend on special features of these sorts of proposition. I shall, for example, argue that no one can render false a law of physics; but I shall not argue that this is the case because laws of physics are *true*, but because of other features that they possess.

It is obvious that the proposition expressed by 'Aristotle could have rendered the last true proposition asserted by Plato false', is a proposition that we should be hard put to express without using the idiom of rendering propositions false, or, at least, without using some very similar idiom. We shall find this new idiom very useful in discussing the relation between free will (a thesis about abilities) and determinism (a thesis about certain propositions).

III

 I shall now imagine a case in which a certain man, after due deliberation, refrained from performing a certain contemplated act. I shall then argue that, if determinism is true, then that man *could not have* performed that act. Because this argument will not depend on any features peculiar to our imagined case, the incompatibility of free will and determinism *in general* will be established, since, as will be evident, a parallel argument could easily be constructed for the case of any agent and any unperformed act.

Here is the case. Let us suppose there was once a judge who had only to raise his right hand at a certain time, T, to prevent the execution of a sentence of death upon a certain criminal, such a hand-raising being the sign, according to the conventions of the judge's country, of a granting of special clemency. Let us further suppose that the judge – call him 'J' – refrained from raising his hand at that time, and that this inaction resulted in the criminal's being put to death. We may also suppose that the judge was unbound, uninjured, and free from paralysis; that he decided not to raise his hand at T only after a period of calm, rational, and relevant deliberation; that he had not been subjected to any 'pressure' to decide one way or the other about the criminal's death; that he was not under the influence of drugs, hypnosis, or anything of that sort; and finally, that there was no element in his deliberations that would have been of any special interest to a student of abnormal psychology.

Now the argument. In this argument, which I shall refer to as the 'main argument', I shall use 'T_0' to denote some instant of time earlier than J's birth, 'P_0' to denote the proposition that expresses the state of the world at T_0, 'P' to denote the proposition that expresses the state of the world at T, and 'L' to denote the conjunction into a single proposition of all laws of physics. (I shall regard L itself as a law of physics, on the reasonable assumption that if A and B are laws of physics, then the conjunction of A and B is a law of physics.) The argument consists of seven statements, the seventh of which follows from the first six:

(1)   If determinism is true, then the conjunction of P_0 and L entails P.

(2)   If J had raised his hand at T, then P would be false.

(3)   If (2) is true, then if J could have raised his hand at T, J could have rendered P false.[7]

(4)   If J could have rendered P false, and if the conjunction of P_0 and L entails P, then J could have rendered the conjunction of P_0 and L false.

(5)   If J could have rendered the conjunction of P_0 and L false, then J could have rendered L false.

(6) J could not have rendered L false.

(7)   If determinism is true, J could not have raised his hand at T.
∴

That (7) follows from (1) through (6) can easily be established by truth-functional logic. Note that all conditionals in the argument except for (2) are truth-functional. For purposes of establishing the *validity* of this argument, (2) may be regarded as a simple sentence. Let us examine the premises individually.

(1)   This premise follows from the definition of determinism.

(2)   If J had raised his hand at T, then the world would have been in a different state at T from the state it was in fact in. (See our second condition on the content of 'the state of the world'.) And, therefore, if J had raised his hand at T, some contrary of P would express the state of the world at T. It should be emphasized that 'P' does not *mean* 'the proposition that expresses the state of the world at T'. Rather, 'P' *denotes* the proposition that expresses the state of the world at T. In Kripke's terminology, 'P' is being used as a *rigid designator*, while 'the proposition that expresses the state of the world at T' is perforce non-rigid.[8]

(3)   Since J's hand being raised at T would have been sufficient for the falsity of P, there is, if J could have raised his hand, at least one condition sufficient for the falsity of P that J could have produced.

(4)   This premise may be defended as an instance of the following general principle:

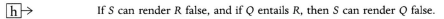

If S can render R false, and if Q entails R, then S can render Q false.

This principle seems to be analytic. For if Q entails R, then the denial of R entails the denial of Q. Thus, any condition sufficient for the falsity of R is also sufficient for the falsity of Q. Therefore, if there is some condition that S

---

[7]   'J could have raised his hand at T' is ambiguous. It might mean either (roughly) 'J possessed, at T, the ability to raise his hand', or 'J possessed the ability to bring it about that his hand rose at T'. If J was unparalyzed at T but paralyzed at all earlier instants, then the latter of these would be false, though the former might be true. I mean 'J could have raised his hand at T' in the latter sense.

[8]   See Saul Kripke, 'Identity and Necessity', in *Identity and Individuation* (ed. by Milton K. Munitz), New York (1971).

can produce that is sufficient for the falsity of R, there is some condition (that same condition) that S can produce that is sufficient for the falsity of Q.

(5)   This premise may be defended as an instance of the following general principle, which I take to be analytic:

> If Q is a true proposition that concerns only states of affairs that obtained before S's birth, and if S can render the conjunction of Q and R false, then S can render R false.

Consider, for example, the propositions expressed by

> The Spanish Armada was defeated in 1588.

and

> Peter van Inwagen never visits Alaska.

The conjunction of these two propositions is quite possibly true. At any rate, let us assume it is true. Given that it is true, it seems quite clear that I can render it false if and only if I can visit Alaska. If, for some reason, it is not within my power ever to visit Alaska, then I *cannot* render it false. This is a quite trivial assertion, and the general principle (above) of which it is an instance is hardly less trivial. And it seems incontestable that premise (5) is also an instance of this principle.

(6)   I shall argue that if anyone *can* (i.e., has it within his power to) render some proposition false, then that proposition is not a law of physics. This I regard as a conceptual truth, one of the data that must be taken account of by anyone who wishes to give an analysis of 'can' or 'law'. It is this connection between these two concepts, I think, that is at the root of the incompatibility of free will and determinism.

In order to see this connection, let us suppose that both of the following are true:

(A)   Nothing ever travels faster than light.
(B)   Jones, a physicist, can construct a particle accelerator that would cause protons to travel at twice the speed of light.

It follows from (A) that Jones will never exercise the power that (B) ascribes to him. But whatever the reason for Jones's failure to act on his ability to render (A) false, it is clear that (A) and (B) are consistent, and that (B) entails that (A) is not a law of physics. For given that (B) is true, then Jones is able to conduct an experiment that would falsify (A); and surely it is a feature of any proposition that is a physical law that no one *can* conduct an experiment that would show it to be false.

Of course, most propositions that look initially as if they might be physical laws, but which are later decided to be nonlaws, are rejected because of experiments that are actually performed. But this is not essential.

In order to see this, let us elaborate the example we have been considering. Let us suppose that Jones's ability to render (A) false derives from the fact that he has discovered a mathematically rigorous proof that under certain conditions C, realizable in the laboratory, protons would travel faster than light. And let us suppose that this proof proceeds from premises so obviously true that all competent physicists accept his conclusion without reservation. But suppose that conditions C never obtain in nature, and that actually to produce them in the laboratory would require such an expenditure of resources that Jones and his colleagues decide not to carry out the experiment. And suppose that, as a result, conditions C are never realized and nothing ever travels faster than light. It is evident that if all this were true, we should have to say that (A), while *true*, is not a law of physics. (Though, of course, 'Nothing ever travels faster than light except under conditions C' might be a law.)

The laboratories and resources that figure in this example are not essential to its point. If Jones *could* render some proposition false by performing *any* act he does not in fact perform, even such a simple act as raising his hand at a certain time, this would be sufficient to show that that proposition is not a law of physics.

This completes my defense of the premises of the main argument. In the final part of this paper, I shall examine objections to this argument suggested by the attempts of various philosophers to establish the compatibility of free will and determinism.

IV

The most useful thing a philosopher who thinks that the main argument does not prove its point could do would be to try to show that some premise of the argument is false or incoherent, or that the argument begs some important question, or contains a term that is used equivocally, or something of that sort. In short, he should get down to cases. Some philosophers, however, might continue to hold that free will and determinism, in the sense of Part I, are compatible, but decline to try to point out a mistake in the argument. For (such a philosopher might argue) we have, in everyday life, *criteria* for determining whether an agent could have acted otherwise than he did, and these criteria determine the *meaning* of 'could have acted otherwise'; to know the meaning of this phrase is simply to know how to apply these criteria. And since these criteria make no mention of determinism, anyone who thinks that free will and determinism are incompatible is simply confused.[9]

---

[9] Cf. Antony Flew, 'Divine Omniscience and Human Freedom', *New Essays in Philosophical Theology* (ed. by Antony Few and Alasdair MacIntyre), London (1955), pp. 149–51 in particular.

As regards the argument of Part III (this philosopher might continue), this argument is very complex, and this complexity must simply serve to hide some error, since its conclusion is absurd. We must treat this argument like the infamous 'proof' that zero equals one: It may be amusing and even instructive to find the hidden error (if one has nothing better to do), but it would be a waste of time to take seriously any suggestion that it is sound.

Now I suppose we do have 'criteria', in some sense of this overused word, for the application of 'could have done otherwise', and I will grant that knowing the criteria for the application of a term can plausibly be identified with knowing its meaning. Whether the criteria for applying 'could have done otherwise' can (as at least one philosopher has supposed[10]) be taught by simple ostension is another question. However this may be, the 'criteria' argument is simply invalid. To see this, let us examine a simpler argument that makes the same mistake.

$\boxed{j}\mapsto$ Consider the doctrine of 'predestinarianism'. Predestinarians hold (i) that if an act is foreseen it is not free, and (ii) that all acts are foreseen by God. (I do not claim that anyone has ever held this doctrine in precisely this form.) Now suppose we were to argue that predestinarianism must be compatible with free will, since our criteria for applying 'could have done otherwise' make no reference to predestinarianism. Obviously this argument would be invalid, since predestinarianism is incompatible with free will. And the only difference I can see between this argument and the 'criteria' argument for the compatibility of free will and determinism is that predestinarianism, unlike determinism, is *obviously* incompatible with free will. But, of course, theses may be incompatible with one another even if this incompatibility is not obvious. Even if determinism cannot, like predestinarianism, be seen to be incompatible with free will on the basis of a simple formal inference, there is, nonetheless, a conceptual connection between the two theses (as we showed in our defense of premise (6)). The argument of Part III is intended to draw out the implications of this connection. There may well be a mistake in the argument, but I do not see why anyone should think that the very idea of such an argument is misconceived.

$\boxed{k}\mapsto$ It has also been argued that free will *entails* determinism, and, being itself a consistent thesis, is *a fortiori* compatible with determinism. The argument, put briefly, is this. To say of some person on some particular occasion that he acted freely is obviously to say at least that *he* acted on that occasion. Suppose, however, that we see someone's arm rise and it later turns out that there was *no cause whatsoever* for his arm's rising. Surely we should have to say that *he* did not really raise his arm at all. Rather, his arm's rising was a mere chance happening, that, like a muscular twitch, had nothing to do with *him*, beyond the fact that it happened to involve a part of his body. A necessary condition for this person's really having raised his hand is that *he*

---

[10]   Flew, *loc. cit.*

caused his hand to rise. And surely 'he caused' means 'his character, desires, and beliefs caused'.[11]

I think that there is a great deal of confusion in this argument, but to expose this confusion would require a lengthy discussion of many fine points in the theory of agency. I shall only point out that if this argument is supposed to refute the conclusion of Part III, it is an *ignoratio elenchi*. For I did not conclude that free will is incompatible with the thesis that every event has a cause, but rather with determinism as defined in Part I. And the denial of this thesis does not entail that there are uncaused events.

Of course, one might try to construct a similar but relevant argument for the falsity of the conclusion of Part III. But, so far as I can see, the plausibility of such an argument would depend on the plausibility of supposing that if the present movements of one's body are not completely determined by physical law and the state of the world before one's birth, then these present movements are not one's own doing, but, rather, mere random happenings. And I do not see the least shred of plausibility in this supposition.

$\boxed{1}\!\!\rightarrow$ I shall finally consider the popular 'conditional analysis' argument for the compatibility of free will and determinism. According to the advocates of this argument – let us call them 'conditionalists' – what statements of the form:

(8) S could have done X

mean is:

(9)   If S had chosen to do X, S would have done X.[12]

For example, 'Smith could have saved the drowning child' means, 'If Smith had chosen to save the drowning child, Smith would have saved the drowning child.' Thus, even if determinism is true (the conditionalists argue), it is possible that Smith did not save but *could have* saved the drowning child, since the conjunction of determinism with 'Smith did not save the child' does not entail the falsity of 'If Smith had chosen to save the child, Smith would have saved the child'.

Most of the controversy about this argument centers around the question whether (9) is a correct analysis of (8). I shall not enter into the debate about whether this analysis is correct. I shall instead question the relevance of this

[11]   Cf. R. E. Hobart, 'Free Will as Involving Determination and Inconceivable Without It', *Mind* (1934); A. J. Ayer, 'Freedom and Necessity', in his collected *Philosophical Essays*, New York (1954); P. H. Nowell-Smith, 'Freewill and Moral Responsibility', *Mind* (1948); J. J. C. Smart, 'Free Will, Praise, and Blame', *Mind* (1961).

[12]   Many other verbs besides 'choose' figure in various philosophers' conditional analyses of ability. E.g., 'wish', 'want', 'will', 'try', 'set oneself'. Much of the important contemporary work on this analysis, by G. E. Moore, P. H. Nowell-Smith, J. L. Austin, Keith Lehrer, Roderick Chisholm, and others, is collected in *The Nature of Human Action* (ed. by Myles Brand), Glenview, Ill. (1970). See also 'Fatalism and Determinism', by Wilfrid Sellars, in *Freedom and Determinism* (ed. by Keith Lehrer) New York (1966), pp. 141–74.

debate to the argument of Part III. For it is not clear that the main argument would be unsound if the conditional analysis *were* correct. Clearly the argument is *valid* whether or not (8) and (9) mean the same. But suppose the premises of the main argument were rewritten so that every clause they contain that is of form (8) is replaced by the corresponding clause of form (9) – should we then see that any of these premises is false? Let us try this with premise (6), which seems, *prima facie*, to be the crucial premise of the argument. We have:

(6a)   It is not the case that if *J* had chosen to render *L* false, *J* would have rendered *L* false.

Now (6a) certainly seems true: If someone chooses to render false some proposition *R*, and if *R* is a law of physics, then surely he will fail. This little argument for (6a) *seems* obviously sound. But we cannot overlook the possibility that someone might discover a mistake in it and, perhaps, even construct a convincing argument that (6a) is false. Let us, therefore, assume for the sake of argument that (6a) is demonstrably false. What would this show? I submit that it would show that (6a) does not mean the same as (6), since (6) is, as I have argued, *true*.

The same dilemma confronts the conditionalist if he attempts to show, on the basis of the conditional analysis, that any of the other premises of the argument is false. Consider the argument got by replacing every clause of form (8) in the main argument with the corresponding clause of form (9). If all the premises of this new argument are true, the main argument is, according to the conditionalist's own theory, sound. If, on the other hand, any of the premises of the new argument is false, then (*I* would maintain) this premise is a counterexample to the conditional analysis. I should not be begging the question against the conditionalist in maintaining this, since I have given arguments for the truth of each of the premises of the main argument, and nowhere in these arguments do I assume that the conditional analysis is wrong.

Of course, any or all of my arguments in defense of the premises of the main argument may contain some mistake. But unless the conditionalist could point to some such mistake, he would not accomplish much by showing that some statement he *claimed* was equivalent to one of its premises was false.[13]

---

[13]   For an argument in some respects similar to what I have called the 'main argument', see Carl Ginet's admirable article, 'Might We Have No Choice?' in Lehrer, *op. cit.*, pp. 87–104. Another argument similar to the main argument, which is (formally) much simpler than the main argument, but which is stated in language very different from that of traditional statements of the free-will problem, can be found in my 'A Formal Approach to the Problem of Free Will and Determinism', *Theoria* (1974).

Commentary on van Inwagen

Van Inwagen's short paper, first published in 1975, has become the *locus classicus* for contemporary discussion of the issue of whether or not free will is compatible with determinism. The core of the paper lies in section III, where he presents the 'Consequence Argument', whose conclusion is that if determinism is true, nobody can do otherwise than what they actually do: a claim from which incompatibilism is supposed to follow. Van Inwagen claims that the argument is valid, and argues that each of the premises is true. Sections I and II set the scene by clarifying some core concepts invoked in the argument: 'determinism' and 'law of physics' (section I), and 'can' (section II). Finally, in section IV, having presented the Consequence Argument, he rebuts some possible objections to the argument.

The paper as a whole may seem somewhat dry and pedantic, but do not be tempted to dismiss it as a boring piece of logic-chopping; after all, there is nothing boring about the thesis for which van Inwagen is arguing. The care with which he defines his terms and the apparently water-tight nature of his argument make it very hard to see how one might object to it; and that means that it's going to take a lot of thought to work out where sensible lines of criticism might be found – and, we hope you agree, there is nothing boring about *that*.

1. Look at what van Inwagen says at $\boxed{a} \mapsto$. Why do you think he does not try to establish the truth or falsity of determinism? And why does he say that he is not going to attempt to establish the existence or non-existence of free will?

Section I

Van Inwagen starts out by defining 'determinism'.

2. Say in your own words why van Inwagen says at $\boxed{b} \mapsto$ that without restriction (i), determinism would be 'a mere tautology'.

From $\boxed{c} \mapsto$, he moves on to the question, What is a law of physics? He lays out some standard necessary conditions for a proposition's being a law of physics: it must be true and contingent, it must not entail the existence of some concrete individual, and it must 'support its counterfactuals'. But, he argues, none of these conditions are *sufficient* conditions for a proposition's being a law of physics. The upshot is that he does not know how to *define* (that is, provide necessary *and* sufficient conditions for a proposition's being) a law of nature; but, he claims, this does not matter: he will later appeal to some 'basic and evident' claims about laws of physics that one cannot seriously deny.

3. Explain in your own words why, according to van Inwagen, none of the conditions he lists can be *sufficient* conditions for a proposition's being a law of physics. Provide your own example – as clear a case as you can think of – of a proposition that meets the conditions and yet is not, intuitively, a law of physics.

Section II

Van Inwagen starts, at $\boxed{d}\mapsto$, by making a claim that will turn out to be crucial to his argument for incompatibilism: the claim that 'to deny that men have free will is to assert that what a man *does* do and what he *can* do coincide'.

4. Express this claim in your own words. Does it immediately strike you as plausible or implausible? Why or why not?

We'll come back to this claim later on.

Next, as with the concept 'law of physics', van Inwagen tells us that he will later make some conceptual claims about 'can' (or 'power' or 'ability'), even though he does not know how to *analyse* the concept. Finally, he introduces a locution, '*S* can render... false' (or '*S* could have rendered... false').

5. Express the following in the 'can render/could have rendered false' idiom: (i) Julian had toast for breakfast, but he could have had something else. (ii) Helen had the power to resist the bar of chocolate, even though she actually ate it; (iii) Susan is able to play the violin at this moment, although she isn't; (iv) Gavin could have fixed his bike on Thursday but didn't.

Section III

We now get to the heart of the paper: the Consequence Argument. At $\boxed{e}\mapsto$, van Inwagen tells us that he is going to provide an argument for the claim that a particular person could not have performed a particular act (the claim being that judge *J* could not have raised his hand at *T*), but that 'the incompatibility of free will and determinism *in general* will be established, since... a parallel argument could easily be constructed for the case of any agent and any unperformed act'.

6. Why does van Inwagen suppose, at $\boxed{f}\mapsto$, that the judge was unbound and uninjured, decided after a period of calm deliberation, and so on? What, if anything, would be wrong with the argument if he didn't suppose all this?

The Consequence Argument, which we shall refer to as (CA), is stated at $\boxed{g}\mapsto$. It has six premises – (1) to (6) – and (7) is the conclusion. Van Inwagen does not bother to explain *how* the conclusion follows from the premises; he simply asserts that the validity of (CA) can be 'established by truth-functional logic'. This, you will doubtless be pleased to hear, presents us with a nice logic exercise.

7. (i) Using the letters below to stand for sentences appearing in argument (CA), rewrite the argument using just those letters together with 'and' (&), 'if...then...' (→) and 'not' (¬). (ii) If you have taken an introductory course on truth-functional logic (otherwise known as propositional or sentential calculus), try to prove, by whatever method you have learned, that the argument is indeed valid.

The answer to (i) and an informal demonstration of the validity of (CA) are provided as an appendix at the end of this chapter. If you haven't studied logic, or if you get stuck on either (i) or (ii), take a look and try to follow it.

Sentence letters:
A: Determinism is true
B: The conjunction of P_0 and L entails P
C: If J had raised his hand at T, then P would be false
D: J could have raised his hand at T
E: J could have rendered P false
F: J could have rendered the conjunction of P_0 and L false
G: J could have rendered L false

Notice that, while the conclusion of (CA) makes a claim about a particular individual and a particular act – it says that if determinism is true, judge J could not have raised his hand at T – nothing in the argument relies on any specific features of either the person or the act. If determinism is true, then the conjunction of a complete description of the state of the world at some past time (P_o) and the laws of physics (L) entails not only that judge J raises his arm at T; that conjunction also entails every single fact about what happened or will happen after P_o. For example, if in fact you had toast for breakfast yesterday, then P_o & L entails that you did – and so, by (CA), you could not have done otherwise.

Having presented the Consequence Argument, van Inwagen proceeds to defend each of its premises. Premises (1) to (3) are pretty straightforward; it's premises (4) to (6) that are less straightforward and correspondingly more controversial. A closer look at them will help you to understand exactly how the argument works.

Let's start with premise (4). Van Inwagen says that this premise is simply an instance of a more general principle, stated at $\boxed{h} \rightarrow$, which, he says, 'seems to be analytic'. (If you don't know what 'analytic' means, just think of it as meaning 'necessarily true'; alternatively, look at the definition of 'analytic' in the commentary on Davidson in chapter 3.) Does this principle seem true? The easiest way to convince yourself that it at least looks *prima facie* plausible is to run through a few examples.

8. Think of a case where, intuitively, S can indeed render R false, and then think of some proposition Q, which entails R. Intuitively, can S also render Q false? Now think of a couple more cases and answer the same question. Do your answers confirm van Inwagen's principle or not? If they do confirm it, do you think a counter-example to the principle is possible in principle?

Most likely, you will find it impossible to think of a case where the principle fails to hold. So perhaps van Inwagen is right that the principle is true. (This has been disputed, e.g. by David Lewis (1981). But Lewis's reasons for denying the principle are pretty subtle – he doesn't simply come up with a plausible-seeming counter-example.)

Where are we up to? Well, so far things look like this. Suppose determinism is true. Then $P_o \& L$ entails P (the proposition completely describing the state of the world at time T). So if judge J could have rendered P false (by raising his hand) then, by the principle just discussed, he could have rendered $P_o \& L$ false. Premise (5) says that if J could have rendered $P_o \& L$ false, then he could have rendered L false. Van Inwagen defends this premise by claiming, in effect, that obviously one cannot render P_0 false: one cannot render false any proposition about the distant past. You cannot, for example, render it false that the Spanish Armada was defeated in 1588, or that the Battle of Hastings took place in 1066, or that Ronald Reagan was once President of the USA. It looks like van Inwagen's premise (5) is pretty plausible. So if J could have rendered $P_o \& L$ false, given that he could not have rendered P_o false, it must be the case that he could instead have rendered L false.

So our next question is: could J have rendered L false? More generally, can anyone render any proposition which states a law of physics false? Care is needed here, because there are two mistakes it's easy to make.

First, people sometimes call a scientific hypothesis that was once accepted but has since been proved to be false a 'law'. For example, we talk about 'Newton's Second Law' of motion: force = mass $\times$ acceleration, or $F = ma$. But Newton's Second Law turned out not to be true: it is violated by objects travelling close to the speed of light. However, establishing that Newton's Second Law is false was *not* a matter of rendering a law of physics false. Rather it was a matter of establishing that a certain proposition, $F = ma$, which people *thought* was a law, was not a law at all (even though we still rather confusingly call that proposition 'Newton's Second Law'). Rendering a law false (in van Inwagen's sense) is not the same as refuting or falsifying a scientific hypothesis.

9. Suppose that someone falsifies a previously-accepted scientific hypothesis H, by finding a case where H fails to hold. (Imagine, for instance – to take a toy example – that the hypothesis is that all swans are white, and someone falsifies it by discovering a black swan.) Explain in your own words why this does *not* amount to 'rendering a law false'.

Second, you might be inclined to reason as follows: 'If a proposition states a law of physics, then the proposition *must* be true in order for it to state a genuine law. The fact that the proposition states a law *entails* that the proposition is true. So *of course* we cannot render false any proposition that states a law of physics.' That conclusion would make van Inwagen's claim that we cannot render *L* false trivial.

The above line of reasoning is mistaken. Of course, if we grant that some proposition *P* actually states a law of physics, then we know that, given that assumption, nothing anyone has *actually* done or will ever do will render *P* false, since, by assumption, *P* is *not* false but true (since it states a law). But it isn't a logical consequence of this, just by itself, that nobody *could have* (but didn't) render *P* false.

To see why, compare the case where proposition *P* states some more mundane truth: that Helen had toast for breakfast this morning, say. If we grant that *P* is true, then we know that, given that assumption, nothing anyone has *actually* done or will ever do will render *P* false. But it manifestly isn't a logical consequence of this, just by itself, that nobody *could have* rendered *P* false. The fact that Helen had toast for breakfast entails that she didn't skip breakfast. But it doesn't entail that she was *unable*, at the time, to skip breakfast. After all, if the latter were a logical consequence of the former, we wouldn't need the Consequence Argument in the first place!

Having dealt with a couple of common misconceptions about what it *means* to ask whether anyone can render false a proposition stating a law of physics, we can now get back to van Inwagen's answer to it. He argues at $\boxed{\text{i}} \! \rightarrow$ that the answer is 'no': it is a conceptual truth – a part of what 'law' *means* – that the laws of physics cannot be rendered false.

Van Inwagen is here appealing to a standard claim about the difference between those generalizations that are laws and those that are not. Consider the following two claims:

i)   Nothing ever travels faster than light.
ii) No lump of solid gold weighs (nor ever has weighed, nor ever will weigh) more than 1000 kg.

Both claims are (let's suppose) true; but (again, let's suppose), unlike (ii), (i) states a law of physics: it does not simply *happen* to be true. What might something – in particular, (ii) – merely 'happening to be true' amount to? Well, one way we might try to cash that thought out is by saying that someone *could*, if they had the inclination and enough money, render (ii) false: someone *could* buy vast quantities of gold and make them into a solid lump weighing more than 1000 kg. If (ii) really is true, then nobody *will*, in fact, ever do this. But even though nobody ever has done it or will do it, someone *could* do it.

We might therefore try to articulate what is involved in the fact that (i) does not merely happen to be true by saying that nobody could render (i) false: no matter how much money or ingenuity they had, they would never manage to get something to travel faster than light. It just can't be done. The laws of physics place constraints on what can and can't happen in the world: constraints from which we cannot break free.

If all this sounds utterly obvious to you, then of course you will accept premise (6). It should be noted, however, that some authors have denied that the laws of physics place constraints on us in the sense required for it to be the case that we cannot render them false (see for example Beebee and Mele 2002).

All in all, though, (CA) is looking sound (a sound argument is a valid argument with true premises – and so has a true conclusion). The premises really do all seem true, and the argument is certainly valid. (We have mentioned in passing that some philosophers have attempted to deny premise (4) or premise (6), but it would take us too far afield to spell out the details of those attempts; you might like to chase them up for yourself.)

> 10. Write down (i) the thesis of incompatibilism, and (ii) the conclusion of (CA). You'll notice that they are not the same. What additional claim needs to be established in order to infer (i) from (ii)? Do you think the claim is true? Why or why not? Compare your answer to your answer to question 4 above.

Looking back to the beginning of section II, you'll see that van Inwagen earlier assumed without argument that 'to deny that men have free will is to assert that what a man *does* do and what he *can* do coincide'. And it is just this assumption – or, to be precise, the weaker assumption that *if* one cannot do otherwise than what one actually does, *then* one does not act freely – that he needs to take him from the conclusion of the consequence argument to the thesis of incompatibilism. And so one way to reject incompatibilism – a way that does not require one to find fault in (CA) – would be to reject that assumption. The next paper, by Dennett, attempts just this move, as we shall see.

Section IV

The final section of the paper deals with three different ways in which one might attempt to argue that free will and determinism are compatible after all.

The first objection to incompatibilism, and van Inwagen's response, can be quite hard to follow, but the basic idea is really quite straightforward, and focuses on what we *mean* when we say, 'so-and-so could have done otherwise'.

> 11. Describe some situations about which it would, intuitively (setting aside worries about incompatibilism), seem correct to say, 'she could have done otherwise', and some situations in which it would intuitively seem incorrect to say this. Compare the two lists. Can you think of any general features that distinguish them? If so, what are they?

Typically, we think of cases involving coercion or compulsion as being cases where one could not have done otherwise. Suppose Sam steals from a shop. We might be inclined to say that he could not have refrained from stealing if he is a kleptomaniac, or if someone was holding a gun to his back and vowed to shoot Sam if he failed to steal anything. In the absence of such features, we would be inclined to say that Sam could have done otherwise.

Now, suppose that these kinds of feature – absence of ordinary kinds of coercion or constraint, say – constitute *criteria* for determining that an agent could have done otherwise: it is just part of the *meaning* of 'could have done otherwise' that an action meeting these criteria counts as an action the agent could have refrained from performing. Then, given that an action can satisfy those criteria whether or not determinism is true, it looks like – given this conception of what it takes to be such that one could have done otherwise – the truth of determinism could not possibly entail that we can never do otherwise than what we actually do. For the truth of determinism does not entail that, for example, everyone who steals from a shop is really a kleptomaniac: some people are kleptomaniacs and some are not, whether or not determinism is true.

> 12. Van Inwagen argues that this argument against incompatibilism is invalid, and he does so, at $\boxed{\text{j}}\mapsto$, by using an analogy with predestinarianism. Try to state his objection to the argument in your own words. Are you convinced? Why or why not?

The second argument for compatibilism van Inwagen discusses, at $\boxed{\text{k}}\mapsto$, says that since free will *entails* determinism, it must be compatible with determinism – otherwise free will would be compatible with neither determinism nor the denial of determinism. So, since the thesis that we have free will is consistent, compatibilism must be true.

> 13. (i) The above argument rests on the premise that free will entails determinism. Sketch the argument van Inwagen proposes for this premise, on behalf of the compatibilist, in your own words. (ii) What is an *ignoratio elenchi*? (Look it up if you don't know.) (iii) Van Inwagen says that 'the denial of determinism does not entail that there are uncaused events'. In other words, he claims that determinism might be false, and yet every event have a cause. Do you agree? Justify your answer.

The final argument for compatibilism, at $\boxed{\text{l}}\mapsto$, appeals to what is standardly called the 'conditional analysis' of 'could have done otherwise'. The argument runs as follows: Since (according to the conditional analysis of 'could have done otherwise') (8) means the same as (9), and (9) can be true even if determinism is true, it follows that (8) can be true even if determinism is true. So determinism is compatible with the thesis that we can sometimes do otherwise than what we actually do.

> 14. State van Inwagen's response to this argument in your own words. Are you convinced by it? Why or why not?

Van Inwagen finishes by making it clear where the burden of proof now lies in the debate between compatibilists and incompatibilists. He has presented an argument for incompatibilism – an argument that looks valid and each of whose premises seems plausible. And he has argued that each of the standard arguments for compatibilism fails. So the burden of proof now lies squarely with the compatibilist: if compatibilism is to be a defensible thesis, there must be something wrong with van Inwagen's argument. The compatibilist thus needs to provide a convincing objection to van Inwagen's argument for incompatibilism.

Daniel Dennett, 'Could Have Done Otherwise' (extract from *Elbow Room*)

1.   Do We Care Whether We Could Have Done Otherwise?

In the midst of all the discord and disagreement among philosophers about free will, there are a few calm islands of near unanimity. As van Inwagen notes:

> Almost all philosophers agree that a necessary condition for holding an agent responsible for an act is believing that the agent *could have* refrained from performing that act. (van Inwagen 1975, p. 189)

But if this is so, then whatever else I may have done in the preceding chapters, I have not yet touched the central issue of free will, for I have not yet declared a position on the "could have done otherwise" principle: the principle that holds that one has acted freely (and responsibly) only if one could have done otherwise. It is time, at last, to turn to this central, stable area in the logical geography of the free will problem. First I will show that this widely accepted principle is simply false. Then I will turn to some residual problems about the meaning of "can" – Austin's frog at the bottom of the beer mug [see chapter one of *Elbow Room*, p. 19].

The "could have done otherwise" principle has been debated for generations, and the favorite strategy of compatibilists – who must show that free will and determinism are compatible after all – is to maintain that "could have done otherwise" does not mean what it seems at first to mean; the sense of the phrase denied by determinism is irrelevant to the sense required for freedom. It is so obvious that this is what the compatibilists *have* to

---

Editors' note: the footnotes have been omitted from this selection.

say that many skeptics view the proffered compatibilist "analyses" of the meaning of "could have done otherwise" as little more than self-deceived special pleading. James (1921, p. 149) called this theme "a quagmire of evasion" and Kant (*Critique of Practical Reason*, Abbot translation 1873, p. 96) called it a "wretched subterfuge."

Instead of rising to the defense of any of the earlier analyses – many of which are quite defensible so far as I can see – I will go on the offensive. I will argue that *whatever* "could have done otherwise" actually means, it is not what we are interested in when we care about whether some act was freely and responsibly performed. There is, as van Inwagen notes, something of a tradition of simply assuming that the intuitions favoring the "could have done otherwise" principle are secure. But philosophers who do assume this do so in spite of fairly obvious and familiar grounds for doubt.

[a] One of the few philosophers to challenge it is Frankfurt, who has invented a highly productive intuition pump that generates counterexamples in many flavors: cases of overdetermination, where an agent deliberately and knowingly chose to do something, but where – thanks typically to some hovering bogeyman – if he hadn't so chosen, the bogeyman would have seen to it that he did the thing anyway (Frankfurt 1969, but see also van Inwagen 1978 and 1983, and Fischer 1982). Here is the basic, stripped-down intuition pump (minus the bells and whistles on the variations, which will not concern us – but only because we will not be relying on them):

> Jones hates Smith and decides, in full possession of his faculties, to murder him. Meanwhile Black, the nefarious neurosurgeon (remember him?), who also wants Smith dead, has implanted something in Jones' brain so that *just in case Jones changes his mind* (and chickens out), Black, by pushing his special button, can put Jones back on his murderous track. In the event Black doesn't have to intervene; Jones does the deed all on his own.

In such a case, Frankfurt claims, the person would be responsible for his deed, since he chose it with all due deliberation and wholeheartedness, in spite of the lurking presence of the overdeterminer whose hidden presence makes it the case that Jones couldn't have done otherwise.

I accept Frankfurt's analysis of these cases (that is, I think they can be defended against the objections raised by van Inwagen, Fischer, and others), and think these thought experiments are useful in spite of their invocation of imaginary bogeymen, for they draw attention to the importance, for responsibility, of the actual causal chain of deliberation and choice running through the agent – whatever may be happening elsewhere.

[b] But Frankfurt's strategy seems to me to be insufficiently ambitious. Although *he* takes his counterexamples to show that the "could have done otherwise" principle – which he calls the principle of alternate possibilities – is irremediably false, his counterexamples are rather special and unlikely

cases, and they invite the defender of the principle to try for a patch: modify the principle slightly to take care of Frankfurt's troublesome cases. Exotic circumstances do little or nothing to dispel the illusion that in the normal run of things, where such overdetermination is lacking, the regnant principle is indeed that if a person could not have refrained (could not have done otherwise), he would not be held responsible. But in fact, I will argue, it is seldom that we even *seem* to care whether or not a person could have done otherwise. And when we do, it is often because we wish to draw the opposite conclusion about responsibility from the one tradition endorses.

"Here I stand," Luther said. "I can do no other." Luther claimed that he could do no other, that his conscience made it *impossible* for him to recant. He might, of course, have been wrong, or have been deliberately overstating the truth. But even if he was – perhaps especially if he was – his declaration is testimony to the fact that we simply do not exempt someone from blame or praise for an act because we think he could do no other. Whatever Luther was doing, he was not trying to duck responsibility.

c→ There are cases where the claim "I can do no other" is an avowal of frailty: suppose what I ought to do is get on the plane and fly to safety, but I stand rooted on the ground and confess I can do no other – because of my irrational and debilitating fear of flying. In such a case I can do no other, I claim, because my rational control faculty is impaired. But in other cases, like Luther's, when I say I cannot do otherwise I mean I cannot because I see so clearly what the situation is and because my rational control faculty is *not* impaired. It is too obvious what to do; reason dictates it; I would have to be

d→ mad to do otherwise, and since I happen not to be mad, I cannot do otherwise. (Notice, by the way, that we say it was "up to" Luther whether or not to recant, and we do not feel tempted to rescind that judgment

e→ when we learn that he claimed he could do no other. Notice, too, that we often say things like this: "If it were up to me, I know for certain what I would do.")

I hope it is true – and think it very likely is true – that it would be impossible to induce me to torture an innocent person by offering me a

f→ thousand dollars. "Ah" – comes the objection – "but what if some evil space pirates were holding the whole world ransom, and promised not to destroy the world if only you would torture an innocent person? Would that be something you would find impossible to do?" Probably not, but so what? That is a vastly different case. If what one is interested in is whether *under the specified circumstances* I could have done otherwise, then the other case mentioned is utterly irrelevant. I claimed it would not be possible to induce me to torture someone *for a thousand dollars*. Those who hold dear the principle of "could have done otherwise" are always insisting that we should look at whether one could have done otherwise in *exactly* the same circumstances. I claim something stronger; I claim that I could not do otherwise even in any roughly similar case. I would *never* agree to torture an innocent person for a thousand dollars. It would make no difference, I claim, what tone of voice the briber used, or whether or not I was tired and hungry, or whether the proposed victim was well illuminated or partially concealed in shadow. I am, I hope, immune to all such offers.

Now why would anyone's intuitions suggest that if I am right, then if and when I ever have occasion to refuse such an offer, my refusal would not count as a responsible act? Perhaps this is what some people think: they think that if I were right when I claimed I could not do otherwise in such cases, I would be some sort of zombie, "programmed" always to refuse thousand-dollar bribes. A genuinely free agent, they think, must be more volatile somehow. If I am to be able to listen to reason, if I am to be flexible in the right way, they think, I mustn't be too dogmatic. Even in the most preposterous cases, then, I must be able to see that "there are two sides to every question." I must be able to pause, and weigh up the pros and cons of this suggested bit of lucrative torture. But the only way I could be consti- tuted so that I can always "see both sides" – no matter how preposterous one side is – is by being constituted so that *in any particular case* "I could have done otherwise."

That would be fallacious reasoning. Seeing both sides of the question does not require that one not be overwhelmingly persuaded, in the end, by one side. The flexibility we want a responsible agent to have is the flexibility to recognize the one-in-a-zillion case in which, thanks to that thousand dollars, not otherwise obtainable, the world can be saved (or whatever). But the general capacity to respond flexibly in such cases does not at all require that one "could have done otherwise" *in the particular case*, but only that under some variations in the circumstances – the variations that matter – one would do otherwise.

It might be useful to compare two cases that seem quite different at first, but belong on a continuum.

1. Suppose I know that if I ever see the full moon, I will probably run amok and murder the first person I see. So I make careful arrangements to have myself locked up in a windowless room on several nights each month. I am thus rendered *unable* to do the awful things I would do otherwise. Moreover, it is thanks to my own responsible efforts that I have become unable to do these things. A fanciful case, no doubt, but consider the next case, which is somewhat more realistic.

2. Suppose I know that if I ever see a voluptuous woman walking unescorted in a deserted place I will probably be overcome by lust and rape her. So I educate myself about the horrors of rape from the woman's point of view, and enliven my sense of the brutality of the crime so dramatically that if I happen to encounter such a woman in such straits, I am *unable* to do the awful thing I would have done otherwise. (What may convince me that I would otherwise have done

this thing is that when the occasion arises I experience a considerable inner tumult; I discover myself shaking the bars of the cage I have built for myself.) Thanks to my earlier responsible efforts, I have become quite immune to this rather more common sort of possession; I have done what had to be done to render certain courses of action *unthinkable* to me. Like Luther, I *now* can do no other.

Suppose – to get back all the way to realism – that our parents and teachers know that if we grow up without a moral education, we will become selfish, untrustworthy and possibly dangerous people. So they arrange to educate us, and thanks to their responsible efforts, our minds recoil from thoughts of larceny, treachery and violence. We find such alternatives unthinkable under most normal circumstances, and moreover have been taught to think ahead for ourselves and to contribute to our own moral development. Doesn't a considerable part of being a responsible person consist in making oneself unable to do the things one would be blamed for doing if one did them? Philosophers have often noted, uneasily, that the difficult moral problem cases, the decisions that "might go either way," are not the only, or even the most frequent, sorts of decisions for which we hold people responsible. They have seldom taken the hint to heart, however, and asked whether the "could have done otherwise" principle was simply wrong.

i ⊢→   I grant that we do indeed often ask ourselves whether an agent could have done otherwise – and in particular whether or not we ourselves could have done otherwise – in the wake of some regrettable act. But we never show any interest in trying to answer the question we have presumably just asked! Defenders of the principle suppose that there is a sense of "could have done otherwise" according to which, if determinism is true, no one ever could have done otherwise than he did. Suppose they are right that there is such a sense. Is it the sense we intend when we use the words "could he have done otherwise?" to inaugurate an inquiry into an agent's responsibility for an act he committed? It is not. In pursuing such inquiries we manifestly ignore the sort of investigations that would have to be pursued if we really were interested in the answer to that question, the metaphysicians' question about whether or not the agent was completely determined by the state of the universe at that instant to perform that action.

j ⊢→   If our responsibility really did hinge, as this major philosophical tradition insists, on the question of whether we ever could do otherwise than we in fact do *in exactly those circumstances,* we would be faced with a most peculiar problem of ignorance: it would be unlikely in the extreme, given what now seems to be the case in physics, that anyone would ever know whether anyone has ever been responsible. For today's orthodoxy is that indeterminism reigns at the subatomic level of quantum mechanics, so in the absence of any general and accepted argument for universal determinism, it is possible for all we know that our decisions and actions are truly the magnified, macroscopic effects of quantum-level indeterminacies occurring in our brains. But it is also possible, for all we know, that even though indeterminism reigns in our brains at the subatomic quantum mechanical level, our macroscopic decisions and acts are all themselves determined; the quantum effects could just as well be self-canceling, not amplified (as if by organic Geiger counters in the neurons). And it is extremely unlikely, given the complexity of the brain at even the molecular level (a complexity for which the word "astronomical" is a vast understatement), that we could ever develop good evidence that any particular act was such a large-scale effect of a critical subatomic indeterminacy. So if someone's responsibility for an act did hinge on whether, at the moment of decision, that decision was (already) determined by a prior state of the world, then barring a triumphant return of universal determinism in microphysics (which would rule out all responsibility on this view), the odds are very heavy that we will never have *any* reason to believe of any particular act that it was or was not responsible. The critical difference would be utterly inscrutable from every macroscopic vantage point, and practically inscrutable from the most sophisticated microphysical vantage point imaginable.

Some philosophers might take comfort in this conclusion, but I would guess that *only* a philosopher could take comfort in it. To say the very least it is hard to take seriously the idea that something that could matter so much could be so magnificently beyond our ken. (Or look at the point another way: those who claim to know that they have performed acts such that they could have done otherwise in exactly those circumstances must admit that they proclaim this presumably empirical fact without benefit of the slightest shred of evidence, and without the faintest hope of ever obtaining any such evidence.)

Given the sheer impossibility of conducting any meaningful investigation into the question of whether or not an agent could have done otherwise, what can people think they are doing when they ask that question in particular cases? They must take themselves to be asking some other question. They are right; they are asking a much better question. (If a few people have been asking the unanswerable metaphysical question, they were deluded into it by philosophy.) The question people are really interested in asking is a better question for two reasons: it is usually empirically answerable, and its answer matters. For not only is the traditional metaphysical question unanswerable; its answer, even if you knew it, would be useless.

What good would it do to know, about a particular agent, that on some occasion (or on every occasion) he could have done otherwise than he did? Or that he could not have done otherwise than he did? Let us take the latter case first. Suppose you knew (because God told you, presumably) that when Jones pulled the trigger and murdered his wife at time t, he could *not* have done otherwise. That is, given Jones' microstate at t and the complete microstate of Jones' environment (including the gravitational effects of distant stars, and so on) at t, no other Jones-trajectory was possible than the trajectory he took. If Jones were ever put back into exactly that state again, in exactly that circumstance, he would pull the trigger again. And if he were put in that state a million times, he would pull the trigger a million times.

Now if you learned this, would you have learned anything about Jones? Would you have learned anything about his character, for instance, or his likely behavior on merely similar occasions? No. Although people are physical objects which, like atoms or ball bearings or bridges, obey the laws of physics, they are not only more complicated than anything else we know in the universe, they are also designed to be so sensitive to the passing show that they never can be in the same microstate twice. One doesn't even have to descend to the atomic level to establish this. People learn, and remember, and get bored, and shift their attention, and change their interests so incessantly, that it is as good as infinitely unlikely that any person is ever in the same (gross) *psychological* or *cognitive* state on two occasions. And this would be true even if we engineered the surrounding environment to be "utterly the same" on different occasions – if only because the second time around the agent would no doubt think something that went unthought the first time, like "Oh my, this all seems so utterly familiar; now what did I do last time?" (see chapter two [of *Elbow Room*], p. 33)

There is some point in determining how a bridge is caused to react to some very accurately specified circumstances, since those may be circumstances it will actually encounter *in its present state* on a future occasion. But there would be no payoff in understanding to be gained by determining the micro-causation of the behavior of a human being in some particular circumstance, since he will certainly never confront that micro-circumstance again, and even if he did, he would certainly be in a significantly different reactive state at the time.

Learning (from God, again) that a particular agent was *not* thus determined to act would be learning something equally idle, from the point of view of character assessment or planning for the future. As we saw in chapter five, the undetermined agent will be no more flexible, no more versatile, no more sensitive to nuances, no more reformable, than his deterministic cousin.

So if anyone is interested at all in the question of whether or not one could have done otherwise in *exactly* the same circumstances (and internal state), this will have to be a particularly pure metaphysical curiosity – that is to say, a curiosity so pure as to be utterly lacking in any ulterior motive, since the answer could not conceivably make any noticeable difference to the way the world went.

Why, though, does it still seem as if there ought to be a vast difference, somehow visible from the ordinary human vantage point, between a world in which we could not do otherwise and a world in which we could? Why should determinism still seem so appalling? Perhaps we are misled by the

God's-eye-view image, *"sub specie aeternitatis,"* in which we spy our own life-trajectories in space and time laid out from birth to death in a single, fixed, rigid, unbranching, four-dimensional "space-time worm," pinned to the causal fabric and unable to move. (Causation, in Hume's fine metaphor, is "the cement of the universe" (Mackie 1974), so perhaps we see our entire lives as *cast in concrete*, trapped like a fossil in the unchanging slab of space-time.)

What we would like, it seems, is for someone to show us that we can *move about* in that medium. But this is a confusion; if we feel this yearning it is because we have forgotten that time is one of the dimensions we have spatialized in our image. Scanning from left to right is scanning from past to future, and a vertical slice of our image captures a single moment in time. To have elbow room in that medium – to be able to wiggle and squirm in between the fixed points of birth and death for instance – would not be to have the power to choose in an undetermined way, but to have the power to choose two or more courses *at one time*.

Is that what we want – to have our cake and eat it too? To have chosen *both* to marry and to remain unmarried, *both* to pull the trigger and to drop the gun? If that is the variety of free will we want, then whether or not it might be worth wanting, we can be quite confident that it must elude us – unless, perhaps, we adopt Everett's many-worlds interpretation of quantum mechanics, in which case it just might follow that we do lead a zillion lives (though our many alter egos, alas, could never get together and compare notes)!

[k]→   If we let go of that fantasy and ask what we really, soberly want, we find a more modest hope: while there are indeed times when we would give anything to be able to go back and undo something in the past, we recognize that the past is closed for us, and we would gladly settle for an "open future." But what would an open future be? A future in which our deliberation is effective: a future in which if I decide to do A then I will do A, and if I decide to do B then I will do B; a future in which – since only one future is possible – the only possible thing that can happen is the thing I decide in the end to do.

2.   What We Care About

If it is unlikely then that it matters whether or not a person could have done otherwise (when we look microscopically closely at the causation involved) what is the other question that we are really interested in when we ask "but could he have done otherwise?"

Once more I am going to use the tactic of first answering a simpler question about simpler entities. Consider a similar question that might arise about our deterministic robot, the Mark 1 Deterministic Deliberator.

By hypothesis, it lives its entire life as a deterministic machine on a deterministic planet, so that whatever it does, it could not have done otherwise, if we mean that in the strict and metaphysical sense of those words that philosophers have concentrated on. Suppose then that one fine Martian day it makes a regrettable mistake; it concocts and executes a scheme that destroys something valuable – another robot, perhaps. I am not supposing, for the moment, that it can regret anything, but just that its designers, back on Earth, regret what it has done, and find themselves wondering a wonder that might naturally be expressed: *could it have done otherwise?*

They know it is a deterministic system, of course, so they know better than to ask the metaphysical question. Their question concerns the design of the robot; for in the wake of this regrettable event they may wish to redesign it slightly, to make this *sort* of event less likely in the future. What they want to know, of course, is what information the robot was relying on, what reasoning or planning it did, and whether it did "enough" of the right sort of reasoning or planning. Of course in one sense of "enough" they know the robot did not do enough of the right sort of thing; if it had, it would have done the right thing. But it may be that the robot's design in this case could not really be improved. For it may be that it was making optimal use of optimally designed heuristic procedures – but this time, unluckily, the heuristic chances it took didn't pay off. Put the robot in a *similar* situation in the future, and thanks to no more than the fact that its pseudo-random number generator is in a different state, it will do something different; in fact it will usually do the right thing. It is tempting to add: it *could* have done the right thing on this occasion – meaning by this that it was well enough designed, at that time, to have done the right thing (its "character" is not impugned). Its failure depended on nothing but the fact that something *undesigned* (and unanticipatable) happened to intervene in the process in a way that made an unfortunate difference.

A heuristic program is not guaranteed to yield the "right" or sought-after result. Some heuristic programs are better than others; when one fails, it may be possible to diagnose the failure as assignable to some characteristic weakness in its design. But even the best are not foolproof, and when they fail, as they sometimes must, there may be no reason at all for the failure: as Cole Porter would say, it was just one of those things.

Such failures are not the only cases of failures that will "count" for the designers as cases where the system "could have done otherwise." If they discover that the robot's failure, on this occasion, was due to a "freak" bit of dust that somehow drifted into a place where it could disrupt the system, they may decide that this was such an unlikely event that there is no call to redesign the system to guard against its recurrence. They will note that, in the micro-particular case, their robot could not have done otherwise; moreover, if (by remotest possibility) it ever found itself in *exactly* the same circumstance again, it would fail again. But the designers will realize that they have no rational interest in doing anything to improve the design of the robot. It failed on the occasion, but its design is nevertheless above reproach. There is a difference between being optimally designed and being infallible. [See chapter seven of *Elbow Room*.]

Consider yet another sort of case. The robot has a ray gun that it fires with 99.9 percent accuracy. That is to say, sometimes, over long distances, it fails to hit the target it was aiming at. Whenever it misses, the engineers want to know something about the miss: was it due to some *systematic* error in the controls, some foible or flaw that will keep coming up, or was it just one of those things – one of those "acts of God" in which, in spite of an irreproachable execution of an optimally designed aiming routine, the thing just narrowly missed? There will always be such cases; the goal is to keep them to a minimum – consistent with cost-effectiveness of course. Beyond a certain point, it isn't worth caring about errors. Quine (1960, pp. 182 and 259) notes that engineers have a concept of more than passing philosophical interest: the concept of "don't-cares" – the cases that one is rational to ignore. When they are satisfied that a particular miss was a don't-care, they may shrug and say: "Well, it could have been a hit."

What concerns the engineers when they encounter misperformance in their robot is whether or not the misperformance is a telling one: does it reveal something about a pattern of systematic weakness, likely to recur, or an inappropriate and inauspicious linking between sorts of circumstances and sorts of reactions? Is this *sort* of thing apt to happen again, or was it due to the coincidental convergence of fundamentally independent factors, highly unlikely to recur? To get evidence about this they ignore the micro-details, which will never be the same again in any case, and just average over them, analyzing the robot into a finite array of *maros*copically defined states, organized in such a way that there are links between the various degrees of freedom of the system. The question they then ask is this: are the links the right links for the task?

This rationale for ignoring micro-determinism (wherever it may "in principle" exist) and squinting just enough to blur such fine distinctions into probabilistically related states and regions that can be *treated as* homogeneous is clear, secure, and unproblematic in science, particularly in engineering and biology, as we have seen. (See Wiener 1948 and Wimsatt 1980.) That does not mean, of course, that this is also just the right way to think of people, when we are wondering if they have acted responsibly. But there is a lot to be said for it.

 Why do we ask "could he have done otherwise?" We ask it because something has happened that we wish to interpret. An act has been performed, and we wish to understand how the act came about, why it came about, and what meaning we should attach to it. That is, we want to know what conclusions to draw from it about the future. Does it tell us anything about the agent's character, for instance? Does it suggest a criticism of the agent that might, if presented properly, lead the agent to improve his ways in some regard? Can we learn from this incident that this is or is not an agent who can be trusted to behave similarly on similar occasions in the future? If one held his character constant, but changed the circumstances in minor – or even major – ways, would he almost always do the same lamentable sort of thing? Was what we have just observed a "fluke," or was it a manifestation of a "robust" trend – a trend that persists, or is constant, over an interestingly wide variety of conditions?

When the agent in question is oneself, this rationale is even more plainly visible. Suppose I find I have done something dreadful. *Who cares* whether, in exactly the circumstances and state of mind I found myself, I could have done something else? I didn't do something else, and it's too late to undo what I did. But when I go to interpret what I did, what do I learn about myself? Ought I to practice the sort of maneuver I botched, in hopes of making it more reliable, less vulnerable to perturbation, or would that be wasted effort? Would it be a good thing, so far as I can tell, for me to try to adjust my habits of thought in such sorts of cases in the future?

Knowing that I will always be somewhat at the mercy of the considerations that merely happen to occur to me as time rushes on, knowing that I cannot entirely control this process of deliberation, I may take steps to bias the likelihood of certain sorts of considerations routinely "coming to mind" in certain critical situations. For instance, I might try to cultivate the habit of counting to ten in my mind before saying anything at all about Ronald Reagan, having learned that the deliberation time thus gained pays off handsomely in cutting down regrettable outbreaks of intemperate commentary. Or I might decide that no matter how engrossed in conversation I am, I must learn to ask myself how many glasses of wine I have had every time I see someone hovering hospitably near my glass with a bottle. This time I made a fool of myself; if the situation had been quite different, I certainly would have done otherwise; if the situation had been virtually the same, I might have done otherwise and I might not. The main thing is to see to it that I will jolly well do otherwise in similar situations in the future.

That, certainly, is the healthy attitude to take toward the regrettable parts of one's recent past. It is the self-applied version of the engineers' attitude toward the persisting weaknesses in the design of the robot. Of course if I would rather find excuses than improve myself, I may dwell on the fact that I don't *have* to "take" responsibility for my action, since I can always imagine a more fine-grained standpoint from which my predicament looms larger than I do. (If you make yourself really small, you can externalize virtually everything.)

In chapter seven I will say more about the rationale for being generous with one's self-ascriptions of responsibility. But for now I will just draw attention to a familar sort of case in which we hover in the vicinity of asking whether we really could have done otherwise, and then (wisely) back off.

One often says, after doing something awful, "I'm terribly sorry; I simply never thought of the consequences; it simply didn't occur to me what harm I was doing!" This looks almost like the beginning of an excuse – "Can I help it what occurs to me and what doesn't?" – but healthy self-controllers shun this path. They *take* responsibility for what might be, very likely is, just an "accident," just one of those things. That way, they make themselves less likely to be "accident" victims in the future.

Commentary on Dennett

The title of Dennett's chapter (from which we have omitted the final section and the footnotes) tells us where in the compatibilism/incompatibilism dispute his attention will be focused – and you don't have to get very far into it to realize that he is defending compatibilism. In particular, his target is the incompatibilist claim that it *matters* – that it matters for moral responsibility and for free will – whether or not we can do otherwise (raise our arms, say) *given the exact conditions* that we happen to be in, down to the tiniest detail. Dennett's overall claim is that this just does not, and should not, matter at all.

The chapter is considerably more free-wheeling than van Inwagen's paper. While this undoubtedly makes Dennett's chapter more of a pleasure to read through, it also makes it considerably harder to tell exactly what he is up to. Roughly, though, the text breaks down as follows. In the first section, Dennett argues that when it comes to moral responsibility, it simply does not matter whether or not we could have done otherwise, in the incompatibilist's sense of 'could have done otherwise' (or even in a more relaxed sense of 'could have done otherwise'). In the second section, he argues that there is a sense of 'could have done otherwise' that does matter to us, but that the ability to do otherwise in this sense does not require the falsity of determinism.

Section 1

Dennett starts out by noting that most philosophers are agreed that the ability to do otherwise is a necessary condition for moral responsibility. (Recall the discussion of moral responsibility and free will in the introduction to this chapter.) He then, at [a]↦, briefly describes Harry Frankfurt's case of the 'nefarious neurosurgeon' (Frankfurt 1969) – a case which Frankfurt, Dennett and many others take to refute the claim that moral responsibility requires the ability to do otherwise. (Van Inwagen mentions Frankfurt's paper in passing in his footnote 3.)

1. (i) Explain in your own words exactly why the case of the nefarious neurosurgeon allegedly demonstrates that moral responsibility does not require the ability to do otherwise. (ii) Do you think it does demonstrate this? Why or why not? (iii) Dennett says at [b]↦ that Frankfurt's strategy is 'insufficiently ambitious'. Explain why he says this.

Dennett provides an example of an everyday case where, he claims, the inability to do otherwise does not undermine moral responsibility: the case of Martin Luther, a German theologian whose writings, which questioned the authority of the Pope, inspired the Reformation in the sixteenth century. When pressed to publicly renounce his views, Luther said that he could not do so unless those views were shown, by appeal to reason and the Bible, to be false. When Luther (reputedly) said, 'Here I stand. I can do no other', he was saying that he was unable to recant. But – as Dennett points out – Luther was clearly not thereby 'trying to duck responsibility'.

> 2. (i) At $\boxed{c}\mapsto$, Dennett distinguishes between two kinds of case where it seems right to say that one could not have done otherwise. Describe the distinction in your own words. What claim is Dennett implicitly making about what *is* important for moral responsibility? (ii) How does your answer relate to Dennett's claim, just before $\boxed{b}\mapsto$, that the 'actual causal chain of deliberation running through the agent' is important for responsibility?

Dennett also makes an important claim (at $\boxed{d}\mapsto$) about our use of the expression, 'it was up to me'. Our intuitions about whether or not something was 'up to me' tend to go along with our intuitions about whether or not we are morally responsible for it. ('It's not *my* fault you didn't get the job; it wasn't up to me.') It therefore serves the incompatibilist's cause to claim that to say that something is up to me is to say that I could have done otherwise (since in that case, if determinism is true, nothing is ever up to me). Dennett alleges that 'I am able to do otherwise' does not mean the same as 'it is up to me'.

> 3. How does Dennett try to justify this claim? Are you convinced?
> 4. Dennett points out at $\boxed{e}\mapsto$ that we often say things like, 'if it were up to me, I know for certain what I would do'. Suppose that 'it is up to me whether or not I do X' means 'I *could* do X, and I *could* refrain from doing X' (in the incompatibilist's sense of 'could'). Could 'if it were up to me, I know for certain what I would do' be true? Why or why not?

Dennett next turns his attention to the question of what kind of 'flexibility we want the responsible agent to have' ($\boxed{g}\mapsto$). He argues that it is *not* the 'flexibility' that would arise from its being genuinely undetermined by the past and the laws whether, in a particular case, one tortures an innocent person and pockets the $1,000 bribe, or whether one doesn't accept the bribe. We want some other kind of flexibility – a kind that does not require that in this particular case, or even in a range of similar cases, we genuinely might go either way.

> 5. Explain in your own words what kind of flexibility Dennett thinks we want the responsible agent to have. What is the relevance of the case of the evil space pirates (at $\boxed{f}\mapsto$) to this kind of flexibility?

In the page or so from h ↦, Dennett proposes that in fact moral responsibility actually consists, in large part, in educating ourselves and our children in such a way as to render us unable to do otherwise in certain kinds of case (and when education fails us, we can always lock ourselves up!).

6. Van Inwagen concedes, in footnote 4 of his paper, that there are cases where we apparently do not judge the inability to do otherwise to render one morally unaccountable. (Suppose you lock yourself in a room at 3 pm to stop yourself murdering someone who you know will be in the vicinity at 3.30 pm. Intuitively, you deserve praise for failing to murder them – even though at the relevant time (3.30 pm) you could not have murdered them.) But van Inwagen evidently takes this concession to be consistent with the general claim that responsibility requires the ability to do otherwise. (i) Read the footnote, and then describe how you think those two claims might be reconciled with one another. (ii) Do you think van Inwagen needs to deny Dennett's claim about moral education? Why or why not?

Dennett's topic for most of the rest of this section, from i ↦, is what we mean when we ask whether or not someone could have done otherwise. He starts, at j ↦, by going on the offensive against the incompatibilist, arguing that if moral responsibility really did hinge on whether they could have done otherwise in the sense presupposed by the incompatibilist, 'we would be faced with a most peculiar problem of ignorance'.

7. Explain exactly what the 'problem of ignorance' is. Do you think this is really a problem for the incompatibilist? If not, why not?

Dennett's conclusion is that we do not ordinarily mean what the incompatibilist claims we mean: we do not mean that in *exactly* the same circumstances, they could have done otherwise. (What, then, *do* we mean? Dennett will address this question later on.)

8. What is Dennett's argument for the conclusion that 'could have done otherwise' doesn't ordinarily mean 'could have done otherwise in *exactly* the same circumstances'? Can you think of any objections that an incompatibilist might raise?

The section ends with Dennett saying, at k ↦, that what we want is an 'open future'. And he tells us what an open future would be: 'a future in which if I decide to do A then I will do A, and if I decide to do B then I will do B ...'

9. Compare this claim with the conditional analysis of 'can' discussed in the final section of van Inwagen's paper. What do you think the incompatibilist's response to Dennett's claim about what an 'open future' consists in would be?

Section 2

The major thesis for which Dennett has argued so far is that responsibility does not require the ability to do otherwise. He has also made some suggestive claims about what responsibility *does* require (see your answers to questions 2, 5 and 9 above). In particular, he has claimed (see $\boxed{i} \mapsto$) that 'could have done otherwise', as we ordinarily use this expression, does not mean what the incompatibilist takes it to mean. He now turns to providing an account of what 'could have done otherwise', as ordinarily used, *does* mean. Or rather, he attempts to say what sort of answer we are looking for when we ask whether someone could have done things differently.

Dennett starts out by discussing the 'Mark I Deterministic Deliberator' – a make-believe machine introduced in the previous chapter of his book. Think of the Deterministic Deliberator (or 'DD' for short) as a robot with artificial intelligence, designed and constructed by scientists, that is sent to investigate another planet – Mars, say. DD is far more sophisticated than any robots that currently exist, and can think about options, make decisions, plan ahead, and so on – though in a pretty rudimentary way compared to humans. (You might be inclined to think that robots can't *really* think or decide or make plans because they don't *really* have minds. In that case, you'll have to think of the robot as merely simulating thought, decision, and so on, in the sense that (say) it tends to behave in similar ways to the ways we might behave given similar inputs: it learns from experience that it will sink if it steps in that nasty green slime, that some obstacles can be pushed out of the way but it needs to walk around others, and so on.)

As its name implies, DD is, by hypothesis, fully deterministic. However, it does sometimes employ heuristic procedures which depend on a 'pseudo-random number generator': a program that generates sequences of numbers that are apparently random – in practice there's no way to predict what the next number will be – but are in fact produced by a perfectly deterministic process. (Think of shuffling a deck of cards. It doesn't take much shuffling for the order of the cards to be completely unpredictable by the players, but card-shuffling, for all we know, is a completely deterministic process. At any rate, when it comes to playing the game, it doesn't matter at all whether the order of the cards is due to a deterministic or an indeterministic process.)

At $\boxed{1} \mapsto$, Dennett claims that it makes perfectly good sense for the scientists back home, having discovered that DD has done something unfortunate – destroyed another robot, say – to wonder whether it could have done otherwise: whether it could have refrained from destroying the other robot.

Granted that it is reasonable for the scientists to ask this question, we need to ask: what exactly is it that they want to know when they ask it? One thing they apparently can't be asking is whether in *exactly* the same circumstances DD could do otherwise. The scientists know that DD is deterministic, and so they already know the answer to *that* question.

10. What, according to Dennett, *are* the scientists interested in finding out when they ask whether DD could have done otherwise?

Note that Dennett is employing a classic philosophical technique in this part of the paper. He takes a simpler case – the case of DD – and draws some conclusions from it. (The scientists can't reasonably be interested in whether DD could do otherwise in *exactly* those circumstances.) He then claims that our own (more complex) case is relevantly similar to the simpler case, and that we should therefore draw the same conclusions in our own case. (*We* can't reasonably be interested in whether *we* could do otherwise in exactly the same circumstances.)

11. Do you think the case of DD and our own case *are* relevantly similar, in a way that justifies drawing the same conclusion in each case? Why or why not?
12. At $\boxed{m}\mapsto$, Dennett tells us why he thinks we ask whether someone could have done otherwise. Do you agree with him? What consequences does your answer have for the principle that moral responsibility requires the ability to do otherwise in van Inwagen's sense of 'ability to do otherwise'?

Further Reading

An excellent place to start is Watson 1983: a collection of many of the classic papers on the topic of free will. Other, more recent collections include O'Connor 1995 and Ekstrom 2001. Some papers that have been especially influential are Frankfurt 1969, which claims to provide a counter-example to the thesis that free action requires the ability to do otherwise; Lewis 1981, which argues that the Consequence Argument is flawed; Mele 1999, which provides an argument (known as the 'problem of luck') against those who claim that free will is compatible with *in*determinism; and Kane 1999 – an attempt to solve the problem of luck. Dennett 1984 (of which the text reproduced above is the first two sections of chapter 6) and Fischer 1994 are reasonably accessible book-length treatments of free will.

Essay Questions

1. Does moral responsibility require the ability to do otherwise?
2. Does Dennett succeed in establishing that there is a sense of 'could have done otherwise' that is (i) compatible with determinism and (ii) relevant to free will?
3. Is the Consequence Argument sound?
4. What kind of 'flexibility' does an agent need in order to be morally responsible?

5. Does Frankfurt's 'nefarious neurosurgeon' case establish that what is required for free will is the 'actual causal chain of deliberation and choice running through the agent' rather than the ability to do otherwise?

Appendix: Answer to Question 7 (van Inwagen): The Validity of the Consequence Argument

(a) Using the sentence letters provided, the argument looks like this:

(1)   A→B
(2)   C
(3)   C→(D→E)
(4)   (E&B)→F
(5)   F→G
(6)   ¬G

Conclusion:

(7)   A→¬D

(b) Here's one (informal) way to demonstrate that the argument is valid:

We can show that the conclusion, A→¬D, is true if we can show that A&D is false: that is, if we can prove ¬(A&D). This is because ¬(A&D) entails A→¬D. You can demonstrate this easily using truth-tables. But you should be able to see it anyway: ¬(A&D) says that at least one of A and D is false. So, given this, if A is true then D must be false: A→¬D.

So we want to prove ¬(A&D). One way to do this is to show that A&D entails a contradiction, since nothing that entails a contradiction can be true. So let's assume A&D. If we can derive a contradiction from this assumption, then we will have shown that A→¬D is true (because A&D is false). So here goes:

Step i: Assume A&D.

Step ii: Look at premise (1) of the Consequence Argument. Since A is true (by step i), by (1) we can infer B (by *modus ponens*[1]). Remember this for later.

Step iii: Premises (2) and (3) together obviously entail D→E (by *modus ponens*). We've already assumed D (at step i), so we can infer E.

---

[1]   *Modus ponens* is just a fancy name for the following logical principle: Suppose that *X* is true, and suppose that if *X* is true, then *Y* is true as well. Then *Y* must be true. (Suppose that Mary was born in 1985, and that if Mary was born in 1985 then she is older than Jane. It follows that Mary is older than Jane.)

Step iv: Now look at premise (4). We've just inferred E, and we already inferred B at step ii. So we've got E&B. So, by (4), we can infer F.

Step v: Given premise (5), together with F (which we established at step iv), we can infer G (by *modus ponens* again).

Step vi: We've just established G. But premise (6) tells us that ¬G. So we've derived a contradiction: G&¬G. So – assuming the truth of all 6 premises of the Consequence Argument – our initial assumption, A&D, must be false: it entails a contradiction. So we can infer ¬(A&D).

Step vii: ¬(A&D) entails A→¬D (see above). So we can infer A→¬D, which is the conclusion of the Consequence Argument. QED.

3

Realism and Anti-realism

Introduction

Realism, anti-realism and relativism

The question we shall be asking in this chapter is this: when we talk about items such as tables, trees and people, do we succeed in making claims about a reality that is mind-independent? This question concerns our discourse about *the external world in general*: to ask it is to consider the entirety of our talk about the world, to go *global*. According to the doctrine we shall call 'global realism' – by contrast with *local* versions of realism concerning, say, our moral or aesthetic talk – our discourse about the external world genuinely describes a reality that owes neither its existence nor its character to the way in which we represent it. On this view, our language functions like a

> map of the world. Maps can better or worse represent the terrain which they concern. But nothing about that terrain will owe its existence, or character, to the institution of cartography or to the conventions and techniques therein employed. (Wright 1992: 2)

For the global realist, then, our external-world talk maps a realm that has its nature *anyway* – whether or not our language represents it as such. By contrast, global anti-realists, as their name suggests, set their face against this picture. For an anti-realist, our language determines the nature of what is there: we succeed only in talking about things as *conceptualized* (or experienced or whatever) *by us*.

Anti-realists may come in different stripes. However, for the time being we have in mind a *particular species* of anti-realist challenge: that of *relativism*. The relativist believes that different systems of representation represent, not a single, mind-independent reality in different ways, but different, mind-dependent reali*ties*.

It is this latter position that is Davidson's quarry in the extract that follows this introduction, so we shall begin by attempting to shed light upon it by drawing an analogy between the global relativist's position and that taken up by one species of local relativist: the relativist about morals.

An analogy: moral relativism

Moral relativism is the product of a fact and a philosophical thesis. The fact is that different cultures can have radically different ethical opinions to our own. (For example, the practice of *suttee* – the immolation of a widow on her husband's funeral pile – is thought to be morally acceptable in certain Hindu cultures but tends to be frowned upon from a Judaeo-Christian perspective.) The accompanying philosophical thesis is this: there can be *irresolvable disputes* on such matters as the moral status of suttee: disputes that would persist 'once all the facts are in'. Once this latter claim has been made, it is tempting to think that the divergence in ethical beliefs across cultures is a symptom of a deeper, metaphysical truth: namely, that

(1)   Moral facts are 'relative to our culture'.

Claim (1) – the thesis that moral statements are only ever true or false *relative* to a particular, culturally specific, overarching moral 'conceptual scheme' – is the version of moral anti-realism that is moral relativism. The moral relativist does not deny that there are moral facts; she simply denies that they are suitably mind-independent for the realist: such facts, she claims, are nothing but the products of particular cultures. This, she argues, is why it is a mistake to think that the moral beliefs of one culture can be legitimately evaluated from the moral standpoint of another culture. Someone from a Judaeo-Christian perspective criticizing *suttee* would, in effect, be committed to denying (1), for they would be committed to holding that there is a cross-cultural fact of the matter about whether or not *suttee* is morally acceptable, which is just what (1) denies.

It is a very large philosophical question whether there are any good *arguments* which take us from the apparent existence of irresolvable ethical disputes to (1). But for the time being, you should note that (1) is implicitly committed to a claim about *meaning*:

(2)   The meanings of moral terms differ from one culture to another.

To see this, imagine a culture whose members, by and large, assent to a claim *p* which we translate as 'rape is sometimes morally acceptable'. Now, if our translation is completely accurate – if their claim *p* really does mean 'rape is sometimes morally acceptable' – then it looks like moral relativism can't get off the ground. For it is just a conceptual truth that two sentences with the very same meaning cannot differ in truth-value. So if 'rape is sometimes morally acceptable' (as uttered by us) is *false*, then *p* (as uttered by the members of our imaginary culture) *must be false too*. Or – to put it the other way around – if *p* is true, then 'rape is sometimes morally acceptable' must be true too.

That ethical relativism requires (2) is very important. For it amounts to this: moral relativism can only be true – that is, moral facts can only be culturally dependent – if we *cannot adequately translate* moral claims made by members of one culture into the language of another culture. If we *can* adequately translate moral claims from the language of one culture into the language of another, then we will simply be in the position of *disagreeing* with members of the other culture about what the moral facts are – and that is precisely to accept that there *are* culture-independent moral facts that we are disagreeing about. To put the point in a way prevalent in the literature, moral relativism requires that 'moral languages' – the bits of natural language used to express moral claims – are, to use Thomas Kuhn's expression, 'incommensurable' (Kuhn 1962). And what this means is that if relativism is true, the 'irresolvable disputes' that initially motivated the move towards relativism turn out not to be *disputes* at all. People who *appear* to be arguing about whether *suttee* can be morally justified are, as it happens, using words with incommensurable meanings, and hence talking at cross purposes rather than really disagreeing.

Global relativism and the dualism of scheme and content

Let us now return to the position taken up by the global relativist. In an analogous way to that in which the moral relativist takes there to exist culturally specific *moral* conceptual schemes, the global relativist approaches her position by first of all claiming that we have a more basic, global conceptual scheme: a way of carving up reality that is enshrined in the concepts by which we think about it. For example, we divide furniture up by focusing on what it can be used for (a chair is something that can be sat on, a table is something you can put your dinner or whatever on, a desk is something you sit at in order to read or write, etc.). We divide animals up according to biological classifications: tigers, lions and leopards are all cats; foxes, wolves and spaniels are all dogs, etc. We divide up the larger items in the universe according to various astronomical categories: planets, moons, asteroids, comets, etc. And so on.

So far so good: we categorize the world in various ways, using a wide variety of concepts that make up what we might call our conceptual scheme. Why might this idea push us towards global relativism? The beginning of an answer is provided by the fact that, once we reflect upon our way of carving up reality, it is tempting to conclude that this way of doing it is not *demanded* by the world as it is in itself. As Kant (1781/1787) noted, our representations of the world in perception and thought are not simply the result of reality *imprinting* itself upon our minds. Rather, our way of conceptualizing the world – the way in which we organize the raw data of sensory experience – *reflects* the way our minds work. Our conceptual scheme is, perhaps, nothing more than the way that *we* carve up reality: the way in which creatures with our particular sensory apparatus, and with brains that are 'hardwired' like ours, *happen* to do it.

The position we have been describing is, in essence, the 'dualism of scheme and content' bequeathed to us by Kant (1781/1787: A 50–1/B 74–5). As Kant saw it, how the world seems to us is not simply determined by the 'given' element to experience: the raw sensory content that we take in passively through our senses. Our representations of the world are also determined by the conceptual scheme that we bring to such content: the scheme whose nature is itself determined by how our minds happen to work.

Kant has taken a stand here on the question of what it is that a conceptual scheme is taken to organize or fit: he takes a conceptual scheme to organize, or fit, *experience*. But as we shall see in Davidson's paper, a believer in scheme/content dualism need not agree with Kant on this question: she may take our conceptual scheme to carve up *reality* rather than our experience of reality. However, for the time being at least, we can harmlessly put this difference to one side. For the key point to establish now is that once we accept the dualism of scheme and content, global relativism would seem to be closing in on us fast. For to admit that our conceptual scheme reflects features of ourselves would seem to suggest its *contingency*. Presumably, aliens inhabiting very, very different environments, with very, very different sensory and cognitive apparatus, might carve the universe up in a very, very different way to the way we carve it up.[1] But if such a state of affairs is possible – as it seems to be – then the global relativist has gained an important foothold. For surely, she will argue, the best we can possibly achieve, in thinking and talking about the world, is a conception of the world *as-conceptualized-by-us*. And, given that our imagined aliens conceptualize the world in a completely different way, we cannot really make sense of the idea that one or other group – whether it's us or them – has got it right and the other group has got it wrong. Since alternative conceptual schemes are possible, it would be nothing short of cosmic prejudice to insist that *our* way of seeing the world is the correct way.

It is at this point that it becomes highly tempting to take the relativist's way out. Our beliefs and the imagined alien creature's beliefs are on a par, says the global relativist: while we and the aliens each regard our respective beliefs as true, this is only because we make our claims from within different, and incommensurable, conceptual schemes. In reality, there are no facts independent of conceptual schemes; there are no *absolute* truths. Facts depend upon conceptual schemes, and there are as many distinct sets of facts – one might say 'worlds' – as there are schemes. The world we represent is *our* world: the world of our conceptual framework. Given the dualism of scheme and content, it would seem that we cannot form a pure representation of the world – a view from nowhere – unstained by our arbitrary, distinctively human, concepts.

'The linguistic turn' and incommensurability

For Kant, the central elements of our conceptual scheme – the concepts he calls 'the categories' – are mental capacities to organize the data of raw sense experience,

---

[1]   Although Kant, for one, would deny this. For Kant, the scheme he describes is, necessarily, the form of any possible experience (1781/7: A 93/B 126).

hard-wired into the mind's faculty of understanding. But the elements of a conceptual scheme need not be thought of in this way. Contemporary philosophers may well find Kant's non-linguistic 'take' on concepts unsatisfactory for all sorts of reasons, not least because it seems to render problematic the relation between language and thought. If concepts are non-linguistic mental items, then language must merely be thought's clothing, an account which brings with it the difficulty of explaining both how it is possible to think without language and how language could come to express thought. For reasons such as this, it has become common to regard conceptual schemes, not as frameworks of *concepts*, but as systems of *sentences*: that is, *languages*. Thus Quine, the most influential recent propounder of the notion of a conceptual scheme, claims that such a scheme is 'a fabric of sentences accepted in science as true, however provisionally' (Quine 1981: 41).

With this linguistic slant on the notion of a conceptual scheme having been taken, we can now return to the case of our imagined aliens and ask the question: what would it be for these creatures to have a different conceptual scheme from us, and, hence, for global relativism to be true? Given our earlier discussion of moral relativism, the answer should be obvious. We and the aliens differ in our respective conceptual schemes just in case there is no way of translating what our imagined aliens say about the world into our own language (English, as it happens). The relativist has to think of our language and the aliens' language as incommensurable, and hence has to regard it as impossible for one of us and an alien to engage in a genuine *dispute*. Otherwise it will turn out that the aliens will simply differ from us (if at all) by believing some claims we reject, and rejecting some claims we believe – and those disputed claims will, precisely, be *disputed* claims: claims about the world-independent-of-anyone's-conceptual-scheme. Once more, then, and as we noted in our discussion of moral relativism, we see that the relativist starts out by imagining ways of carving up the world that *conflict* with our own, and then reconstrues the apparent disagreement as incommensurability.

Davidson on the very idea of a conceptual scheme

So is the game up for the realist? Does the apparent ease with which we can conceive of there being different ways of conceptualizing reality that are incommensurable with each other propel us towards global relativism? Not according to Davidson. For Davidson, as we shall see, denies that the very idea of a conceptual scheme makes sense.

At least one part of Davidson's argument would seem to go as follows. As we now know, to conceive of an alternative conceptual scheme is to conceive of a language that is untranslatable into our own. But it is just this idea, Davidson argues, that we can make no sense of. For we can only get a grip on the notion of *truth* in the case of *our own language*. Consequently, we can only take the noises coming from someone else's mouth as being capable of being true (or false) in so far as we suppose that they are saying something that could in principle be translated into our own language. If this condition of translatability were not met, we could not regard them as expressing truths, and hence (since to make an assertion is to say something that might in principle be true) we could not view them as language-speakers at all. If the noises coming from another creature's mouth are in principle incapable of being translated by us, then we cannot regard these noises as *linguistic*.

Clearly, if Davidson is right, then global relativism is doomed. Given that conceptual schemes are systems of sentences accepted as true, the relativist must say that there can be alternative such systems that are true but untranslatable into our own tongue. But it is Davidson's charge that such a supposition is unintelligible: a creature making sounds that we cannot in principle translate cannot be said to be expressing truths (or falsehoods). The conceptual connection between truth and translatability has seen to this.

As a result of taking this stand against relativism, Davidson counts himself as a realist. He is, after all, arguing against a thesis (namely, that there could be different, incommensurable conceptual schemes) that needs to be true in order for relativism – a brand of anti-realism – to be true. But is Davidson's argument sound? And is Davidson's position deserving of the epithet 'realist'? Nagel answers both of these questions in the negative.

Nagel's attack on 'idealism'

Davidson, in attacking the idea that there could be creatures with a different conceptual scheme from ours, takes himself to be arguing for a version of realism. (He is, after all, attacking a version of relativism, which is a kind of anti-realism.) Nagel's view of Davidson's position is very different. Davidson quite explicitly says that he is 'giving up dependence on the concept of an uninterpreted reality' (see $\boxed{y} \mapsto$ in Davidson's piece). According to Nagel, in denying the intelligibility of there being a way the world is in itself that is 'carved up' by our conceptual scheme, Davidson actually ends up defending a pernicious form of anti-realism. Nagel believes that 'the world extends beyond the reach of our minds' in the sense that 'our grasp on the world is limited not only in respect of what we can know but also in respect of what we can conceive' ($\boxed{a} \mapsto$ in Nagel's piece). In other words, he believes that the way the world is could in principle be utterly different to the way we actually do, or indeed could in principle, conceive of it. It is this thesis that Nagel takes to define 'realism' and so, inasmuch as Davidson's attack on scheme–content dualism involves a repudiation of this idea, Nagel takes Davidson to count as an enemy of realism. Indeed, if Nagel is right, Davidson's anti-realism is more extreme than that of the scheme–content dualist. The scheme–content dualist, in taking it to be possible for there to be different ways of conceptualizing reality, presupposes (even if she herself does not see it this way) that there is a way the world is in itself – a world beyond these various conceptual schemes – which these said schemes carve up. As Nagel sees it, in denying that such an idea makes sense, Davidson thereby sets his face against a properly robust realism.

Nagel's target, however, is not limited to Davidson. An anti-realist, on Nagel's understanding of the term, is anyone who denies that we can make sense of the notion that there are, or could be, facts or things whose existence or nature is utterly ungraspable by us. Consider the notion of 'reality' deployed by the scheme–content dualist described above: reality is that which *our* conceptual scheme carves up into cats, planets, hydrogen atoms, and so on, but which *other* conceptual schemes might carve up differently. A different kind of anti-realist – one who is not a scheme–content dualist – will deny that there is any real content to the notion of 'reality' thus deployed. After all, this kind of anti-realist will say, we can say nothing at all about the *nature* of this 'reality'. For as soon as we attempt to say something about what this reality may or may not be like, we deploy our concepts, and so are speaking about reality-as-conceptualized-by-us, and not about reality-as-it-is-independently-of-our-conceptual-scheme. So what could we possibly *mean* by claiming that there is or might be such a scheme-independent reality? The answer, according to the kind of anti-realism Nagel is attacking, is: nothing at all. It simply makes no sense to claim that there is a way the world is, independently of the concepts or language we deploy, or could in principle deploy, to describe it.

Whether or not Nagel is right to cast Davidson as an anti-realist of this kind, there are many other philosophers who are arguably (or, in some cases, explicitly) members of this category – for example, Thomas Kuhn (1962), Hilary Putnam (1981), and Richard Rorty (1989), and indeed anyone who counts themselves as a 'postmodernist'. Nagel's target is thus a very large one indeed; and, at least in so far as it includes the postmodernist movement, his target includes a philosophical position that has had a huge influence, not just on philosophy but on many other academic disciplines.

Moreover, it is not stretching the truth too far to say that post-modernism poses a threat to the legitimacy of metaphysics itself. If, for example, one thinks of scientific enquiry on the one hand, and talk of moral responsibility on the other, as simply different and incommensurable (and so non-competing) ways of talking, one thereby throws into question whether there is even a *prima facie* 'problem' of free will. Similarly, if one denies that any sense can be made of the thought that our talk and thought about the world latches on to how things mind-independently are, one will be inclined to regard the dispute about whether 'universals' exist (the topic of chapter 5), and the dispute about whether objects 'endure' or 'perdure' (the topic of chapter 6), with detached bemusement. In one sense, then, Nagel is fighting for the right of metaphysics to exist as a serious branch of philosophical enquiry.

Donald Davidson, 'On the Very Idea of a Conceptual Scheme'

Philosophers of many persuasions are prone to talk of conceptual schemes. Conceptual schemes, we are told, are ways of organizing experience; they are systems of categories that give form to the data of sensation; they are points of view from which individuals, cultures, or periods survey the passing scene. There may be no translating from one scheme to another, in which case the beliefs, desires, hopes and bits of knowledge that characterize one person have no true counterparts for the subscriber to another scheme. Reality itself is relative to a scheme: what counts as real in one system may not in another.

Even those thinkers who are certain there is only one conceptual scheme are in the sway of the scheme concept; even monotheists have religion. And when someone sets out to describe "our conceptual scheme," his homey task assumes, if we take him literally, that there might be rival systems.

[a] → Conceptual relativism is a heady and exotic doctrine, or would be if we could make good sense of it. The trouble is, as so often in philosophy, it is hard to improve intelligibility while retaining the excitement. At any rate that is what I shall argue.

[b] → We are encouraged to imagine we understand massive conceptual change or profound contrasts by legitimate examples of a familiar sort. Sometimes an idea, like that of simultaneity as defined in relativity theory, is so important that with its addition a whole department of science takes on a new look. Sometimes revisions in the list of sentences held true in a discipline are so central that we may feel that the terms involved have changed their meanings. Languages that have evolved in distant times or places may differ extensively in their resources for dealing with one or another range of phenomena. What comes easily in one language may come hard in another, and this difference may echo significant dissimilarities in style and value.

But examples like these, impressive as they occasionally are, are not so extreme but that the changes and the contrasts can be explained and described using the equipment of a single language. Whorf, wanting to demonstrate that Hopi incorporates a metaphysics so alien to ours that Hopi and English cannot, as he puts it, "be calibrated," uses English to convey the contents of sample Hopi sentences. Kuhn is brilliant at saying what things were like before the revolution using – what else? – our postrevolutionary idiom. Quine gives us a feel for the "pre-individuative phase in the evolution of our conceptual scheme," while Bergson tells us where we can go to get a view of a mountain undistorted by one or another provincial perspective.

[c] → The dominant metaphor of conceptual relativism, that of differing points of view, seems to betray an underlying paradox. Different points of view make sense, but only if there is a common coordinate system on which to plot them; yet the existence of a common system belies the claim of dramatic incomparability. What we need, it seems to me, is some idea of the considerations that set the limits to conceptual contrast. There are extreme suppositions that founder on paradox or contradiction; there are modest examples we have no trouble understanding. What determines where we cross from the merely strange or novel to the absurd?

d→   We may accept the doctrine that associates having a language with having a conceptual scheme. The relation may be supposed to be this: if conceptual schemes differ, so do languages. But speakers of different languages may share a conceptual scheme provided there is a way of translating one language into the other. Studying the criteria of translation is therefore a way of focussing on criteria of identity for conceptual schemes. If conceptual schemes aren't associated with languages in this way, the original problem is needlessly doubled, for then we would have to imagine the mind, with its ordinary categories, operating with a language with *its* organizing structure. Under the circumstances we would certainly want to ask who is to be master.

Alternatively, there is the idea that *any* language distorts reality, which implies that it is only wordlessly if at all that the mind comes to grips with things as they really are. This is to conceive language as an inert (though necessarily distorting) medium independent of the human agencies that employ it; a view of language that surely cannot be maintained. Yet if the mind can grapple without distortion with the real, the mind itself must be without categories and concepts. This featureless self is familiar from theories in quite different parts of the philosophical landscape. There are, for example, theories that make freedom consist in decisions taken apart from all desires, habits and dispositions of the agent; and theories of knowledge that suggest that the mind can observe the totality of its own perceptions and ideas. In each case, the mind is divorced from the traits that constitute it; a familiar enough conclusion to certain lines of reasoning, as I said, but one that should always persuade us to reject the premisses.

We may identify conceptual schemes with languages, then, or better, allowing for the possibility that more than one language may express the same scheme, sets of intertranslatable languages. Languages we will not think of as separable from souls; speaking a language is not a trait a man can lose while retaining the power of thought. So there is no chance that someone can take up a vantage point for comparing conceptual schemes by temporarily shedding his own. Can we then say that two people have different conceptual schemes if they speak languages that fail of intertranslatability?

e→   In what follows I consider two kinds of case that might be expected to arise: complete, and partial, failures of translatability. There would be complete failure if no significant range of sentences in one language could be translated into the other; there would be partial failure if some range could be translated and some range could not (I shall neglect possible asymmetries.) My strategy will be to argue that we cannot make sense of total failure, and then to examine more briefly cases of partial failure.

f→   First, then, the purported cases of complete failure. It is tempting to take a very short line indeed: nothing, it may be said, could count as evidence that some form of activity could not be interpreted in our language that was not at the same time evidence that that form of activity was not speech behavior. If this were right, we probably ought to hold that a form of activity that cannot be interpreted as language in our language is not speech behavior. Putting matters this way is unsatisfactory, however, for it comes to little more than making translatability into a familiar tongue a criterion of languagehood. As fiat, the thesis lacks the appeal of self-evidence; if it is a truth, as I think it is, it should emerge as the conclusion of an argument.

The credibility of the position is improved by reflection on the close relations between language and the attribution of attitudes such as belief, desire and intention. On the one hand, it is clear that speech requires a multitude of finely discriminated intentions and beliefs. A person who asserts that perseverance keeps honor bright must, for example, represent himself as believing that perseverance keeps honor bright, and he must intend to represent himself as believing it. On the other hand, it seems unlikely that we can intelligibly attribute attitudes as complex as these to a speaker unless we can translate his words into ours. There can be no doubt that the relation between being able to translate someone's language and being able to describe his attitudes is very close. Still, until we can say more about *what* this relation is, the case against untranslatable languages remains obscure.

It is sometimes thought that translatability into a familiar language, say English, cannot be a criterion of languagehood on the grounds that the relation of translatability is not transitive. The idea is that some language, say Saturnian, may be translatable into English, and some further language, like Plutonian, may be translatable into Saturnian, while Plutonian is not translatable into English. Enough translatable differences may add up to an untranslatable one. By imagining a sequence of languages, each close enough to the one before to be acceptably translated into it, we can imagine a language so different from English as to resist totally translation into it. Corresponding to this distant language would be a system of concepts altogether alien to us.

This exercise does not, I think, introduce any new element into the discussion. For we should have to ask how we recognized that what the Saturnian was doing was *translating* Plutonian (or anything else). The Saturnian speaker might tell us that that was what he was doing or rather, we might for a moment assume that that was what he was telling us. But then it would occur to us to wonder whether our translations of Saturnian were correct.

$\boxed{\text{g}} \rightarrow$ According to Kuhn, scientists operating in different scientific traditions (within different "paradigms") "live in different worlds." Strawson's *The Bounds of Sense* begins with the remark that "It is possible to imagine kinds of worlds very different from the world as we know it."[1] Since there

---

[1] Peter Strawson, *The Bounds of Sense*, London, 1966, p. 15.

is at most one world, these pluralities are metaphorical or merely imagined. The metaphors are, however, not at all the same. Strawson invites us to imagine possible non-actual worlds, worlds that might be described, using our present language, by redistributing truth values over sentences in various systematic ways. The clarity of the contrasts between worlds in this case depends on supposing our scheme of concepts, our descriptive resources, to remain fixed. Kuhn, on the other hand, wants us to think of different observers of the same world who come to it with incommensurable systems of concepts. Strawson's many imagined worlds are seen (or heard) – anyway described – from the same point of view; Kuhn's one world is seen from different points of view. It is the second metaphor we want to work on.

$\boxed{h} \mapsto$ The first metaphor requires a distinction within language of concept and content: using a fixed system of concepts (words with fixed meanings) we describe alternative universes. Some sentences will be true simply because of the concepts or meanings involved, others because of the way of the world. In describing possible worlds, we play with sentences of the second kind only.

$\boxed{i} \mapsto$ The second metaphor suggests instead a dualism of quite a different sort, a dualism of total scheme (or language) and uninterpreted content. Adherence to the second dualism, while not inconsistent with adherence to the first, may be encouraged by attacks on the first. Here is how it may work.

$\boxed{j} \mapsto$ To give up the analytic–synthetic distinction as basic to the understanding of language is to give up the idea that we can clearly distinguish between theory and language. Meaning, as we might loosely use the word, is contaminated by theory, by what is held to be true. Feyerabend puts it this way:

> Our argument against meaning invariance is simple and clear. It proceeds from the fact that usually some of the principles involved in the determinations of the meanings of older theories or points of view are inconsistent with the new...theories. It points out that it is natural to resolve this contradiction by eliminating the troublesome...older principles, and to replace them by principles, or theorems, of a new...theory. And it concludes by showing that such a procedure will also lead to the elimination of the old meanings.[2]

$\boxed{k} \mapsto$ We may now seem to have a formula for generating distinct conceptual schemes. We get a new out of an old scheme when the speakers of a language come to accept as true an important range of sentences they previously took to be false (and, of course, vice versa). We must not describe this change simply as a matter of their coming to view old falsehoods as truths, for a truth is a proposition, and what they come to accept, in

[2]   Paul Feyerabend, "Explanation, Reduction, and Empiricism," in *Scientific Explanation, Space, and Time: Minnesota Studies in the Philosophy of Science*, Vol. III, Minneapolis, 1962, p. 82.

accepting a sentence as true, is not the same thing that they rejected when formerly they held the sentence to be false. A change has come over the meaning of the sentence because it now belongs to a new language.

This picture of how new (perhaps better) schemes result from new and better science is very much the picture philosophers of science, like Putnam and Feyerabend, and historians of science, like Kuhn, have painted for us. A related idea emerges in the suggestion of some other philosophers, that we could improve our conceptual lot if we were to tune our language to an improved science. Thus both Quine and Smart, in somewhat different ways, regretfully admit that our present ways of talking make a serious science of behavior impossible. (Wittgenstein and Ryle have said similar things without regret.) The cure, Quine and Smart think, is to change how we talk. Smart advocates (and predicts) the change in order to put us on the scientifically straight path of materialism; Quine is more concerned to clear the way for a purely extensional language. (Perhaps I should add that I think our *present* scheme and language are best understood as extensional and materialist.)

If we were to follow this advice, I do not myself think science or understanding would be advanced, though possibly morals would. But the present question is only whether, if such changes were to take place, we should be justified in calling them alterations in the basic conceptual apparatus. The difficulty in so calling them is easy to appreciate. Suppose that in my office of Minister of Scientific Language I want the new man to stop using words that refer, say, to emotions, feelings, thoughts and intentions, and to talk instead of the physiological states and happenings that are assumed to be more or less identical with the mental riff and raff. How do I tell whether my advice has been heeded if the new man speaks a new language? For all I know, the shiny new phrases, though stolen from the old language in which they refer to physiological stirrings, may in his mouth play the role of the messy old mental concepts.

The key phrase is: for all I know. What is clear is that retention of some or all of the old vocabulary in itself provides no basis for judging the new scheme to be the same as, or different from, the old. So what sounded at first like a thrilling discovery – that truth is relative to a conceptual scheme – has not so far been shown to be anything more than the pedestrian and familiar fact that the truth of a sentence is relative to (among other things) the language to which it belongs. Instead of living in different worlds, Kuhn's scientists may, like those who need Webster's dictionary, be only words apart.

Giving up the analytic–synthetic distinction has not proven a help in making sense of conceptual relativism. The analytic–synthetic distinction is however explained in terms of something that may serve to buttress conceptual relativism, namely the idea of empirical content. The dualism of the synthetic and the analytic is a dualism of sentences some of which are true (or false) both because of what they mean and because of their empirical content, while others are true (or false) by virtue of meaning alone, having no empirical content. If we give up the dualism, we abandon the conception of meaning that goes with it, but we do not have to abandon the idea of empirical content: we can hold, if we want, that *all* sentences have empirical content. Empirical content is in turn explained by reference

m⟩→ to the facts, the world, experience, sensation, the totality of sensory stimuli, or something similar. Meanings gave us a way to talk about categories, the organizing structure of language, and so on; but it is possible, as we have seen, to give up meanings and analyticity while retaining the idea of language as embodying a conceptual scheme. Thus in place of the dualism of the analytic–synthetic we get the dualism of conceptual scheme and empirical content. The new dualism is the foundation of an empiricism shorn of the untenable dogmas of the analytic–synthetic distinction and reductionism – shorn, that is, of the unworkable idea that we can uniquely allocate empirical content sentence by sentence.

n⟩→ I want to urge that this second dualism of scheme and content, of organizing system and something waiting to be organized, cannot be made intelligible and defensible. It is itself a dogma of empiricism, the third dogma. The third, and perhaps the last, for if we give it up it is not clear that there is anything distinctive left to call empiricism.

The scheme–content dualism has been formulated in many ways. Here are some examples. The first comes from Whorf, elaborating on a theme of Sapir's. Whorf says that:

o⟩→ ...language produces an organization of experience. We are inclined to think of language simply as a technique of expression, and not to realize that language first of all is a classification and arrangement of the stream of sensory experience which results in a certain world-order...In other words, language does in a cruder but also in a broader and more versatile way the same thing that science does...We are thus introduced to a new principle of relativity, which holds that all observers are not led by the same physical evidence to the same picture of the universe, unless their linguistic backgrounds are similar, or can in some way be calibrated.[3]

Here we have all the required elements: language as the organizing force, not to be distinguished clearly from science; what is organized, referred to variously as "experience," "the stream of sensory experience," and "physical evidence"; and finally, the failure of intertranslatability ("calibration"). The failure of inter-translatability is a necessary condition for difference of conceptual schemes; the common relation to experience or the evidence is what is supposed to help us make sense of the claim that it is languages or schemes that are under consideration when translation fails. It is essential to this idea

[3] Benjamin Lee Whorf, *Language, Thought and Reality: Selected Writings of Benjamin Lee Whorf*, ed. J.B. Carroll, New York, 1956, p. 55.

that there be something neutral and common that lies outside all schemes. This common something cannot, of course, be the *subject matter* of contrasting languages, or translation would be possible. Thus Kuhn has recently written:

> Philosophers have now abandoned hope of finding a pure sense-datum language . . . but many of them continue to assume that theories can be compared by recourse to a basic vocabulary consisting entirely of words which are attached to nature in ways that are unproblematic and, to the extent necessary independent of theory. . . Feyerabend and I have argued at length that no such vocabulary is available. In the transition from one theory to the next words change their meanings or conditions of applicability in subtle ways. Though most of the same signs are used before and after a revolution – e.g. force, mass, element, compound, cell – the ways in which some of them attach to nature has somehow changed. Successive theories are thus, we say, incommensurable.[4]

"Incommensurable" is, of course, Kuhn and Feyerabend's word for "not intertranslatable." The neutral content waiting to be organized is supplied by nature.

Feyerabend himself suggests that we may compare contrasting schemes by "choosing a point of view outside the system or the language." He hopes we can do this because "there is still human experience as an actually existing process"[5] independent of all schemes.

The same, or similar, thoughts are expressed by Quine in many passages: "The totality of our so-called knowledge or beliefs . . . is a man-made fabric which impinges on experience only along the edges . . .";[6] " . . . total science is like a field of force whose boundary conditions are experience";[7] "As an empiricist I . . . think of the conceptual scheme of science as a tool . . . for predicting future experience in the light of past experience."[8] And again:

> We persist in breaking reality down somehow into a multiplicity of identifiable and discriminable objects . . . We talk so inveterately of objects that to say we do so seems almost to say nothing at all; for how else is there to talk? It is hard to say how else there is to talk, not because our objectifying pattern is an invariable trait of human nature, but because we are bound to adapt any alien pattern to our own in the very process of understanding or translating the alien sentences.[9]

---

[4]   Thomas Kuhn, "Reflection on my Critics" in *Criticism and the Growth of Knowledge*, eds. I. Lakatos and A. Musgrave, Cambridge, 1970, pp. 266, 267.
[5]   Paul Feyerabend, "Problems of Empiricism," in *Beyond the Edge of Certainty.* ed. R.G. Colodny. Englewood Cliffs, New Jersey, 1965, p. 214.
[6]   W.V.O. Quine, "Two Dogmas of Empiricism," reprinted in *From a Logica' Point of View,* 2nd edition. Cambridge, Mass., 1961, p. 42.
[7]   Ibid.
[8]   Ibid., p. 44.
[9]   W.V.O. Quine, "Speaking of Objects," reprinted in *Ontological Relativity and Other Essays.* New York, 1969, p. 1.

The test of difference remains failure or difficulty of translation: "...to speak of that remote medium as radically different from ours is to say no more than that the translations do not come smoothly."[10] Yet the roughness may be so great that the alien has an "as yet unimagined pattern beyond individuation."[11]

[p]→ The idea is then that something is a language, and associated with a conceptual scheme, whether we can translate it or not, if it stands in a certain relation (predicting, organizing, facing or fitting) to experience (nature, reality, sensory promptings). The problem is to say what the relation is, and to be clearer about the entities related.

The images and metaphors fall into two main groups: conceptual schemes (languages) either *organize* something, or they *fit* it (as in "he warps his scientific heritage to fit his...sensory promptings"[12]). The first group contains also *systematize, divide up* (the stream of experience); further examples of the second group are *predict, account for, face* (the tribunal of experience). As for the entities that get organized, or which the scheme must fit, I think again we may detect two main ideas: either it is reality (the universe, the world, nature), or it is experience (the passing show, surface irritations, sensory promptings, sense data, the given).

[q]→ We cannot attach a clear meaning to the notion of organizing a single object (the world, nature etc.) unless that object is understood to contain or consist in other objects. Someone who sets out to organize a closet arranges the things in it. If you are told not to organize the shoes and shirts, but the closet itself, you would be bewildered. How would you organize the Pacific Ocean? Straighten out its shores, perhaps, or relocate its islands, or destroy its fish.

A language may contain simple predicates whose extensions are matched by no simple predicates, or even by any predicates at all, in some other language. What enables us to make this point in particular cases is an ontology common to the two languages, with concepts that individuate the same objects. We can be clear about breakdowns in translation when they are local enough, for a background of generally successful translation provides what is needed to make the failures intelligible. But we were after larger game: we wanted to make sense of there being a language we could not translate at all. Or, to put the point differently, we were looking for a criterion of languagehood that did not depend on, or entail, translatability into a familiar idiom. I suggest that the image of organizing the closet of nature will not supply such a criterion.

How about the other kind of object, experience? Can we think of a language organizing *it*? Much the same difficulties recur. The notion of

---

[10] Ibid., p. 25.
[11] Ibid., p. 24.
[12] "Two Dogmas of Empiricism," p. 46.

organization applies only to pluralities. But whatever plurality we take experience to consist in – events like losing a button or stubbing a toe, having a sensation of warmth or hearing an oboe – we will have to individuate according to familiar principles. A language that organizes *such* entities must be a language very like our own.

Experience (and its classmates like surface irritations, sensations and sense data) also makes another and more obvious trouble for the organizing idea. For how could something count as a language that organized *only* experiences, sensations, surface irritations or sense data? Surely knives and forks, railroads and mountains, cabbages and kingdoms also need organizing.

This last remark will no doubt sound inappropriate as a response to the claim that a conceptual scheme is a way of coping with sensory experience; and I agree that it is. But what was under consideration was the idea of *organizing* experience, not the idea of *coping with* (or fitting or facing) experience. The reply was apropos of the former, not the latter, concept. So now let's see whether we can do better with the second idea.

[r] ⊢→ When we turn from talk of organization to talk of fitting we turn our attention from the referential apparatus of language – predicates, quantifiers, variables and singular terms – to whole sentences. It is sentences that predict (or are used to predict), sentences that cope or deal with things, that fit our sensory promptings, that can be compared or confronted with the evidence. It is sentences also that face the tribunal of experience, though of course they must face it together.

[s] ⊢→ The proposal is not that experiences, sense data, surface irritations or sensory promptings are the sole subject matter of language. There is, it is true, the theory that talk about brick houses on Elm Street is ultimately to be construed as being about sense data or perceptions, but such reductionistic views are only extreme, and implausible, versions of the general position we are considering. The general position is that sensory experience provides all the *evidence* for the acceptance of sentences (where sentences may include whole theories). A sentence or theory fits our sensory promptings, successfully faces the tribunal of experience, predicts future experience, or copes with the pattern of our surface irritations, provided it is borne out by the evidence.

In the common course of affairs, a theory may be borne out by the available evidence and yet be false. But what is in view here is not just actually available evidence; it is the totality of possible sensory evidence past, present and future. We do not need to pause to contemplate what this might mean. The point is that for a theory to fit or face up to the totality of possible sensory evidence is for that theory to be true. If a theory quantifies over physical objects, numbers or sets, what it says about these entities is true provided the theory as a whole fits the sensory evidence. One can see how, from this point of view, such entities might be called posits. It is reasonable to call something a posit if it can be contrasted with something that is not. Here the something that is not is sensory experience – at least that is the idea.

The trouble is that the notion of fitting the totality of experience, like the notions of fitting the facts, or being true to the facts, adds nothing intelligible to the simple concept of being true. To speak of sensory experience rather than the evidence, or just the facts, expresses a view about the source or nature of evidence, but it does not add a new entity to the universe against which to test conceptual schemes. The totality of sensory evidence is what we want provided it is all the evidence there is; and all the evidence there is is just what it takes to make our sentences or theories true. Nothing, however, no *thing*, makes sentences and theories true: not experience, not surface irritations, not the world, can make a sentence true. *That* experience takes a certain course, that our skin is warmed or punctured, that the universe is finite, these facts, if we like to talk that way, make sentences and theories true. But this point is put better without mention of facts. The sentence "My skin is warm" is true if and only if my skin is warm. Here there is no reference to a fact, a world, an experience, or a piece of evidence.[13]

Our attempt to characterize languages or conceptual schemes in terms of the notion of fitting some entity has come down, then, to the simple thought that something is an acceptable conceptual scheme or theory if it is true. Perhaps we better say *largely* true in order to allow sharers of a scheme to differ on details. And the criterion of a conceptual scheme different from our own now becomes: largely true but not translatable. The question whether this is a useful criterion is just the question how well we understand the notion of truth, as applied to language, independent of the notion of translation. The answer is, I think, that we do not understand it independently at all.

We recognize sentences like " 'Snow is white' is true if and only if snow is white" to be trivially true. Yet the totality of such English sentences uniquely determines the extension of the concept of truth for English. Tarski generalized this observation and made it a test of theories of truth: according to Tarski's Convention T, a satisfactory theory of truth for a language L must entail, for every sentence s of L, a theorem of the form "s is true if and only if p" where "s" is replaced by a description of s and "p" by s itself if L is English, and by a translation of s into English if L is not English.[14] This isn't, of course, a definition of truth, and it doesn't hint that there is a single definition or theory that applies to languages generally. Nevertheless, Convention T suggests, though it cannot state, an important feature common to

[13] These remarks are defended in my "True to the Facts," *The Journal of Philosophy*, Vol. 66 (1969), pp. 748–64.

[14] Alfred Tarski, "The Concept of Truth in Formalized Languages," in *Logic, Semantics, Metamathematics*, Oxford, 1956.

all the specialized concepts of truth. It succeeds in doing this by making essential use of the notion of translation into a language we know. Since Convention T embodies our best intuition as to how the concept of truth is used, there does not seem to be much hope for a test that a conceptual scheme is radically different from ours if that test depends on the assumption that we can divorce the notion of truth from that of translation.

w|→ Neither a fixed stock of meanings, nor a theory-neutral reality, can provide, then, a ground for comparison of conceptual schemes. It would be a mistake to look further for such a ground if by that we mean something conceived as common to incommensurable schemes. In abandoning this search, we abandon the attempt to make sense of the metaphor of a single space within which each scheme has a position and provides a point of view. . . . [Davidson then goes on to discuss the possibility of languages that are partially untranslatable.]

x|→ It would be wrong to summarize by saying we have shown how communication is possible between people who have different schemes, a way that works without need of what there cannot be, namely a neutral ground, or a common coordinate system. For we have found no intelligible basis on which it can be said that schemes are different. It would be equally wrong to announce the glorious news that all mankind – all speakers of language, at least – share a common scheme and ontology. For if we cannot intelligibly say that schemes are different, neither can we intelligibly say that they are one.

y|→ In giving up dependence on the concept of an uninterpreted reality, something outside all schemes and science, we do not relinquish the notion of objective truth – quite the contrary. Given the dogma of a dualism of scheme and reality, we get conceptual relativity, and truth relative to a scheme. Without the dogma, this kind of relativity goes by the board. Of course truth of sentences remains relative to language, but that is as objective as can be. In giving up the dualism of scheme and world, we do not give up the world, but reestablish unmediated touch with the familiar objects whose antics make our sentences and opinions true or false.

Commentary on Davidson

Davidson, as we noted in the Introduction to this chapter, aims to undermine global relativism by arguing that the very idea of a conceptual scheme, and with it scheme/content dualism, make no sense. To this end, the first three paragraphs of Davidson's paper see him swiftly characterizing his target: what he calls 'conceptual relativism' but which we know as 'global relativism'. At a|→, Davidson is equally clear about the strategy he will employ: he will argue, not that conceptual relativism is false, but that it is *unintelligible*: it *would be* a heady and exotic doctrine, *if* we could make sense of it; but, he intimates, we can't.

Davidson's argument for this thesis has been immensely influential since his paper was first published in 1974, not least because it promises to sweep away in double-quick time what many have seen as a bothersome doctrine. None the less, the argument is, at times, compressed – not to mention controversial – so it will be useful to break it down into its component stages.

Davidson starts his argument, in the two paragraphs beginning at $\boxed{b} \mapsto$, by applying pressure to some of the examples to which global relativists appeal. When it comes to the kinds of examples that have been used to make the relativist's case – such as the idea that the Hopi language embodies a distinct conceptual scheme by virtue of not having any words that refer to what we call 'time' – Davidson points out that we actually find it relatively easy to characterize putatively variant conceptual schemes in our terms. Indeed, Benjamin Whorf, a defender of the kind of relativism Davidson wants to resist, ironically seems to prove this in remarks such as the following:

> The Hopi conceive time and motion in the objective realm in a purely operational sense – as a matter of the complexity and magnitude of operations connecting events – so that the element of time is not separated from whatever element of space enters into the operations. (Whorf 1956: 63)

In seeming to be able to characterize the metaphysics embodied by the Hopi language so easily, Whorf just demonstrates that what we have here is not an alternative scheme at all, but a *disagreement* about the nature of reality between the Hopi speakers and English speakers. As we saw in the Introduction, if languages are inter-translatable, then what we have is not a difference in scheme but a difference in opinion.

Having made this point, Davidson continues, at $\boxed{c} \mapsto$, by suggesting that one of the leading metaphors used by relativists – that of differing *points of view* – in fact works *against* relativism. Distinct points of view must be points of view *on* a common something; and if they are to be understood as such, then there must be a common perspective from which they can be understood as variant perspectives on the same thing. But if this is right, then the variant perspectives cannot be variant schemes.

1. (i) Try to imagine a group of people who carve up the world in a very different way from ourselves. Perhaps they take the world to be populated by objects such as '"half a horse and a piece of river", "my ear and the moon", and other products of a surrealist imagination' (Kolakowski 1968: 47–8). Do you think that such 'surrealist' people might manage to theorize about the world, and get around in it, as successfully as we do? Why or why not? (ii) Does the fact that we can describe such a possible situation mean that such people merely have different *opinions* about the world from us? Why or why not?

In the three paragraphs following $\boxed{d} \mapsto$, Davidson addresses two questions: first, what must the relativist take conceptual schemes to be?; and, second, what is it for two people to have different conceptual schemes? His answer to the first question is one with which we are, by now, familiar: conceptual scheme are languages (or, better, sets of inter-translatable languages). Here Davidson takes the linguistic turn that we plotted in the Introduction. Given his answer to the first question, his answer to the second question is no less familiar: he decides to work with the hypothesis that two people have different schemes when they speak languages that fail of inter-translatability.

At $\boxed{e}\mapsto$, Davidson goes on to distinguish two possible strengths of untranslatability: complete (in which no significant range of sentences in one language can be translated into the other) and partial (in which some sentences can be translated). In his view, we can make sense of neither phenomenon and, as a result, can make no sense of the idea of alternative conceptual schemes. In the extract we are reading, only the case against complete failures of translatability is made.

So what is wrong with the idea that there could be wholly incommensurable (that is, untranslatable) languages? At $\boxed{f}\mapsto$, Davidson is swift in offering his core objection. We could not, he suggests, ever be in a position to judge that some (apparent) linguistic behaviour were the behaviour of a being speaking an untranslatable language. As he himself puts it,

> nothing, it may be said, could count as evidence that some form of activity could not be interpreted in our language that was not at the same time evidence that that form of activity was not speech behavior.

However, Davidson admits that this claim – in essence, that languages are necessarily translatable into a familiar tongue – is far from obvious, and hence must be argued for rather than merely asserted. In what follows, Davidson provides such an argument.

2. Davidson's conclusion, as advertised at $\boxed{a}\mapsto$, is that the very idea of alternative conceptual schemes to ours (that is, of languages untranslatable into our own) makes no sense. But look once more at his claim quoted above. This says that we could not have *evidence* that a being is speaking an untranslatable language. Do you think it follows from this that the notion of such an untranslatable language is literally *unintelligible*? Why or why not?

As we saw at $\boxed{d}\mapsto$, the question of whether there can be alternative conceptual schemes has become the question of whether there can be untranslatable languages. The conceptual relativist must therefore give us an account of what it is for something to be a language that does not presuppose its translatability into some other language. So, with a view to approaching this issue, Davidson considers two different metaphors at $\boxed{g}\mapsto$. First, one might imagine, from the same point of view, other kinds of worlds or 'alternative universes' – worlds radically different from our own; or, second, one might imagine a single world as seen from different points of view (that is, by means of incommensurable systems of concepts).

When it comes to the first metaphor – that is, our imagining different kinds of world from the same point of view – Davidson implicitly claims, at $\boxed{j}\mapsto$, that it commits us to there being a sharp 'analytic/synthetic distinction': a distinction between sentences that are true purely by virtue of the meanings of the words (analytic truths) and sentences that are true by virtue of how the world is (synthetic truths). But what exactly is Davidson getting at here, and why is it important? These are difficult questions, but we shall try to answer them both in the next five paragraphs.

To see why the first metaphor embodies a commitment to the analytic/synthetic distinction, consider how you would set about imagining a radically different universe to our own. In doing so, you will *describe* that universe 'using our present language', as Davidson puts it. You might, for example, imagine a universe with disc-shaped rather than spherical planets, with people who are utterly incapable of feeling guilt or remembering what happened to them more than four days ago, with small, rat-like beings who can predict the future with certainty and communicate with the dead, or whatever you like. In describing your imagined alternative universe in this way, you are, in effect, constructing a 'theory' about that universe: you are making claims about what that universe is like, just as a theory about the actual world consists of a collection of claims about what the actual world is like. And you are taking it for granted that the words you use – like 'person' or 'planet' or 'rat' or 'guilt' – do not change their meanings when you switch from describing how things actually are to describing the imaginary universe. That is, you are taking it for granted that the *meanings* of your words are independent of your theory *about* the world: one *language* can be used to construct radically different *theories*.

Davidson's key point is that such a thought-experiment embodies the analytic/synthetic distinction. For, in taking language to be independent from theory, it thereby commits us to the idea that some sentences – the 'analytic' ones – are true no matter *how* the world is, while others – the 'synthetic' sentences – depend for their truth or falsity upon how the world is. 'All bachelors are unmarried', for example, will still be true in the bizarre universe described in the previous paragraph; one thing you *won't* be able to imagine is that in your imagined universe there are married bachelors. By contrast, the synthetic sentence, 'Nobody can communicate with the dead', though actually true, would be false in the imagined bizarre universe, while the similarly synthetic 'Planets are disc-shaped' would be true in that universe but is actually false.

> 3. Think of some examples of sentences that are, intuitively, analytic, and sentences that are intuitively synthetic, and describe the difference between the two kinds of sentence in your own words.

We shall return to the first metaphor's commitment to the analytic/synthetic distinction presently. For the time being, let us consider the second metaphor: the metaphor of seeing the same world from different points of view. Davidson says at $\boxed{i} \mapsto$ that this second metaphor suggests 'a dualism of total scheme (or language) and uninterpreted content'. And his idea here is that this second metaphor says that we have something 'uninterpreted' – this might be the flow of experience, say, or perhaps just the world itself – and then a conceptual scheme, with concepts like 'planet', 'person', 'guilt' and 'rat' – which we impose upon that uninterpreted content. According to this picture, different schemes – different 'points of view' – might divide up that content in different and incommensurable ways, so that the language used by users of a different scheme cannot adequately be translated into our own.

Here, then, is a metaphor that might, in principle, help us to get a handle on the notion of one language that cannot be translated into another, and this gets us back to Davidson's central concern: *can* we get a handle on that notion?

We can now return to the thrust of Davidson's argument in this part of the text. Davidson says that 'adherence to the second dualism [that is, the dualism of scheme and content, or "scheme–content dualism", as we are calling it], while not inconsistent with adherence to the first, may be encouraged by attacks on the first' ($\boxed{i} \mapsto$). In other words, Davidson suggests that the rejection of the analytic/synthetic distinction *might* be thought to provide a good reason to uphold scheme-content dualism, and with it the doctrine of conceptual relativism.

At this point, we need to switch back to the first metaphor and its commitment to the analytic/synthetic distinction. W. V. Quine famously rejected the analytic/synthetic distinction in his 'Two Dogmas of Empiricism' (1951). And to follow Quine, as Davidson points out at $\boxed{j} \mapsto$, is to 'give up the idea that we can clearly distinguish between theory and language': our theory about how things *are* is not independent of what the words we use to describe how things are *mean*. Now, Davidson does not explicitly say here that he agrees with Quine that the analytic/synthetic distinction *should* be rejected, but he clearly does not want to claim that it should be retained. And so he needs to argue that the rejection of that distinction does not, in fact, provide any grounds for accepting conceptual relativism. This is what he now proceeds to do.

At $\boxed{k} \mapsto$, Davidson explains why the conceptual relativist (or what we called the 'global relativist' in the Introduction) might now, having rejected the analytic/synthetic distinction, have 'a formula for generating distinct conceptual schemes'. For example, when scientists abandoned Newtonian physics in favour of relativistic physics, they stopped thinking of space and time as radically different things and started thinking of the world in terms of 'space-time'. One *might* think that they came 'to view old falsehoods as truths', and *vice versa*: they used to believe that space and time had certain properties, and they then rejected those old claims and began to believe different claims about space and time – claims that they previously believed to be false. However, once we have abandoned the analytic/synthetic distinction, it is tempting to think that this is not what happened at all. Perhaps what happened instead was that expressions like 'space' and 'time' *changed their meaning*, so that the claims they previously rejected are not the very same claims as the ones they started to accept. This conception of what is going on – one shared by Kuhn (1962), Feyerabend (1965) and others – becomes possible once one grants that the meanings of one's words are not independent of one's theory about the world: changes in what we believe might go hand-in-hand with changes in the meanings of the words we use to express those beliefs.

4. Try to describe in your own words the connection between (i) upholding the analytic/synthetic distinction, and (ii) thinking of radical changes in our theories as being *merely* a matter of 'coming to view old falsehoods as truths' (and *vice versa*).

However, in the four paragraphs following $\boxed{k}\mapsto$ Davidson explains why he is unconvinced by this suggestion. The problem, he thinks, is that we still do not have any *grounds* for thinking that the new 'scheme' is really a different scheme from the old one. For example, a materialist about the mind could recommend that people replace their talk of emotions, feelings, desires and the like with words picking out brain states and events; but even if people changed the way in which they spoke, this would not of itself show that they were no longer talking of emotions, feelings and desires. They could merely be using the new words to express the same old psychological concepts. As Davidson nicely puts it at $\boxed{l}\mapsto$, 'Instead of living in different worlds, Kuhn's scientists may, like those who need Webster's dictionary, be only words apart'. He thus takes himself to have shown that, contrary to what one might have thought, abandoning the analytic–synthetic distinction provides no grounds at all for believing in conceptual relativism.

Davidson now goes back on the offensive, and returns to his central theme: that conceptual relativism is not only ungrounded but unintelligible. He is going to argue, from $\boxed{n}\mapsto$, that scheme–content dualism – the dualism 'of organizing system and something waiting to be organized' – 'cannot be made intelligible and defensible', and so neither can the kind of relativism that is underpinned by scheme–content dualism.

Recall that the 'content' part of scheme–content dualism is supposed to be something 'uninterpreted'. As Davidson puts it at $\boxed{m}\mapsto$, the notion of 'empirical content' is supposedly 'explained by reference to the facts, the world, experience, sensation, the totality of sensory stimuli, or something similar'. The basic gist of Davidson's argument is going to be as follows. If we think that there is a 'dualism' of (that is, a distinction between) 'scheme' and 'content', then, whatever we think the 'content' is (the world, experience, or whatever), we have to provide an intelligible account of what the *relation* between scheme and content is supposed to be. (See the paragraph at $\boxed{p}\mapsto$.) But no genuinely comprehensible account of the nature of this relation is in the offing. And so scheme–content dualism, in the end, cannot be made intelligible.

The first proposal that Davidson considers comes from the quotation from Whorf at $\boxed{o}\mapsto$. Whorf says that 'language produces an organization of experience ... language first of all is a classification and arrangement of the stream of sensory experience which results in a certain world-order'. So the claim here is that the 'stream of sensory experience' – the content – is 'organized' or 'classified' or 'arranged' by language. Whorf then goes on to state the relativist position he takes to follow from this: 'all observers are not led by the same physical evidence to the same picture of the universe, unless their linguistic backgrounds are similar, or can in some way be calibrated'.

6. Explain in your own words what you think Whorf means (or at least what Davidson takes him to mean) by 'same picture of the universe' and 'calibrated'.

Davidson's argument against Whorf's claim that language 'organizes' experience, or indeed the other candidate for the notion of 'content', namely 'the world, nature etc.', happens in the four paragraphs from $\boxed{q}$ ↦. He starts out by arguing that we 'cannot attach a clear meaning to the notion of organizing a single object (the world, nature etc.) unless that object is understood to contain or consist in other objects'.

7. (i) Explain the closet analogy Davidson uses in the paragraph at $\boxed{q}$ ↦. (ii) Why must a scheme–content dualist think that what needs organizing – the 'content' – is (or is analogous to) 'a single object'? (If you think the 'content' could consist in a plurality of objects, try to say which distinct objects these would be – but beware, you are not allowed to invoke your own conceptual scheme to do this!)

Having dispatched the notion of 'organization', Davidson turns his attention, at $\boxed{r}$ ↦, to the thought that perhaps our conceptual scheme 'fits' or 'faces' or 'copes with' experience. The first stage in his argument against this proposal takes place in the passage from $\boxed{s}$ ↦ to $\boxed{t}$ ↦; and what he claims to establish here is that the claim that our conceptual scheme or theory fits or faces up to or copes with experience is really just the claim that our theory is *true*.

8. (i) Explain Davidson's argument in this passage in your own words. (ii) Do you think he succeeds in establishing that a theory's 'fitting' (etc.) experience is just a matter of that theory's being true?

Given what Davidson takes himself to have just established, it turns out that 'something is an acceptable conceptual scheme or theory if it is [largely] true'; and so 'the criterion of a conceptual scheme different from our own now becomes: largely true but not translatable' ($\boxed{u}$ ↦).

9. Explain in your own words exactly why the criterion 'becomes: largely true but not translatable'.

We now, at last, come to the final stage of Davidson's argument. If the criterion of a conceptual scheme different from our own is that that scheme is 'largely true but not translatable', then we can only make sense of the notion of a different conceptual scheme if we can 'understand the notion of truth, as applied to language, independent of the notion of translation' – since we have to be able to make sense of the idea of a scheme being true-but-untranslatable. And here is the problem: according to Davidson, we do *not* understand the notion of truth independently of the notion of translation.

Quite why this is so is explained in the compressed paragraph at $\boxed{v}$ ↦. Davidson's argument is technical and quite hard to follow, but amounts, we think, to this. Our concept of truth, for a language, cannot be grasped independently of the concept of translation. This much is evident in the fact that to understand the concept of truth for a language, *L*, one must know that, for every sentence *s* of *L*, *s* is true if and only if *p*, where '*s*' is a description of *s* and '*p*' is replaced by *s* itself (if *L* is English), or by a *translation* of *s* into English (if *L* is a language other than English). Presuming that *L* is English, then, grasp of the concept of truth consists in knowing that 'Tibbles is grey' is true if and only if Tibbles is grey, that 'Tiddles is a tabby' is true if and only if Tiddles is a tabby, and so on.

What does this show? According to Davidson, the moral to be drawn is that our concept of what is true cannot outstrip what we can assert in either our own language or any translatable language. And this is because we cannot conceive of a sentence's being true unless we can imagine it taking the place of '*s*' in a sentence of the form '*s* is true if and only if *p*' in which '*p*' takes the place of a sentence of our language. Our grasp of the concept of truth consists in our being disposed to accept the instances of '*s* is true if and only if *p*', but the place of '*p*' can only be taken by *a sentence we can understand*. It thus follows that our concept of truth only has application to a language that we can understand or to a language that can be translated into a language that we can understand. To (try to) conceive of true but untranslatable sentences is to try to stretch our concept of truth beyond its breaking point.

> 10. What do you make of the Davidson's argument here? Does it depend on there being *no more* to the concept of truth than its featuring in the '*s* is true if and only if *p*' schema? If so, should we accept the argument?
> 11. Think about the structure of Davidson's argument against scheme–content dualism. Has he shown that it is *impossible* to give an account of the relation between scheme and content according to which distinct conceptual schemes are possible, or has he shown something weaker than this?

In the paper's final two paragraphs, from $\boxed{x}\mapsto$, Davidson sums up the state of play as he sees it. Given the soundness of his argument against the (would-be) relativist's attempt to distinguish conceptual schemes, it follows that we cannot intelligibly say that schemes are different. We have found no means of distinguishing between such schemes. But this also means that we cannot say that we all share the same conceptual scheme: for if we cannot find a means to distinguish them, we cannot say that we all share one. Relativism turns out to be, not false, but unintelligible.

In the article's final paragraph, from $\boxed{y}\mapsto$, Davidson addresses the question of whether his view counts as realist: whether, in other words, a notion of 'objective truth' has been preserved. He thinks so: inasmuch as an anti-realist position – relativism – has been repudiated, realism has been defended. In saying that we have 'unmediated touch with the familiar objects whose antics make our sentences and opinions true or false', Davidson is claiming that our sentences and opinions are capable of representing how things stand in a world of mind-independent objects.

On the other hand, his central argument against relativism has been that no sense can be made of the idea of different conceptual schemes 'organizing' or 'fitting' something that stands outside all conceptual schemes. He takes himself to have shown that we should abandon the search for what he calls at $\boxed{w}\!\!\rightarrow$ 'a theory-neutral reality', and in so doing, he says, 'we abandon the attempt to make sense of the metaphor of a single space within which each scheme has a position and provides a point of view'.

> **12.** Thinking about Davidson's argument against scheme–content dualism, what, according to him, is wrong with thinking that there is a 'single space' within which each scheme 'provides a point of view'?

At $\boxed{y}\!\!\rightarrow$, Davidson states baldly that he has given up 'dependence on the concept of an uninterpreted reality, something outside all schemes and science'. And he seems to be saying here that, at bottom, it is the notion of 'uninterpreted reality' that makes no sense.

> **13.** (i) Do you think a *realist* should claim that the notion of 'uninterpreted reality' makes no sense? Why or why not? (ii) What concept of 'realism' does the answer you just gave presuppose? In other words, what would it *take* to be a realist or an anti-realist according to the conception of realism you appealed to in answering (i)?

Thomas Nagel, 'Thought and Reality' (extract from *The View from Nowhere*)

1. Realism

I have at various points expressed commitment to a form of realism, and must now say more about it. In simple terms it is the view that the world is independent of our minds, but the problem is to explain this claim in a nontrivial way which cannot be easily admitted by everyone, and thereby to show how it conflicts with a form of idealism that is held by many contemporary philosophers.

Realism makes skepticism intelligible. In the last chapter we discussed skepticism with regard to knowledge. Here I want to introduce another form of skepticism – not about what we know but about how far our $\boxed{a}\!\!\rightarrow$ thoughts can reach. I shall defend a form of realism according to which our grasp on the world is limited not only in respect of what we can know but also in respect of what we can conceive. In a very strong sense, the world extends beyond the reach of our minds.[1]

---

[1] This thesis is also defended by Fodor (1983: 120–6).

b→   The idealism to which this is opposed holds that what there is is what we can think about or conceive of, or what we or our descendants could come to be able to think about or conceive of – and that this is necessarily true because the idea of something that we could not think about or conceive of makes no sense. The "we" is important. I leave aside views, also called idealist, that hold reality to be correlative with mind in a much wider sense – including infinite minds, if there are such things. Perhaps, given any type of world, there could be a mind capable of conceiving it adequately; I have no idea of the limits on possible minds. The realism I am defending says the world may be inconceivable to *our* minds, and the idealism I am opposing says it could not be.

There are more radical forms of idealism than this, such as the view that to exist is to be perceived, or that what exists must be an object of possible experience for us, or that what exists or is the case must be an object of possible knowledge for us, or must be verifiable by us, or that it must be something about which we could have evidence. These views have all found adherents, but I believe that they depend finally on the more general form of idealism I have described, together with different specific views about the conditions of human thought. The common element is a broadly epistemological test of reality – which has never lost its popularity despite the supposed death of logical positivism.

I want to oppose to this general position a different view of the relation of our thoughts to reality, particularly those thoughts that attempt to represent the world objectively. In pursuing objectivity we alter our relation to the world, increasing the correctness of certain of our representations of it by compensating for the peculiarities of our point of view. But the world is in a strong sense independent of our possible representations, and may well extend beyond them. This has implications both for what objectivity achieves when it is successful and for the possible limits of what it can achieve. Its aim and sole rationale is to increase our grasp of reality, but this makes no sense unless the idea of reality is not merely the idea of what can c→   be grasped by those methods. In other words, I want to resist the natural tendency to identify the idea of the world as it really is with the idea of what can be revealed, at the limit, by an indefinite increase in objectivity of standpoint.

It has already been argued that in various respects the pursuit of objectivity can be carried to excess, that it can lead away from the truth if carried out in the wrong way or with respect to the wrong subject matter. That is one way in which objectivity does not correspond to reality: it is not always the best mode of understanding. But human objectivity may fail to exhaust reality for another reason: there may be aspects of reality beyond its reach because they are altogether beyond our capacity to form conceptions of the world. What there is and what we, in virtue of our nature, can think about are different things, and the latter may be smaller than the former. Certainly *we* are smaller, so this should not be surprising. Human objectivity may be able to grasp only part of the world, but when it is successful it should provide us with an understanding of aspects of reality whose existence is completely independent of our capacity to think about them – as independent as the existence of things we can't conceive.

$\boxed{d} \rightarrow$ The idea that the contents of the universe are limited by our capacity for thought is easily recognized as a philosophical view, which at first sight seems crazily self-important given what small and contingent pieces of the universe we are. It is a view that no one would hold except for philosophical reasons that seem to rule out the natural picture.

That picture is that the universe and most of what goes on in it are completely independent of our thoughts, but that since our ancestors appeared on Earth we have gradually developed the capacity to think about, know about, and represent more and more aspects of reality. There are some things that we cannot now conceive but may yet come to understand; and there are probably still others that we lack the capacity to conceive not merely because we are at too early a stage of historical development, but because of the kind of beings we are. About some of what we cannot conceive we are able to speak vaguely – this may include the mental lives of alien creatures, or what went on before the Big Bang – but about some of it we may be unable to say anything at all, except that there might be such things. The only sense in which we can conceive of them is under that description – that is, as things of which we can form no conception – or under the all-encompassing thought "Everything," or the Parmenidean thought "What is."

I am not claiming that much of what we find *positively inconceivable* – what we can see to be *im*possible, like round squares – may nevertheless be possible. Though there may be cases where our strong convictions of positive inconceivability cannot be relied on as evidence of impossibility, I assume they are rare. I am concerned here rather with the admission of possibilities and actualities which are *negatively* inconceivable to us in the sense that we have and can have no conception of them. (This is different from seeing positively that no such conception could be coherent, because, for example, it would involve a contradiction.)

Not everything about the universe must lie in the path of our possible cognitive development or that of our descendants – even if beings like us should exist forever. It is a philosophical problem how we are able to think about those aspects of reality that we can think about. There is also the question of whether we can think about those things 'as they are in themselves' or only 'as they appear to us'. But what there is, or what is the case, does not coincide necessarily with what is a possible object of thought for us. Even if through some miracle we are capable in principle of conceiving of everything there is, that is not what makes it real.

2. Idealism

e ⊢→ The philosophical argument against this natural view is simple. It parallels one of Berkeley's arguments for the view that for unthinking things, to exist is to be perceived. Berkeley claimed that this became evident if we tried to form the idea of an unperceived object. It turns out to be impossible, he said, because as soon as we try to think, for example, of an unperceived tree, we find that all we can do is to call up a perceptual image of a tree, and that is not unperceived.[2]

It would be generally recognized now that this argument involves the mistake of confusing perceptual imagination as the vehicle of thought with a perceptual experience as part of the object of thought. Even if I employ a visual image to think about the tree, that does not mean I am thinking about a visual impression of the tree, any more than if I draw a tree, I am drawing a drawing of a tree (cf. Williams 1966).

A similar mistake would be to argue that we cannot form the thought of something that no one is actually thinking about or the conception of something that no one is conceiving of. Clearly we can think and talk about the possible state of affairs in which no one is thinking or talking about Bishop Berkeley. The fact that we must talk about Berkeley to talk about the situation in which he is not being talked about doesn't make that situation either inexpressible or impossible.

f ⊢→ But the form of idealism with which I am concerned isn't based on this mistake: it is not the view that what there is must be actually conceived or even currently conceivable. Rather it is the position that what there is must be possibly conceivable by us, or possibly something for which we could have evidence. An argument for this general form of idealism must show that the notion of what *cannot* be thought about by us or those like us makes no sense.

The argument is this. If we try to make sense of the notion of what we could never conceive, we must use general ideas like that of something existing, or some circumstance obtaining, or something being the case, or something being true. We must suppose that there are aspects of reality to which these concepts that we *do* possess apply, but to which no other concepts that we *could* possess apply. To conceive simply that such things may exist is not to conceive of them adequately; and the realist would maintain that everything else about them might be inconceivable to us. The idealist reply is that our completely general ideas of what exists, or is the case, or is true, cannot reach any further than our more specific ideas of

g ⊢→ kinds of things that can exist, or be the case, or be true. We do not, in other

---

[2] Berkeley (1710, §§22–3). This is not Berkeley's only argument for idealism, but he says he is "content to put the whole upon this issue."

words, possess a completely general concept of reality that reaches beyond any possible filling in of its content that we could in principle understand.

Or to put the same point in terms of language, as Davidson does, we do not possess a general concept of truth that goes beyond the truth of all possible sentences in any language that we could understand, or that could be translated into a language that we or others like us could understand. Our general idea of what is the case does not transcend the sum of what we could truly assert to be the case. Here is Davidson rejecting the idea of a conceptual scheme that meets the conditions for applying to the world but is different from our own: "The criterion of a conceptual scheme different from our own now becomes: largely true but not translatable. The question whether this is a useful criterion is just the question how well we understand the notion of truth, as applied to a language, independent of the notion of translation. The answer is, I think, that we do not understand it independently at all."[3]

So the argument that parallels Berkeley's is that if we try to form the notion of something we could never conceive, or think about, or talk about, we find ourselves having to use ideas which imply that we could in principle think about it after all (even if we cannot do so now): because even the most general ideas of truth or existence we have carry that implication. We cannot use language to reach beyond the possible range of its specific application. If we attempt to do so, we are either misusing the language or using it to refer to what is conceivable after all.

This argument is not guilty of Berkeley's error. It does not ascribe to the object of thought something which is only an aspect of the vehicle of thought. It does not claim that to exist is to be thought about, or to have $\boxed{h} \mapsto$ been or to be going to be thought about. Nevertheless, it works in a similar way, for it claims that certain attempts to form significant thoughts fail because they run up against boundaries set by the conditions of the possibility of thought. In Berkeley's argument the hypothesis of existence without the mind is said to conflict with the conditions of thought, and the same is said here about the hypothesis of inconceivability. Realists are deluded, in other words, if they think they have the idea of a reality beyond the reach of any possible human thought except that one. If we examine carefully what they take to be that idea, we will discover that it is either the idea of something more fully within our reach, or no idea at all.

$\boxed{i} \mapsto$ To answer this objection it is necessary to dispute the view of thought on which it depends – as with Berkeley's argument. But first let me try to make clear how paradoxical the conclusion of the idealist argument is. An examination of what is wrong with the conclusion may shed some light on

---

[3] Davidson (1974: 194 [$\boxed{u} \mapsto$ in the extract in this book]); note that some realists might wish to accept the "largely true" condition for a different conceptual scheme, provided it could be shown not to conflict with the "not translatable" condition.

what is wrong with the argument. I must say at the outset that I do not have an alternative theory of thought to offer in place of those that support idealism. My argument will be essentially negative. I believe that the statement of a realist position can be rejected as unintelligible only on grounds which would also require the abandonment of other, much less controversial claims. My position is that realism makes as much sense as many other unverifiable statements, even though all of them, and all thought, may present fundamental philosophical mysteries to which there is at present no solution.

j⟶ It certainly seems that I can believe that reality extends beyond the reach of possible human thought, since this would be closely analogous to something which is not only possibly but actually the case. There are plenty of ordinary human beings who constitutionally lack the capacity to conceive of some of the things that others know about. People blind or deaf from birth cannot understand colors or sounds. People with a permanent mental age of nine cannot come to understand Maxwell's equations or the general theory of relativity or Gödel's theorem. These are all humans, but we could equally well imagine a species for whom these characteristics were normal, able to think and know about the world in certain respects, but not in all. Such people could have a language, and might be similar enough to us so that their language was translatable into part of ours.

If there could be people like that coexisting with us, there could also be such people if we did not exist – that is, if there were no one capable of conceiving of these things that they cannot understand. Then their position in the world would be analogous to the one which I have claimed we are probably in.

We can elaborate the analogy by imagining first that there are higher beings, related to us as we are related to the 9-year-olds, and capable of understanding aspects of the world that are beyond our comprehension. Then they would be able to say of us, as we can say of the others, that there are certain things about the world that we cannot even conceive. And now we need only imagine that the world is just the same, except that these higher beings do not exist. Then what they could say if they did exist remains true. So it appears that the existence of unreachable aspects of reality is independent of their conceivability by any actual mind.

Does this analogy work? Or is there some asymmetry between our situation and that of the hypothetical 9-year-olds?

k⟶ An objection might be that in thinking about them I have all along been conceiving of the world – even the world from which we are absent – in terms of what we actually know about it. The features they can't conceive are fully specifiable in our language. It might be held illegitimate to try to explain simply by analogy with this the idea of our own situation in a world that in some respects we can't think about. We cannot talk sense simply by saying that these people are related to the laws of general relativity as we are to some other features of the world – unless independent significance has been given in this statement to the general expression "features of the world." How can an analogy give sense to something that has no sense on its own, apart from the analogy?

[1]→ In response, let me extend the analogy to make room for this general concept, by an addition to the story about the congenital 9-year-olds. Suppose that, in the world in which we do not exist, one of them, call him Realist junior, develops philosophical leanings (why not?) and wonders whether there may be things about the world that he and others like him are incapable of ever finding out about or understanding. Is this impossible? That is, if he were to utter these words (supposing in other respects his language were like part of ours), would it be a mistake to take them as expressing a hypothesis which would in fact be true in that situation? Would he simply be talking nonsense without realizing it? Would he be incapable of thinking in general terms what we know to be true about his situation (what we have stipulated to be true)? Here the analogy goes in the other direction. If we would be talking nonsense by engaging in such speculation, so would he.

The question is whether we can attribute to Realist junior a general concept of reality which applies, though he can never know it, to the laws of general relativity and all the other features of the universe that humans may be capable of comprehending. Can he have, on the basis of the examples of reality with which he is acquainted, a general concept which applies beyond everything with which he and his like could conceivably become acquainted? If he can, then we ourselves can have the same concept, which will apply to features of the universe that we are incapable of comprehending.

[m]→ Suppose Realist junior expands on the idea by speculating that there might be other beings, with capacities that the 9-year-olds lack, who could understand aspects of reality that are inaccessible to them, though intellectual distance would make it impossible for the higher beings to communicate their understanding to the lower. (I assume an intellectual distance great enough so that the lower beings couldn't form a vicarious conception of something by relying to some extent on the judgments of the higher beings. Much of our ordinary conception of the world is vicarious in this sense – depending on the greater expertise or intelligence of other humans. But merely believing there might be something others could understand is not yet a conception of it, not even a vicarious one.)

Admittedly the idea of a higher form of understanding depends for its significance on the idea of something to be understood, and it is in dispute whether they have the latter idea. But it seems very artificial to deny that someone in this position could believe something we know to be not only significant but true: that there are concepts usable by other types of minds, which apply to the world and can be used to formulate truths about it, but which cannot be translated into his language or any language that he can understand. Wouldn't a 9-year-old Davidson who arose among them be wrong?

n⟩ In fact, wouldn't Davidson himself have to say that this lesser Davidson was wrong in denying the intelligibility of realism? How would Davidson's principle of charity be applied to the dispute between Davidson junior and Realist junior? Wouldn't it imply that Realist junior was right, because what he said could be translated into something we would assert, whereas what Davidson junior said couldn't be translated into something we would assert? I'm not sure. The problem is that Davidson's notion of translation seems to be asymmetrical. I might be able to translate a sentence of someone else's language into a sentence of my language, even though he cannot translate my sentence into his. According to Davidson (so far as I can see) I could say that Realist junior was right and Davidson junior wrong, but Realist junior would be wrong to agree with me – as Davidson junior would no doubt point out to him. This doesn't make the doctrine any less paradoxical. And if these consequences are unacceptable with regard to the 9-year-olds, they are unacceptable with regard to us.

This issue recalls the one discussed in chapter 5, section 2 [of Nagel's book], about the intelligibility of skepticism. In both cases the question is how far we can go in forming the idea of a world with which our minds cannot make contact. The general point I wish to make against restrictive o⟩ theories of what is thinkable is this. Every concept that we have contains potentially the idea of its own complement – the idea of what the concept doesn't apply to. Unless it has been shown positively that there cannot be such things – that the idea involves some kind of contradiction (like the idea of things that are not self-identical) – we are entitled to assume that it makes sense even if we can say nothing more about the members of the class, and have never met one.

To be the value of a variable in our universal or existential quantifications it is not necessary to be the referent of a specific name or description in our language, because we already have the general concept of *everything*, which includes both the things we can name or describe and those we can't. Against that background we can speak of the complement of any concept whatever, unless it has been shown to be positively inconceivable. We can speak of 'all the things we can't describe', 'all the things we can't imagine', 'all the things humans can't conceive of', and finally, 'all the things humans are constitutionally incapable of ever conceiving'. The universal quantifier does not have a built-in limitation to what can be designated in some other way. It could even be used to form the idea, 'all the things *no* finite mind could ever form a conception of'. Naturally the possibility of forming these ideas does not guarantee that anything corresponds to them. But in the nature of the case it is unlikely that we could ever have reason to believe that nothing does.

Creatures who recognize their limited nature and their containment in the world must recognize both that reality may extend beyond our conceptual reach and that there may be concepts that we could not understand. The condition is met by a general concept of reality under which one's actual conception, as well as all possible extensions of that conception, falls as an instance. This concept seems to me adequately explained through the idea of a hierarchical set of conceptions, extending from those much more limited than one's own but contained in it to those larger than one's own but containing it – of which some are reachable by discoveries one might make but others, larger still, are not. (The hierarchy could also include parallel conceptions, not intersecting our own but joined with it only in a larger one.) We could ascribe this concept to the philosophical 9-year-olds in our example, and I maintain that it is the same as our general concept of what there is. It seems to me so clear that we have this concept that any theory of thought or reference which implies that we can't have it is for that reason deeply suspect.

The pursuit of a more objective view, by which we place ourselves in the world and try to understand our relation to it, is the primary method of extending and filling out our particular conception of this reality. But the general concept implies that there is no guarantee that the whole of what there is coincides with what we or beings like us could arrive at if we carried the pursuit of objectivity to the limit – to the convergence of views that would come at that mythical point of stupefaction, "the end of inquiry."

There are limits of objectivity as a form of understanding that follow from the fact that it leaves the subjective behind. These are inner limits. There are also outer limits of objectivity that fall at different points for different types of beings, and that depend not on the nature of objectivity but on how far it can be pursued by a given individual. Objectivity is only a way of extending one's grasp of the world, and besides leaving certain aspects of reality behind, it may fail to reach others, even if more powerful forms of objectivity could encompass them.

3.   Kant and Strawson

As with the topic of knowledge, so with the topic of thought, I believe there is a middle ground between skepticism and reductionism. In the case of knowledge, skepticism arises when we reflect that our beliefs inevitably claim to go beyond their grounds. The effort to avoid skepticism by eliminating this gap can lead to reductionism, a reinterpretation of the content of our beliefs in terms of their grounds.

With thought, the problem is the relation between our conceptions and what is possible. Thought purports to represent facts and possibilities beyond itself, and skepticism is the view that our thoughts themselves give us no way of telling whether they correspond enough to the nature of actual and possible reality to be able to make contact with it at all – even to the extent of permitting false beliefs about it. To escape from such skepticism the reductionist reinterprets the domain of possibilities as the domain of what is or could become conceivable to us – thus guaranteeing (finally) that our thoughts can make contact with it.

To explain the intermediate position let me try to locate it in relation to two opposed views: Kant's skepticism and Strawson's reductionism. (Needless to say, this is not a term Strawson would use to describe his own view.) They are related to one another in that Strawson's view is offered as an empiricist criticism of Kant. Since Strawson's reductionism is quite generous, admitting a great deal into the universe of possibilities, it is important to explain what I think it leaves out.

Kant's position is that we can conceive of things only as they appear to us and never as they are in themselves: how things are in themselves remains forever and entirely out of the reach of our thought. "Doubtless, indeed, there are intelligible entities corresponding to the sensible entities; there may also be intelligible entities to which our sensible faculty of intuition has no relation whatsoever; but our concepts of understanding, being mere forms of thought for our sensible intuition, could not in the least apply to them" (Kant 1781/7, B308–9).

Strawson wishes to remove the Kantian opposition between thinking of things as they appear to us and thinking of them as they are in themselves by declaring the latter idea (in its Kantian version) nonsensical. He believes there is an appearance-reality distinction *within* what Kant regards as the world of appearance, but it is basically the distinction between how things appear to us at any particular time or from a particular vantage point, and how they would come to appear as the result of an improved view or further investigation. Application of the distinction depends, he says, on identity of reference plus a corrected view: the world that now appears to me in one way might come, as a result of procedures of corrective revision, to appear to me or others like me in another way – a way that could be seen as a correction of the first. No idea of reality is left standing by this account which could have application to anything outside the range of possible human conception, evidence, or discovery.

Strawson does not claim that the real is coextensive with what we can *actually* form a conception of. Here is what he says:

> In rejecting the senseless dogma that our conceptual scheme corresponds at no point with Reality, we must not embrace the restrictive dogma that Reality is completely comprehended by that scheme as it actually is. We admit readily that there are facts we do not know. We must admit also that there may be *kinds* of fact of which we have, at present, no more conception than our human predecessors had of some kinds of fact admitted in our conceptual

schemes but not in theirs. We learn not only how to answer old questions, but how to ask new ones. The idea of the aspects of Reality which would be described in the answers to the questions we do not yet know how to ask is one which, like the idea of the realm of the noumenal, though not in the same drastic style, limits the claim of actual human knowledge and experience to be "co-extensive with the real".

This seems to be the necessary, and not very advanced, limit of sympathy with the metaphysics of transcendental idealism.[4]

This is, as I have said, a broad interpretation of the range of possibilities. But the extension of reality beyond what we can now conceive is here still thought of as what *we* might come to if we developed new experiences or ways of thinking, and therefore conceptions of new types of individual, property, and relation that would have application on the basis of possible experience. The implied reference to ourselves and our world remains, even if the series of discoveries is thought of as incompletable. That is the basis for Strawson's claim that we cannot be said to know things only as they appear or might appear to us, because the contrasting idea of what never could appear to us is meaningless.

I want to agree with Strawson in denying that we know things *only* as they appear to us, but agree with Kant in holding that how things are in themselves transcends all possible appearances or human conceptions. Our knowledge of the phenomenal world is partial knowledge of the world as it is in itself; but the entire world can't be identified with the world as it appears to us because it probably includes things of which we cannot and never could conceive, no matter how far the human understanding is expanded, as Strawson suggests, in directions we cannot now imagine. The difficulty is to state this in a way that defies idealist reinterpretation; realists always find it hard to say anything with which idealists cannot arrange to agree by giving it their own meaning.

 Let me first explain my disagreement with Kant.[5] I hold the familiar view that secondary qualities describe the world as it appears to us but primary qualities do not. To be red simply is to be something which would appear red to us in normal conditions – it is a property whose definition is essentially relative. But to be square is not simply to be such as to appear square, even though what is square does appear square. Here the appearance of squareness is significantly explained in terms of the effect on us of squareness in objects, which is not in turn analyzed in terms of the appearance of squareness. The red appearance of red things, on the other hand, cannot be noncircularly explained in terms of their redness, because the

[4] Strawson 1966: 42. See also Strawson 1979, where he explicitly endorses the position that scientific realism is acceptable so long as we recognize its relativity to a particular intellectual standpoint.

[5] I am indebted here to Colin McGinn, though he does not explicitly consider the possibility of things we could never conceive of. See McGinn 1983, chs. 6 and 7.

latter is analyzed in terms of the former. To explain why things appear red we have to go outside the circle of color qualities.

The Kantian view that primary qualities, too, describe the world only as it appears to us depends on taking the entire system of scientific explanations of observable phenomena as itself an appearance, whose ultimate explanation cannot without circularity refer to primary qualities since they on the contrary have to be explained in terms of it. Primary qualities are nothing more on this view than an aspect of our world picture, and if that picture has an explanation, it must be in terms of the effect on us of something outside it, which will be for that reason unimaginable to us – the noumenal world.

The view that this must be how things are results from a refusal to distinguish between two ways in which the human point of view enters into our thoughts – as form and as content. The content of a thought may be quite independent of its particular form – independent, for example, of the particular language in which it is expressed. All of our thoughts must have a form which makes them accessible from a human perspective. But that doesn't mean they are all about our point of view or the world's relation to it. What they are about depends not on their subjective form but on what has to be referred to in any explanation of what makes them true.

The content of some thoughts transcends every form they can take in the human mind. If primary qualities were conceivable only from a human point of view, then the ultimate explanation of why the world appears to us in that way could not refer to primary qualities of things in themselves. But if primary qualities can equally well be grasped from a point of view that has nothing subjectively in common with ours, then the description of the world in terms of them is not relative to our point of view; they are not merely aspects of the phenomenal world but can on the contrary be used, by us or by others, to explain the appearance of that world.

The question is whether every possible explanation of our awareness of primary qualities, either perceptual or theoretical, must refer to the primary qualities of things outside us, or whether they disappear from the final explanation by being entirely included, as appearances, in what is to be explained. Unless the latter is true, the analogy with secondary qualities is meaningless. The mere fact that any thoughts we have about primary qualities must be formulated in language and images that we understand does not settle the matter, nor does the fact that any explanation we accept will be ours. It has to be claimed that at the limit, whether or not we are able to reach it, primary qualities *drop out* of the explanation of their appearance.

But there is no reason to believe that reference to primary qualities will disappear from the explanation of the appearance of primary qualities, no matter how complicated we make the "appearance" to be explained. We can't explain the fact that things look spatially extended except in terms of their being extended. And we can't explain the fact that *that* explanation seems true except again in terms of things being extended, their extension affecting us perceptually in certain ways, and the existence of that relation affecting the results of our investigation into the causes of our perceptual impressions of extension. And so on. If each explanation of the appearance of spatial extension in terms of extension in the world is counted as a new, higher-level appearance of extension, then that too has to be explained in terms of extension in the world. However far up we escalate in the series of "appearances" of extension, the extension of things in themselves will keep one step ahead and recur in the explanation of those appearances.[6]

The only thing that can refute this view is a better alternative. There might be one – at some level the explanation of the fact that so far all our theories of the physical world involve spatial extension might conceivably be explained in terms of something entirely different, something which we might or might not be able to grasp. But Kant's nonexplanation in terms of the inconceivable noumenal world is not that better alternative. It is just a placeholder for something beyond our comprehension, and there is no reason to accept it unless the available realist position, ascribing extension to things in themselves, is ruled out as impossible.

But what reason could there be to hold that, granting the intelligibility of the notion of things in themselves, they couldn't be spatially extended? There is no good reason – only a bad Berkeleyan reason: the move from subjectivity of form to subjectivity of content. In other words, it would have to be claimed that because *we have* the conception of primary qualities, detect them through observation, and use them in explanations, they are essentially relative to our point of view, though in a more complex way than secondary qualities are: relative not just to our perceptual point of view, but to our entire cognitive point of view. I believe there is no defense of this position which does not beg the question.

 But it is necessary to mention one Kantian argument for doubting that things in themselves have primary qualities, even though it does not show this to be impossible. The argument is this. Suppose Kant is right to claim that the primary qualities are essential features of our world picture, so that we cannot conceive of a world without them. This doesn't imply that they can't also be features of the world as it is in itself. But it does mean that we could not understand any explanation of the appearance of primary qualities which did not involve the ascription of primary qualities to things in the world. And if any such alternative would be inconceivable to us, the fact that every explanation we come up with involves primary qualities is not very good evidence that no better explanation of some other kind exists.

That is true. On the other hand, whatever may be the limits of our world picture (whether or not it has to include primary qualities), there is no

---

[6] By contrast, the colors of things drop out of explanations very early. We can explain something's looking red to *me* in terms of its being red, but we can't nonvacuously explain the fact that red things generally look red to human beings in terms of their being red.

guarantee that we will be able to find credible explanations of the appearances within those limits at all. To the extent that we do, there is some
reason to think that the picture does describe things in themselves, as far as
it goes. At any rate it may. Moreover, there is remarkable flexibility in our
conception of the kinds of primary qualities there are – far beyond anything
Kant would have imagined to be conceivable – and it has enabled us to
formulate theories of the physical world further and further removed from
immediate experience. If we agree with Kant that the idea of the world as it
is in itself makes sense, then there is no reason to deny that we know
anything about it.

Let me now turn to the other aspect of the view I am trying to defend –
the claim that there are probably things about the world that we (humans)
cannot conceive. This follows naturally from what has already been said. If
our conception of primary qualities is a partial conception of things as they
are in themselves, its existence is a side-effect of the existence of those things:
it results from their effects on each other and on us, together with our
mental activity. What we are able to understand about the world depends on
the relation between us and the rest of it. It appears to us naturally in certain
ways, and with the help of reason and controlled observation we can form
hypotheses about the objective reality underlying those appearances. But
how much of what there is we can in principle reach by these methods is
contingent on our mental makeup and the hypotheses it enables us to
understand. Our capacity for understanding what there is may be only
partial, because where it exists it depends not only on how things are but
on our constitution, and the former is independent of the latter. In this
global picture we are contained in the world and able to conceive some of it
objectively, but much of it may remain constitutionally beyond our reach.
This too, of course, is *our* conception, but that doesn't mean it is only a
higher-order description of the world as it appears to us. To insist otherwise
is to assume that if any conception has a possessor, it must be about the
possessor's point of view – a slide from subjective form to subjective
content. If there are other intelligent beings whose point of view is incom-
mensurate with ours, there is no reason why they should not also see us as
contained in the world in this way.

My disagreement with Strawson, then, is with the way he interprets the
idea that we are embedded in a world larger than we can conceive. What lies
beyond our current understanding is not adequately captured in the idea of
answers to questions we do not yet know how to ask. It may include things
that we or creatures like us could never formulate questions about.

Whether such things are possible is absolutely central, for if they are, they
set a standard of reality independent of the mind, which more familiar things
may also meet. We may then say that the reality of the features of things in
themselves that we have discovered is just as independent of our capacity to
discover them as is the reality of whatever may lie outside our conceptual

reach, actual or possible. In that case what we know or think about when we think about the structure of matter or the physical nature of light or sound is something whose appearance to us in any form is incidental, and whose existence is not merely that of a character in our best theories.

Commentary On Nagel

Nagel's 'Thought and Reality' – chapter 6 of his *The View from Nowhere* (1986) – is very different in style from Davidson's 'On the Very Idea of a Conceptual Scheme'. While the arguments of the latter are condensed and, at times, technical, Nagel's piece is expansive and has the character of an overarching survey of the terrain. None the less, Nagel concerns himself with issues that are no less complex and challenging. And, crucially, one of his morals is that Davidson should be viewed, not as a realist, but as an enemy of the only version of realism worthy of the name.

Section 1

Nagel's article begins, engagingly, by stating as clearly as possible the realism he wishes to defend. Admitting something that we mentioned in the Introduction – namely, that talk of the world's being mind-independent can be interpreted in many different ways – Nagel sets out his own, controversial, version of this thesis at [a]→. His contention is not merely that the world is there to be discovered by us, but that there may be things that we (or any creature past, present or future) could not even *conceive of*. To use his own words, Nagel takes our grasp on the world to be limited, not simply 'in respect of what we can know', but also 'in respect of what we can conceive'. Our representations of the world become more objective as they abstract from peculiarities in our point of view: peculiarities such as our colour-vision. But it would be a mistake to think that the world *just is* what can be revealed by an indefinite increase in objectivity: for there may be facts that are beyond our ken even when our representations are optimally objective ([c]→).

As Nagel makes clear at [b]→, the main point of his piece is to defend this conception of mind/world relations against contemporary forms of what he terms 'idealism'. An idealist, for Nagel, is anyone who denies the realist doctrine he has just elucidated: anyone who identifies the facts with what we can conceive of. Significantly, as will emerge in the couple of pages from [f]→, Nagel takes Davidson to be an idealist in this sense. Although Davidson is concerned to rebut the threat posed to realism by conceptual relativism, to Nagel's mind he does so by weakening realism illegitimately.

> 1. At this point, look again at the paragraph immediately preceding [v]→ and the final two paragraphs of Davidson's piece. Which version of realism – Davidson's or Nagel's – do you find more intuitive? (That is, which philosophical position – not which conception of 'realism' – do you find more intuitive?) Why?

One question you might be tempted to ask at this point is why Nagel finds his robust version of realism so attractive. Why is Davidson's realism not up to snuff? One answer is given immediately, at $\boxed{d}\mapsto$. Nagel here claims that his strong realism is the *default position*: the position that must be accepted unless it is defeated by philosophical argument. And his reason for thinking this is that it seems 'crazily self-important given what small and contingent pieces of the universe we are' to suppose that we are capable of conceiving of the complete inventory of the universe.

> 2. How convinced are you by Nagel's claim that he occupies the default position? Is our ordinary sense of 'mind-independence' so robust?

Section 2

Early on in section 2, starting at $\boxed{e}\mapsto$, Nagel discusses, and rejects, an infamous argument from Berkeley for a strongly idealist thesis: the thesis that unthinking things – familiar worldly objects such as trees, stones, tables and the like – cannot exist without being perceived by someone. The argument in question states that we can form no idea of an unperceived object, for the simple reason that if we try to call such a thing to mind we bring to mind a *perceptual image* of the object, and to do this is to *perceive* such an image: to see it with the mind's eye, as it were. Nagel's response, in the paragraph following $\boxed{e}\mapsto$, is swift. The fact that I call to mind a perceptual image of an object does not mean that I am really thinking about the image rather than the object itself. To think otherwise is to slide from the fact (if it is a fact) that one thinks about the tree *by means of having a perceptual image* to the false thesis that this image is the thing that one is thinking about. It is to confuse the *vehicle* of thought with its *content*. (This distinction will re-emerge later.)

Having made this point, Nagel goes on to explain, at $\boxed{f}\mapsto$, that the idealism with which he is concerned does not make *exactly* the same mistake as Berkeley's version. None the less, later on, at $\boxed{h}\mapsto$, Nagel makes it clear that he thinks that it works in the same kind of way as its Berkeleian ancestor, since its key claim is that the attempt to form a conception of there being something of which we cannot conceive is necessarily frustrated. If we try to consider such a possibility, the idealist says, we end up using concepts to characterize this thing which entail that it *is* conceivable after all. As Nagel explains at $\boxed{g}\mapsto$, idealists claim that the reason for this is that 'we do not . . . possess a completely general concept of reality that reaches beyond any possible filling in of its content that we could in principle understand'.

Clearly, Nagel has Davidson in mind here, as he explains in the paragraph immediately following $\boxed{g}\mapsto$. Davidson's claim that our concept of truth cannot extend beyond the truth of sentences in any language we could understand, or sentences that could be translated into a language which we could understand, is a linguistic version of Nagel's target thesis. So the question is: what is wrong with it, according to Nagel? The answer to this question comes in the 10 paragraphs following $\boxed{i}\mapsto$.

In his discussion of Davidson's argument, Nagel starts, at $\boxed{j}\!\mapsto$, by pointing out what he takes to be the implausibility of the idealist's thesis. True enough, we can form no *positive* conception of things of which we cannot conceive; but we *can* entertain the proposition that there could be such things by conceiving of them under the description 'things of which we can have no conception'. Indeed, Nagel goes so far as to give us a recipe for arriving at such a conception. Such a recipe has three steps. First, we are to consider everyday cases in which a group of people are constitutionally unable to think of some of the things that others can think of: cases such as that of a species of people with a permanent mental age equivalent to an ordinary 9-year-old, and who thus lack the capacity to understand some of the things that we understand. Second, we are then to imagine a world in which such people exist and yet we do not. Finally, we are then simply to appreciate an analogy: perhaps our position in the world is akin to that of the 9-year-olds in the recipe's second step. That is, we are to imagine 'higher beings' who stand to us as we do to the 9-year-olds, and which can thus conceive of things that are beyond our comprehension; and we are then to cling on to this notion of a realm of things of which we can have no conception while removing these posited higher beings from the picture. There we have it: the possibility of things of which we can have no conception.

As Nagel explains ($\boxed{k}\!\mapsto$), it might be objected that the analogy is illegitimate. In the case of the 9-year-olds, the features they cannot conceive of *are* specifiable in our language, so one might wonder whether we can extrapolate from this case to a case in which the inconceivable features of reality are *not* specifiable in our language.

In response to this concern, Nagel extends the analogy at $\boxed{l}\!\mapsto$: an extension that he takes to show, eventually, the deeply paradoxical nature of Davidson's position. Returning to the recipe's second step at $\boxed{m}\!\mapsto$, Nagel introduces a 9-year-old realist and a 9-year-old Davidson into the thought-experiment. The 9-year-old realist – situated in a world just like the one which we inhabit – wonders whether there might be aspects of reality of which he could have no notion, but which *could* be understood by higher beings (who, despite this, could not communicate such a conception to 9-year-olds due to the latter's intellectual limitations). Nagel's point is that the 9-year-old realist's hypothesis is *true*: we are examples of such 'higher beings'. A 9-year-old Davidson, who insisted that the hypothesis made no sense, would just be *wrong*.

But now Davidson would seem to have a problem. Davidson must, surely, agree that the 9-year-old realist is right and the 9-year-old Davidson is wrong: there *are* aspects of reality of which the 9-year-old realist can have no notion, and which can be understood by higher beings (namely, us). But Davidson must *also* say that the 9-year-old realist himself would be wrong to agree with us on this matter. For if Davidson's central claim is correct, and if one cannot make sense of the idea of things of which we cannot conceive, then something that is true – namely the claim that there are aspects of reality that the 9-year-old realist cannot grasp – turns out, *for the 9-year-old realist himself*, to make no sense. Imagine the 9-year-old realist saying to you, 'there are aspects of reality I cannot conceive of'. All of us (including Davidson) would surely want to say that what he says is *true*. But Davidson also seems to have to say that, *from his own point of view*, what the 9-year-old realist says makes no sense.

This is our paradox, a paradox caused by the fact that, as Nagel puts it at $\boxed{n}\!\!\mapsto$, 'Davidson's notion of translation seems to be asymmetrical'. *A* may be able to translate *B*'s words, but *B* may not be able to translate *A*'s; and what this means is that one and the same thing can be true and yet supposedly make no sense to someone asserting it. This, Nagel states, is an unacceptable conclusion which is equally unacceptable – across the analogy between the 9-year-olds' situation and our predicament – with regard to us.

> 3. (i) Work through Nagel's objection to Davidson, from $\boxed{j}\!\!\mapsto$ to $\boxed{n}\!\!\mapsto$, step by step, and put it in your own words. (ii) Is it convincing? What, if anything, do you think Davidson could say in reply?

The section ends with Nagel drawing a conclusion from his discussion of the Davidsonian position. According to Nagel, Davidson fails to appreciate that '[e]very concept that we have contains potentially the idea of its own complement – the idea of what the concept doesn't apply to' $(\boxed{o}\!\!\mapsto)$. As long as this complement is not incoherent – as is 'the things that are not identical with themselves', for example – it remains intelligible. This being so, the complement of 'things of which we can conceive' makes sense, even though we can form no positive idea of the things to which it could apply.

> 4. Explain what Nagel means by saying that every concept that we have 'contains potentially the idea of its own complement', and give some examples. Do you think what Nagel says is true of (i) quite a lot of our concepts, but by no means all of them? or (ii) all of our concepts, including the concept of 'things of which we can conceive'? or (iii) all of our concepts *except* the concept of 'things of which we can conceive'? Justify your answer.

Section 3

The final section of the extract from Nagel, the discussion of the views of Kant and Strawson, is also of intrinsic interest since it sheds further light on his own position. One thing that is clear is that the robust realism to which Nagel signs up brings with it the threat of a radical form of scepticism. If the world is in his 'very strong sense' independent of our minds – if, in other words, the world is so mind-independent as to extend beyond what we can even conceive of – then a 'gap' would seem to open up between our representations and the world. Descartes's way of bringing home the force of this sceptical worry was the 'malicious demon' hypothesis (1641: 20). You are to imagine that there is a malicious demon whose purpose in life is to ensure that all of your beliefs about the external world are mistaken, something that he achieves by making it seem to you that there is an external world of chairs, tables, cats and the like, when in fact there is no such thing. The problem Descartes presents us with is this. There is no way of telling that the world is as you take it to be, as opposed to being a chimera created by the malicious demon: either way, your experiences remain the same. Given that this is so, it immediately becomes problematic as to how you can be said to know that you are not being systematically deceived by your sensory experiences and thoughts, something which, in turn, problematizes the idea that you can have *any* knowledge of the nature of the external world (if there is one).

So much for Descartes. Nagel, though, admits that his account of mind/world relations places us in a distinctively Cartesian position. Although Nagel puts the problem less figuratively than Descartes, it is to all intents and purposes the same: perhaps 'our thoughts themselves give us no way of telling whether they correspond enough to the nature of actual and possible reality to be able to make contact with it at all – even to the extent of permitting false beliefs about it' ($\boxed{p}\mapsto$). What should we make of this consequence? One might think that a theory's encouragement of such scepticism counts against it, in which case some form of anti-realism (including Davidson's version of 'realism') will seem attractive.

> 5. Explain how one might argue that Davidson's view precludes the possibility of the world's being so different to the way we think it is that our thoughts are not 'able to make contact with it at all'.

Alternatively, with Nagel, one might suppose that the fact that his variety of realism 'makes scepticism intelligible' ($\boxed{a}\mapsto$) is a sign of its correctness. Elsewhere in *The View from Nowhere* Nagel recommends what he terms a 'heroic' response to scepticism: a response that acknowledges the great gap between thought and reality, but which tries to cross it without artificially narrowing it (1986: 68–9). This was Descartes' own way with the sceptic (1641: Meditations II–VI).

> 6. What *is* the moral we should draw from the fact that Nagel's realism renders scepticism intelligible? Is this a sign of his position's strength, or its weakness?

Given the nature of Nagel's realism – a realism that opens up the conceptual possibility that our thought may fail to make *any* sort of contact with the world – isn't his heroic response to scepticism doomed to failure? Not a bit of it, claims Nagel. As Nagel explains from $\boxed{q}\mapsto$, although he takes our experience of secondary qualities (qualities such as colour, taste and smell) to fail to represent the world as it really is, he believes our primary-quality experience (our representation of a thing's size and shape, for example) to be capable of representing the world as it is in itself. Although our primary-quality concepts are 'essential features of our world picture' ($\boxed{r}\mapsto$) – that is, our conceptual scheme – they are none the less features of the mind-independent world. And the reason why Nagel thinks this is that primary qualities, by contrast with secondary qualities, figure essentially in the explanation of their appearance: while the red appearance of things is explained in terms, roughly, of the texture of things and the properties of light, we can only explain the fact that things look spatially extended (look to have a certain shape, say) in terms of their really *being* extended (having a certain shape). True enough, our primary quality concepts form a central part of our conceptual scheme, but this is a claim about their *form*, not their *content*. These concepts are, of course, accessible from our point of view, but they are not *about* either that point of view or the world's relation to it (as is the case with our secondary-quality concepts).

7. Someone might object to Nagel's view about primary qualities as follows: It just isn't true that the appearance of, say, ovalness is to be explained by reference to the oval shape of the object that appears to us. For *round* objects can perfectly well appear oval to us. Do you think this would be a good objection? Why or why not?

8. Read carefully how Nagel distinguishes between squareness and redness in the three paragraphs from $\boxed{q} \mapsto$. Does this way of drawing the distinction strike you as correct? (In particular, think about the use to which he puts the distinction between form and content.)

Having drawn his distinction between our primary-quality and secondary-quality concepts, Nagel sums up what he takes to be the moral of his discussion of scepticism. We can be sure that primary qualities are *bona fide* constituents of the mind-independent world by virtue of the fact that they pull their weight in explanations of our experience. Hence, there is no reason to deny that we know anything about the 'world as it is in itself' (that is, the world as it really is).

9. Are you convinced by this reply to the sceptical problem? Suppose someone said this: primary qualities figure in what we *take to be* explanations of their appearance; but given Nagel's robust realism, how could we ever know whether such explanations are genuine?

Having defended the claim that we can have knowledge of the world as it is in itself, Nagel returns, from $\boxed{r} \mapsto$ to the end of the extract, to the topic of his robust version of realism. Here Nagel claims that the kind of realist picture he recommends becomes obligatory once we appreciate that the content of our representations is determined not only by how things are, but also by how our minds work. In Nagel's own words, '[o]ur capacity for understanding what there is may be only partial, because where it exists it depends not only on how things are but on our constitution, and the former is independent of the latter'. We are able to describe some aspects of reality that a 9-year-old cannot grasp: we (or at least, some of us) can describe reality as containing curved space-time, sub-atomic particles, DNA, and the like. But there are limits to our cognitive resources; we are, after all, only human. Perhaps the ultimate nature of the sub-atomic realm or the outer reaches of the universe (say) will never be revealed to us, because we are simply not up to the job. Our perspective on the world might not be built for representing the world in its entirety.

10. In the paragraph following ⌐r⌐→ Nagel expresses his conviction that 'we are able to conceive some of [the world] objectively'. Should he be so sure? Suppose someone were to say this: if we bring to bear a conceptual scheme on how things are, this means that we can never conceptualize *the world as it really is*, only *the world as we conceive it*; to represent the world as it really is, we would have to stand outside of our conceptual scheme, which is impossible. What would Nagel say in reply?

11. (i) Sum up the different responses made by Davidson and Nagel to global relativism. (ii) Whose response do you think is superior? Why?

Further Reading

A helpful introduction to realism/anti-realism debates is provided by Kirk 1999. On this subject, Wright 1992 is highly original and thought-provoking, but difficult. A good survey of the conceptual schemes literature is provided by Lynch 1998, ch. 2. A philosopher in tune with Nagel's approach is Bernard Williams. His notion of an 'absolute conception' of reality – a notion similar to Nagel's view from nowhere – is introduced in his 1978 and further discussed in his 1985.

Essay Questions

1. Is Davidson's argument against the very idea of a conceptual scheme sound?
2. What, in your view, is the most plausible version of global realism? Is such realism defensible?
3. What do you understand by 'relativism'? Is there a persuasive argument for this thesis?
4. Do we have 'the concept of an uninterpreted reality, something outside all schemes and science' (Davidson)? What consequences does your answer have for the realism/anti-realism debate?
5. Is the fact that it renders scepticism unintelligible the basis of a good argument for anti-realism?

4

Realism and Nominalism

Introduction

Ontology

This chapter sees us make our first foray into matters *ontological*: the study of what kinds of thing exist. Philosophers who dip into this subject area engage in disputes as to what *our ontology* (the philosophically sanctioned list of the kinds of entity that exist) should include. Most of us would agree that the items we unreflectively call 'things' exist: entities such as individual chairs, pebbles, trees, pillar boxes, and the like. But should our ontology also contain, for example, events (e.g. *the playing of the 1975 Cup Final*), processes (e.g. *The Industrial Revolution*), or states of affairs (e.g. *Eleanor's being female*)? Whether the furniture of the universe includes such entities and, if so, how we should characterize them, are ontological questions.

The ontological dispute with perhaps the longest and most distinguished pedigree – what has become known as the 'problem of universals' – is our topic in the current chapter. The issue is this: should our ontology include universals as well as particulars? But before you can get to grips with the two texts grappling with this question, you need to know what is at stake in this quarrel: that is, you must be clear about the supposed nature of the disputed entities – universals – and you must understand how they are supposed to differ from particulars.

Particulars and universals

Just now we said that most of us would agree that the world contains what we unreflectively call 'things'. Such things – the items we can perceive, trip over and bang into – are a subset of *particulars*. But, of course, two or more such particulars may be of the same *type*: two distinct pillar boxes may both be *red*, *cylindrical* and *metallic*, for example. *Universals*, if there exist such entities, are *reified* characteristics. That is, they are entities in their own right, so that the mass or shape of a pillar box is an additional entity to the pillar box itself. What is more, universals are entities with a special feature: *repeatability*. At any give moment in time, one and the same universal may be possessed (philosophers tend to say 'instantiated' or 'exemplified') by more than one particular. So, the idea is this: if two or more pillar boxes are both red, this consists in the fact that there is a single entity – the universal *redness* – that is instantiated by all of them. There is a single entity that is *literally shared* by each pillar box.

Here, then, we have the crux of the distinction between particulars and universals. Universals, we have just noted, are repeatable: the very same universal can be wholly present in more than one place at one time (e.g. redness can be wholly present in a pillar box in Manchester and, simultaneously, in a cricket ball in Durban). Particulars, by contrast, are unrepeatable: if there is a pillar box in Manchester and a pillar box in London, we automatically have two distinct pillar boxes and not one, multiply-located pillar box. (Of course, we could saw a particular pillar box in half and locate one half in Manchester and the other half in London. But even so, the pillar box will not be multiply located in the appropriate sense, since the pillar box will not be *wholly* present in either location.)

Realism, nominalism and the problem of the one over the many

In the previous chapter we introduced you to realism about the external world: the doctrine that things such as tables, trees and people exist and are mind-independent. In a related use of the term 'realism', realism about universals is the thesis that universals – repeatable entities – exist. From now on, when we use the word 'realism', we mean realism about *universals*.

One thing is for sure: realism about universals is highly controversial. Opposed to the realist is the nominalist: someone who follows Locke (1690: II.iii.10) in thinking that 'all things that exist are only particulars'. Our first text sees Michael Devitt pressing the nominalist's case against one particular argument for realism; David Armstrong replies to Devitt from a staunchly realist perspective.

Typically, a realist will claim that the explanation of certain obvious facts requires us to posit entities of the kind in question. (To use the standard jargon, she will say that such explanations require an *ontological commitment* to such entities.) So what are the obvious facts to which a realist is likely to appeal? The fact most commonly appealed to by realists is that distinct particulars may be of the same *type* or *kind*: and it is the thought that this phenomenon stands in need of further explanation – that there is a *problem* of the one over the many – that is the chief concern of Devitt and Armstrong in our selected texts. As we have noted already, two red pillar boxes are distinct entities and yet they are both red: they share a *nature*, in some sense. The realist believes that the fact that the two particulars share a nature stands in need of *explanation*, and that only a commitment to universals can provide us with a plausible such explanation. In other words, the realist takes both of the following claims to be true:

(A)   We need to explain *what it is* for two particulars to be of the same type (e.g. for two pillar boxes both to be red);

(B)   The only satisfying explanation of what it is for two particulars to be of the same type is that they share a universal.

Nominalists – opponents of realism – fall into one of two categories, depending on which of the above two claims they deny. Many nominalists accept (A), but deny (B), claiming that sameness of type admits of an explanation that avoids ontological commitment to universals. Along these lines, it has been suggested that our two pillar boxes are red by virtue of, for example, the same predicate – 'is red' – being true of both; or by virtue of both pillar boxes being members of the class of all the things that are red; or by virtue of both pillar boxes resembling a paradigm red thing. (For a detailed discussion of these options, see Armstrong 1989, chs. 1–3.) Devitt, however, following W. V. Quine (1948), takes another path, denying (A). In his view, as you will see, the problem is chimerical. The fact that both of our pillar boxes are red does not stand in need of explanation, and so does not require us to admit universals into our ontology.

Predication and paraphrase

In the previous section we explained that realists will typically claim that the problem of the one over the many can only have a realist solution. But it is important to appreciate that the fact that distinct individuals may share a nature – that is, be of the same type – is not the only fact to which a realist may appeal to motivate her position. She may also think that aspects of our language-use require us to believe in the existence of universals, as we shall now see.

A second phenomenon to which a realist may appeal – in addition to sharedness of nature – is that of *predication*. A predicate is a form of words that is used to describe something, examples of predicates being the italicized expressions in the following sentences:

(C)   Manchester *is rainy*.
(D)   Socrates *is snub-nosed*.
(E)   Ingmar *is happy*.

In each of (C) to (E), the predicate is used to *describe* the item picked out by a name ('Manchester', 'Socrates', 'Ingmar'). Realists find it tempting to suppose that predicates are akin to names, serving to 'introduce' or 'express' entities: universals. The idea is something like this. The role of 'is rainy' in (C) – like the role of the name 'Manchester' – is to represent something in the world: its purpose is not purely formal as is the case for words like 'and', 'or' and 'if'. But, since we apply 'is rainy' to places other than Manchester, and since, in doing so, we mean the same thing by the predicate, the realist recommends that we should treat it as expressing a universal: raininess. Consequently, when it comes to each of (C) to (E), the realist says that in *describing* an object as rainy, snub-nosed or happy, we are saying that an object instantiates a universal. And this reading is supposedly demonstrated by the fact that each of (C) to (E) can be paraphrased in such a way as to bring the hidden reference to a universal out into the open:

(C★)   Manchester instantiates raininess;
(D★)   Socrates instantiates snub-nosedness;
(E★)   Ingmar instantiates happiness.

In each of (C★) to (E★) there is a noun ('raininess', 'snub-nosedness', 'happiness') that would seem to be doing the job of referring to a universal. Predication, Armstrong urges at $\boxed{d}\!\!\to$ in his article, must be taken with 'ontological seriousness'.

The final fact whose explanation may be taken by a realist to commit us to the existence of universals is also linguistic. It is this: there are true sentences that ostensibly involve reference to universals, sentences such as:

(F)   Red is a colour;
(G)   Humility is a virtue;

and

(H)   He has the same virtues as his father.

Clearly, the nominalist must deny that this apparent reference to universals is real. And the obvious strategy for doing so would be to argue, first, that there are paraphrases of (F) to (H) that involve no such ostensible reference, and, second, that these paraphrases are *more basic* than the sentences they paraphrase: that is, that the existence of such paraphrases demonstrates the ostensible reference to universals in (F) to (H) to be apparent only. Consider a similar strategy for dealing with

(I)   The average family has 1.7 children.

It is obviously absurd to think that there exists an actual family that has 1.7 children, and yet (I) is true. Consequently, to reveal how (I) can be true without committing us to the existence of such a queer entity, we may paraphrase (I) as

(J)   The total number of children divided by the total number of families is 1.7.

Evidently, (J) does not commit us to the existence of an actual family with 1.7 children. Paraphrase has been used to show what the ontological commitments of (I) really are. There are, however, problems in applying this strategy of paraphrase to the case of sentences – such as (F) to (H) – that appear to commit us ontologically to universals. Even Devitt accepts that such paraphrases might be hard to come by. And, in any case, it is unclear what the rules of the game are for deciding which of a pair of sentences reveals the true ontological commitments of the other.

A problem for realism

The previous section ended with a problem for nominalism. But the realist has to face up to (at least) one problem too, as Devitt briefly explains at $\boxed{e}\!\!\rightarrow$. For what the realist must do is explain what it is for a particular to instantiate a universal, something that it is none too easy to do. For if, as it seems natural to think, instantiation is a *relation*, I, that obtains between a and F, then the realist will have to treat I as a universal, and, consequently, will have to posit a *new* instantiation relation, I^*, to hold between I and its relata. But here a vicious regress threatens, since, by the same reasoning, I^*, too, can only be a universal and, as a result, subject to the very same problem. What this demonstrates is that instantiation cannot be a relation. But now the question is this: can the realist explain the nature of instantiation in non-relational terms without lapsing into obscurantism? Armstrong – perhaps the most influential recent realist – takes up this issue at $\boxed{g}\!\!\rightarrow$ in his article. Devitt – as one would expect of a committed nominalist – thinks realism is stumped.

Michael Devitt, ' "Ostrich Nominalism" or "Mirage Realism"?'*

David Armstrong's approach to "the problem of universals" has a contemporary gloss: he leaves it to "total science ... to determine what universals there are." Nevertheless his conception of the problem shows him to be a devotee of the "old-time" metaphysics. The problem is the traditional one allegedly posed by the premise of "Plato's One over Many argument": "Many different particulars can all have what appears to be the same nature" (p. xiii).[1] It is a pity that Armstrong takes no serious account of the "new" metaphysics of W. V. Quine and others according to which there is no such problem as Armstrong seeks to solve.[2] In my view this Quinean position is a much stronger rival to Armstrong's Realism about universals than the many others he carefully demolishes.

The universals we are concerned with here are properties (what Quine calls "attributes") and relations. "Realists" believe in them, "Nominalists" don't. After outlining five versions of Nominalism, Armstrong mentions the Quinean position as a possible sixth under the title "Ostrich or Cloak-and-dagger Nominalism":

*I am indebted to Elizabeth Prior for help with the first draft of this paper and to David Armstrong and Frank Jackson for helpful comments on that draft.

[1]   Such references are to *Nominalism and Realism: Universals and Scientific Realism, Volume 1*; Cambridge: University, 1978.

[2]   See particularly Quine's discussion in "On What There Is," *From a Logical Point of View*; New York: Harper Torchbooks, 1963; pp. 9–14. Quine's discussion is largely aimed at a position like Armstrong's ("For 'McX' read 'McArmstrong' ": Elizabeth Prior).

I have in mind those philosophers who refuse to countenance universals but who at the same time see no need for any reductive analyses of the sorts just outlined. There are no universals but the proposition that a is *F* is perfectly all right as it is. Quine's refusal to take predicates with any ontological seriousness seems to make him a Nominalist of this kind. (p. 16)

Worse, these philosophers are guilty of trying to have it both ways: denying universals whilst, *prima facie*, unashamedly making use of them. They commit the sin of failing to answer "a compulsory question in the examination paper" (p. 17). In Quinean language, they fail to face up to their ontological commitments.

Ostriches are reputed to ignore problems by putting their heads in the sand. Mirages are another feature of desert life: people see things that aren't there. An "Ostrich Nominalist" is a person who maintains Nominalism whilst ignoring a problem. A "Mirage Realist" is a person who adopts Realism because he sees a problem that isn't there. My major thesis is as follows:

1.   To maintain Nominalism whilst ignoring the One over Many argument is not to be an Ostrich Nominalist; rather to adopt Realism because of that argument is to be a Mirage Realist.

Establishing this thesis would not, of course, show Realism to be unjustified (let alone false): there might be problems independent of the One over Many argument for which Realism is a possible solution. Armstrong thinks there are. I agree. To the extent that he is responding to those problems he is not a Mirage Realist. My thesis about him is as follows:

2.   Armstrong is largely though not entirely a Mirage Realist.

Correspondingly, a Nominalist could be an Ostrich by putting his head in the sand as *real* problems loom. However correct his stand on the One over Many argument he could *otherwise* commit the sin that Armstrong complains of. I don't know whether there are any Ostrich Nominalists, but the only philosopher Armstrong alleges (tentatively) to be one, Quine, is not:

3.   Quine is not an Ostrich Nominalist.

Argument for Thesis 1

According to Armstrong, the problem posed by the One over Many argument is that of explaining "how numerically different particulars can nevertheless be identical in nature, all be of the same 'type' " (p. 41). What phenomena are supposed to need explaining here? I take it that what Armstrong is alluding to is the common habit of expressing, assenting to, and believing, statements of the following form:

(1)   *a* and *b* have the same property (are of the same type), *F*-ness.

To settle ontological questions we need a criterion of ontological commitment. Perhaps Quine's criterion has difficulties, but something along that line is mandatory. The key idea is that a person is committed to the existence of those things that must exist for the sentences he accepts to be true. What must exist for a given sentence to be true is a semantic question to which our best theory may give no answer in which we have confidence. Furthermore the sentence may, by its use of quantifiers or singular terms, suggest an answer which the person would want to resist. Hence, in my view, the importance of Quine's mention of paraphrase in this context. Suppose the given sentence seems to require for its truth the existence of *G*'s yet the person can offer another sentence, which serves his purposes well enough, and which is known not to have that requirement. This is known because our semantic theory can be applied to this other sentence, in a way that it cannot to the given sentence, to show that the sentence can be true even though *G*'s do not exist. We can then say that the person's apparent commitment to *G*'s in the given sentence arises from "a mere manner of speaking"; he is not really committed to them.

Now in the ordinary course of conversation a Quinean is prepared to express or assent to the likes of (1). (1) seems to require the existence of an *F*-ness for it to be true. So he appears committed to that existence. To this extent the One over Many argument does pose a problem to the Quinean Nominalist, but it is a negligible extent. He has a suitable paraphrase readily to hand:

(2)   *a* and *b* are both *F.*

When the ontological chips are down, he can drop (1). There is no problem about identities in nature beyond a trivial one of paraphrase.

Armstrong will not be satisfied by this, of course: "You have simply shifted the problem. In virtue of what are *a* and *b* both *F*?" The Quinean sees only a trivial problem here too. It is in virtue of the following:

(3)   *a* is *F*;
(4)   *b* is *F.*

Armstrong will still be dissatisfied: "In virtue of what is *a* (or *b*) *F*?" If the One over Many argument poses a problem it is this. That was historically the case and, though Armstrong always *states* the problem in terms of identities in nature, it is the case for him too.[3] *If there is no problem for the Nominalist in (3) and (4) as they stand then he has an easy explanation of identities in nature.*

The Realist who accepts the One over Many problem attempts to solve it here by claiming the existence of a universal, F-ness, which both *a* and *b* have. The Nominalist who accepts the problem attempts to solve it without that claim. The Quinean rejects the problem.

 The Quinean sees no problem for Nominalism in the likes of (3) because there is a well-known semantic theory which shows that (3) can be true without there being any universals:

(3) is true if and only if there exists an *x* such that '*a*' designates *x* and '*F*' applies to *x*.

So (3) can be true without the existence of F-ness. There is no refusal here "to take predicates with any ontological seriousness." The Quinean thinks that there *really must exist something* (said as firmly as you like) that the predicate '*F*' applies to. However that thing is not a universal but simply an object. Further, in denying that this object need have properties, the Quinean is not denying that *it really is F* (or G, or whatever). He is not claiming that it is "a bare particular." He sees no need to play that game.

The Realist may reply that this is a mistaken statement of the truth conditions of (3) and that the correct one *does* require the existence of F-ness for (3)'s truth. Until a good argument for this reply is produced the Quinean is entitled to go on thinking he has no problem.

All of this is not to say that there is nothing further about (3), or about *a* being *F*, that might need explanation. I can think of four possible problems here. None of them pose any special difficulty for the Nominalist: they are irrelevant to "the problem of universals."

(i) We might need to explain what *caused a* to be *F*. (ii) We might need to explain what was *the purpose* of *a* being *F*. Nobody interested in "the problem of universals" is likely to confuse their problem with (i) or (ii) and so I shall set them aside immediately.

It is not so easy to keep the next two problems distinct from "the problem of universals." (iii) If '*F*' is not a fundamental predicate then as reductivists we might need to explain what *constitutes a* being *F*: perhaps we will want to be told that it is in virtue of being *G*, where '*G*' is some physical predicate (*a* is a gene in virtue of being a DNA molecule). (iv) We might need to explain the *semantics* of '*F*': we might want to know what makes it the case that '*F*' applies to *a*.

The traditional "problem of universals" has often appeared in a misleading semantic guise: how can '*F*' "be applied to an indefinite multiplicity of

[3]   See, e.g., his remarks on Ostrich Nominalism (quoted above) and his discussion of the varieties of Nominalism, pp. 12–16.

particulars" (p. xiii; Armstrong does not approve of this way of putting the problem)? The strictly semantic problem of multiplicity does not have anything to do with universals. We need to explain the link between 'F' and all F things in virtue of which the former applies to the latter. This is not different *in principle* from explaining the link between 'a' and one object, a, in virtue of which the former designates the latter. The explanation of 'F' 's application depends on a theory of one semantic relation, application, the explanation of 'a' 's designation depends on a theory of another, designation. A feature of the explanations will be that it is F things that are linked to 'F', and a that is linked to 'a'. The F-ness of F things and the a-ness of a need not go unexplained in the semantics. Thus I think it is part of a good explanation of the link between 'tiger' and the many objects that it applies to that those objects are genetically of a certain sort. So the semantic problem may require *some* answer to the question: in virtue of what is a F? But the answer required is of type (iii), a reductivist answer.

 In denying that there is any problem for the Nominalist about (3) it is important to see that we are not denying the reductivist problem (iii), nor the semanticist problem (iv), nor some combination of (iii) and (iv). What we are denying can be brought out vividly by taking 'F' to be a fundamental predicate, say a physical predicate. Then there is no problem (iii): we have nothing to say about what makes a F, it just *is* F; that is a basic and inexplicable fact[4] about the universe. Problem (iv) remains: it is the problem of explaining the link between the predicate 'F' and that basic fact. Nothing else remains to be explained.

Why be dissatisfied with this? Explanation must stop somewhere. What better place than with a fundamental physical fact of our world?

Armstrong feels that we need to go further. How can we tell who is right? There is one sure sign that explanation has not gone far enough: an explanation that goes further. Thus if Armstrong's Realist response to the One over Many argument is a genuine explanation then there must be a genuine problem here to be explained. My final remarks in support of thesis 1 will consider Armstrong's response.

One Realist response, but not Armstrong's, to the One over Many argument runs as follows: a is F in virtue of having the property F-ness. We explain (3) by

(5) a has F-ness.

An obvious question arises: how is (5) to be explained? The Realist feels that the one-place predication (3) left something unexplained, yet all he has done to explain it is offer a two-place predication (a relational statement). If there

---

[4]   Lest an uncharitable reader should take this talk as committing me to the existence of facts, let me hasten to add that such talk is a mere manner of speaking, eliminable at the cost of style and emphasis.

is a problem about *a being F* then there is at least an equal problem about *a having F-ness*. Furthermore, the point of this manoeuvre for the Realist is to commit us to universals. In ontology, the less the better. Therefore this sort of Realist makes us ontologically worse off without explanatory gain. Any attempt by him to achieve explanatory power by explaining (5) seems doomed before it starts: it will simply raise the same problem as (5); he is in a vicious regress. If there is a problem about (3) this sort of Realist *cannot* solve it.

Armstrong calls the doctrine we have just considered "relational Immanent Realism," and rejects it for reasons not unconnected to mine (pp. 104–7). In its place he offers us "non-relational Immanent Realism." This doctrine is obscure. Armstrong offers us (5), or the similar, '*F-ness is in a*,' and simply *declares* it to be non-relational and inexplicable: particulars are not *related* to universals but bonded to them in a metaphysical unity (pp. 108–11). We have just seen that (5), taken at face value, cannot explain any problem about (3): it is a relational statement and so any problem for (3) is a probem for it. Armstrong avoids this grievous difficulty for Realism by fiat: (5) is not to be taken at face value. How then is it to be taken? Do we have even the remotest idea of what the words 'in' and 'have' mean here if they are not construed as relational predicates? Armstrong's Realism replaces the explanatory failings of relational Realism with a complete mystery. I suspect that Armstrong views sentences like (5) as attempts to speak the unspeakable: to talk about "the link" between particulars and universals without saying they are related. (Note the scare-quotes around 'in' on p. 108 and the use of a special hyphenating device on p. 111.)

Talk of "particulars" and "universals" clutters the landscape without adding to our understanding. We should rest with the basic fact that *a* is *F*. Even the alleged unity of particular and universal can be captured without mystery: a predication must involve both a singular term and a predicate; drop either partner and you say nothing. For the Nominalist the unity of predication is an unexciting linguistic fact. The move to relational Realism loses the unity. Armstrong's non-relational Realism attempts to bring it back with metaphysical glue. These are "degenerating problem shifts" (Lakatos).

Armstrong sees the One over Many argument as posing a problem for Nominalism and offers a Realist solution. If his solution were real then the problem would be real. The solution is not real. So it throws no doubt on my earlier argument that the problem is not real.

Indeed the Quinean can gain much comfort from Armstrong's book: it is a powerful argument for thesis 1. We have just demonstrated the failings of Armstrong's response to the One over Many argument. Armstrong himself carefully, and convincingly, demolishes every other known response to it. This chronicle of two thousand years of failure makes the task seem hopeless. The alternative view that there is no problem to solve becomes very attractive.

I take my major thesis to be established:

1.　To maintain Nominalism whilst ignoring the One over Many argument is not to be an Ostrich Nominalist; rather to adopt Realism because of that argument is to be a Mirage Realist.

Even if there *are* universals they cannot form part of a solution to the One over Many problem, because that problem is a mirage.

Argument for Thesis 2

[h]→　The arguments for theses 2 and 3 will be brief.

It follows from thesis 1 that in so far as Armstrong adopts Realism because of the One over Many argument, he is a Mirage Realist. At the beginning of his book he indicates that he sees that argument as the main one for universals (p. xiii). When he talks of "the problem of universals" it is the problem allegedly posed by that argument that he is referring to (e.g. p. 41). Almost the whole book is taken up with the consideration of responses to that argument. Armstrong is largely a Mirage Realist.

In one chapter, drawing on the ideas of Arthur Pap and Frank Jackson, Armstrong offers quite independent reasons for Realism (pp. 58–63).[5] We all assent to; express, believe, statements like the following:

(6)　Red resembles orange more than it resembles blue:
(7)　Red is a colour;
(8)　He has the same virtues as his father;
(9)　The dresses were of the same colour.

Unlike (3) these seem to require the existence of properties for them to be true. Whether or not they are sufficient for Realism depends on whether or not we can find acceptable paraphrases without that commitment. There is nothing illusory about this problem for a Nominalist. Armstrong is not entirely a Mirage Realist. So,

2.　Armstrong is largely though not entirely a Mirage Realist.

Argument for Thesis 3

For Quine to be an Ostrich Nominalist would be for him to ignore the ontological problem posed by his acceptance of statements like (6) to (9).

---

[5]　Given the importance Armstrong attaches to the One over Many argument for Realism, this chapter's title, "Arguments for Realism," is misleading.

A priori it is unlikely that this would be so. Quine, more than any other philosopher, has pointed out what constitutes an ontological commitment and has preached against ignoring such. Philosophers, like others, can fail to practise what they preach, but I suggest that it is unlikely that Quine would fail here, about as unlikely as that he would confuse use and mention.

A quick glance through *Word and Object*[6] shows that he does not fail. In a section on abstract terms he considers, e.g., the sentence,

(10)   Humility is a virtue,

a sentence that raises much the same problem as Armstrong's (8), and sees it as committing him to the existence of "an abstract object" (p. 119), in fact to "an attribute," what Armstrong would call "a property." He goes on to "deplore that facile line of thought" that allows us to ignore this (pp. 119–20). He considers ways to paraphrase away this apparent commitment to attributes and admits the difficulties (pp. 121–3). The issues are postponed until Chapter VII. He does not there discuss sentences like (6) to (10) directly, so far as I can see, but his strategy for them is clear enough: all talk of attributes is to be dispensed with in favour of talk of eternal open sentences or talk of classes (p. 209). Whatever the merits of this approach it is not the behaviour of an Ostrich. So,

3.   Quine is not an Ostrich Nominalist.

Commentary on Devitt

Michael Devitt is admirably clear about the objectives of his brief article. Primarily, he aims to defend the second kind of nominalism set out in the Introduction to this chapter: the kind of nominalism that denies (A) (see the Introduction above). According to Devitt, there is no genuine problem of the one over the many, and so the realist cannot motivate her position by portraying it as this problem's best solution. As Devitt explains, Armstrong has called this position 'ostrich nominalism', an epithet chosen to make Armstrong's point that philosophers, such as Quine, who defend it ignore a genuine philosophical question. Devitt denies that he and Quine are behaving like ostriches. It is Armstrong who is mistaken in thinking that the problem of the one over the many is genuine.

So why does Devitt think that the problem of the one over the many is not genuine? The answer to this question is to be found in the five paragraphs from $\boxed{a}\vdash$. As we saw in the Introduction, Armstrong believes that the fact that two numerically distinct particulars are of the same type is a phenomenon that demands explanation. Devitt starts by asking what precise phenomena constitute the *explananda* – the

[6]   W. V. Quine, *Word and Object*; Cambridge, MA: MIT, 1960.

phenomena to be explained – and his answer is that it is our readiness to assert sentences of the form:

(1)   *a* and *b* have the same property, *F*-ness,

sentences whose truth seems to require the existence of universals (in this case, *F-ness*). Devitt's response is simple enough: the apparent ontological commitment to *F*-ness in (1) can be paraphrased away. For (1) simply amounts to

(2)   *a* and *b* are both *F*.

According to Devitt, we should stick with (2) and, 'when the ontological chips are down', resist any temptation to come out with (1). An apparently deep problem disappears once the correct direction of paraphrase has been established. The fact that *a* and *b* are both *F* is not the kind of fact that requires us to posit a universal *F*-ness: *a* and *b* are both *F*, and no more need be said.

> 1. Has Devitt given us a decisive reason for taking (2) to reveal (1)'s ontological commitments (rather than the other way around)? Does Devitt's claim that '[i]n ontology, the less, the better' ($\boxed{f} \rightarrow$) provide such a reason? Have a think about this latter claim. Why, if at all, should we accept it?

Devitt acknowledges that the realist may not be satisfied with stopping here. What, the realist may ask, *explains* the fact that *a* and *b* are both *F*? But for Devitt, someone asking this question could only have failed to understand the meaning of 'and'. For *a* and *b* are both *F* because

(3)   *a* is *F*;

and

(4)   *b* is *F*.

Once more, there is no deep problem to be solved here.

But is there not? The realist may insist that all Devitt has shown is that the problem of the one over the many eventually turns into the problem of what it is for *a* to be *F*. Is not *this* question – 'In virtue of what is *a* F?' – substantial? No, says Devitt. The question 'In virtue of what is *a* F?' admits of no substantial answer: *a* just *is* *F*. In the four paragraphs from $\boxed{c} \rightarrow$ Devitt goes on to defend this latter claim by distinguishing it from substantive questions with which it might be confused. There *are* significant questions concerning *a*'s being *F*; Devitt's point is that they are scientific questions or semantic questions, not ontological ones.

> 2. (a) Explain in your own words questions i to iv. (b) Is Devitt right to distinguish these four questions from the question of the one over the many?

3. At $\boxed{d}\!\!\mapsto$, Devitt considers a case in which *a* is *F* and in which '*F*' is a 'fundamental predicate': one which cannot be further reduced by science. His claim is that 'we have nothing to say about what makes *a F*, it just is *F*; that is, a basic and inexplicable fact about the universe.' But a realist might press the following question at this point: is it coherent to accept that *a* genuinely has characteristics (in other words, that it is not just a featureless blob) but to deny that these characteristics are part of reality (that is, entities)? How do you think Devitt might respond to this question?

The final stage of Devitt's main argument sees him consider a potential response by Armstrong. At $\boxed{e}\!\!\mapsto$ Devitt admits that a realist may well be unhappy with his claim that *a*'s being *F* is an inexplicable fact about the universe. Indeed, she might claim that there must be something about *a* that explains *why* it is *F*, and that this explanation can only be that it genuinely exemplifies the universal *F*-ness. To put it another way, the realist may insist that (3) will have to be explained by

(5)   *a* has *F*-ness.

Now, as we have seen, Devitt denies the reality of the problem to which (5) is posited as a solution. But he accepts that *if* (5) were genuinely to explain (3), his scepticism about the problem would be undermined. For this reason, he sets out to demolish the claim that (5) is genuinely explanatory.

4. Why does Devitt think that (5) cannot explain (3)? In answering this question, you will need to do (at least) two things: explain in your own words the distinction between 'relational Immanent Realism' and 'non-relational Immanent Realism', which Devitt sets out at $\boxed{g}\!\!\mapsto$; and re-read the brief section called 'A problem for realism' in the introduction to this chapter.

Devitt thus holds that the nominalist has no problem with the fact that *a* is *F*. But neither does he think that the nominalist has a problem with the *sentence* '*a* is *F*'. A realist might claim that in asserting (3) – the sentence – we thereby commit ourselves to the existence of universals. As we noted in the Introduction, realists tend to think that predicates 'introduce' or 'express' universals in a way not unlike the way in which names refer to objects. Devitt's reply at, $\boxed{b}\!\!\mapsto$, is simple. Why is (3) true? Because 'is *F*' is true of whatever '*a*' refers to: *a*. Such an explanation commits us to the existence of *a* but not to *F*-ness. Once more, we are in no need of the kind of explanation that might require us to posit universals.

5. Devitt seems to think that this account of predication blunts the charge of not treating predication with due ontological seriousness. But what if a realist were to counter by claiming that Devitt has failed to explain *why* 'is *F*' applies to *a*? The predicate, a realist might say, is true of the object for a *reason*; and this reason is that the object exemplifies the universal *F*-ness. What would Devitt say in reply?

From [h]→, Devitt is careful to point out that he is only arguing that *one* argument for realism – the argument from the one over the many – is unsound.

> 6. (i) Explain in your own words the threat to nominalism Devitt addresses from [h]→. (ii) Take a look at [e]→ in Armstrong's text (below) and, again in your own words, explain why the nominalist should not paraphrase 'Humility is a virtue' as 'Humble persons are virtuous'. (iii) Suppose the nominalist can come up with a paraphrase for any true sentence involving apparent ontological commitment to universals. Will she thereby have demonstrated that our language does not commit us to the existence of universals?

D. M. Armstrong, 'Against "Ostrich" Nominalism: A Reply to Michael Devitt'

I am dissatisfied with my treatment, in volume I of *Universals and Scientific Realism* (Armstrong, 1978), of what I there called "Ostrich" Nominalism. Michael Devitt's vigorous defence of Quine, whom I accused of being such a Nominalist, gives me a second opportunity. (I should like to thank Devitt for comments on earlier drafts, and for the pleasant spirit in which this controversy has been conducted.)

I.   Quine and the "One over Many"

[a]→   I think that the main argument for the existence of universals is Plato's "One over Many." I do not think that it proves straight off that there are universals. But I think that it shows that there is a strong preliminary case for accepting universals. There are various sorts of Nominalists (I spoke of Predicate, Concept, Class, Mereological and Resemblance Nominalists) who seem to perceive the strength of the "One over Many" but who maintain their Nominalism nevertheless. There are, however, Nominalists who deny that the argument has any force. These I christened, tendentiously enough, Ostrich Nominalists. Quine is certainly one who denies the force of the "One over Many."

In chapter 1 of *From a Logical Point of View* (1953 [Quine 1948 in the Bibliography]), that is, the well-known paper "On What There Is," Quine makes a philosopher whom he calls 'McX'[1] advance the "One over Many":

---

[1]   Devitt, following E. Prior, suggests that for the variable 'X' be substituted the name 'Armstrong.' However, Devitt and Prior overlook the fact that 'McArmstrong' is ill-formed. 'Armstrong' is a *Lowland* Scottish name.

> Speaking of attributes, he [McX] says: "There are red houses, red roses and
> sunsets; this much is prephilosophical common sense in which we must all
> agree. These houses, roses and sunsets, then, have something in common;
> and this which they have in common is all I mean by the attribute of redness."
> For McX, thus, there being attributes is even more obvious and trivial than
> the obvious and trivial fact of there being red houses, roses, and sunsets. (pp.
> 9–10.)

In my view, Quine has here made McX considerably overplay his hand.
I would wish to start in a much more cautious way by saying, as I say on
p. xiii, that:

> . . . many different particulars can all have what appears to be the same nature.

and draw the conclusion that, as a result, there is a *prima facie* case for
postulating universals.

Quine, I think, admits or half-admits the truth of this premiss, though in a
back-handed way, when he says, in the course of his assault on McX:

> One may admit that there are red houses, roses and sunsets, but deny, except
> as a popular and misleading manner of speaking, that they have anything in
> common. (p. 10.)

Quine here allows that there is a popular manner of speaking in which
different red things are said to have something in common. But he does not
seem to realize just how ubiquitous such manners of speaking are. We (that
is, everybody) are continually talking about the *sameness* of things. And most
of the time when we talk about the sameness of things we are talking about
the sameness of *different* things. We are continually talking about different
things having the same property or quality, being of the same sort or kind,
having the same nature, and so on.

Philosophers have formalized the matter a little. They draw the enor-
mously useful Peircean distinction between sameness of token and sameness
of type. But they are only formalizing, making explicit, a distinction which
ordinary language (and so, ordinary thought) perfectly recognizes.

G. E. Moore thought, correctly I believe, that there are many facts which
even philosophers should not deny, whatever philosophical account or
analysis they gave of these facts. He gave as an example the existence of
his hands. We can argue about the philosophical account which ought to be
given of material objects, such as Moore's hands. But we should not deny
that there are such things. (He was not arguing that their existence was a
logically necessary or logically indubitable truth.) I suggest that the fact of
sameness of type is a Moorean fact.

b|→ Any comprehensive philosophy must try to give some account of Moor-
ean facts. They constitute the compulsory questions in the philosophical

examination paper. If sameness of type is a Moorean fact, then, because Quine sees no need to give an account of it, he is refusing to answer a compulsory question.

Here is one answer to the question. When we speak of sameness of token, the sameness of the Morning and the Evening star to coin an example, we are speaking of *identity*. But when we speak of sameness of type, of two dresses being the same shade of colour for instance, sameness is merely a matter of *resemblance* (on one view between the dresses, on another between two property-instances). Resemblance is not to be analyzed in terms of identity. Hence *sameness* with respect to token is not the same as (is not identical with) sameness with respect to type. The word "same" is fundamentally ambiguous.

This is not a view which I accept. But it is an attempt to grapple with the problem.

Again, it may be held that sameness of token and sameness of type is sameness in exactly the same sense, *viz.* identity. This Realist view seems to be nearer the truth of the matter. I think it is a bit crude as it stands, because it appears to require recognition of a universal wherever we recognize sameness of type, a universal corresponding to each general word. However, the rightness or wrongness of the answer is not what is in debate here. The point is that the philosophical problem of the nature of sameness of type is faced, not evaded.

By comparison, what does Quine offer us? He simply says:

> That the houses and roses and sunsets are all of them red may be taken as ultimate and irreducible, . . . (p. 10.)

What does he mean by this? This remark might be made by a Realist, or at any rate by a Realist who believes that *redness* is a property. But, of course, Quine is engaged in rejecting Realism, personified by the unfortunate McX.

It is natural to interpret him instead as saying that, although these tokens are all of the same type, yet we have no need to consider what sameness of type is. (And, *a fortiori*, sameness of type is not a matter of identity of property.)

If this is the way to interpret Quine, then is he not an ostrich about types? Like an Oxford philosopher of yore, he keeps on saying that he does not deny that many different objects are all of them red, but what this ostensible sameness is he refuses to explain (except to say it is ultimate and irreducible). Instead, he thrusts his head back into his desert landscape.

But perhaps there is a still deeper level of scepticism in Quine. Perhaps he would object to this foisting upon him of talk about types. Suppose *a* is red and *b* is red, then, Quine might say, we can by a convenient abbreviation say that *a* and *b* are *both* red. If *a* is red and *b* is red and *c* is red, we can by a convenient abbreviation say that *a*, *b* and *c* are *all of them* red. But nothing here justifies talking of sameness of type, unless this too is mere abbreviation.

c→ Such scepticism cannot be maintained. It is true that '*a* and *b* are both red' is an abbreviation of '*a* is red and *b* is red.' But the abbreviation does not hold just for these particular sentences (much less for the above sentence-tokens), but is a rule-governed, projectible, transformation which we are capable of applying to an indefinite multiplicity of sentences. And what is the rule? It goes something like this. Suppose that we are given sentences of the form '*a* is – and *b* is – '. If but only if the two blanks are filled by the *same* predicate, it is permitted to rewrite the sentence as '*a* and *b* are both –,' with that same predicate in the new blank. But 'same predicate' here is a type-notion. It is not meant that the very same predicate-token be plugged successively into the three gaps!

It appears, then, that just to understand phrases like 'are both red' requires that we understand at least what a *predicate*-type is. And if this notion is understood, and at least at a Moorean level accepted, then there can be no bar to understanding, and at least at the Moorean level accepting, type-notions generally. Some account must then be given, reductive or otherwise, of what sameness of type is.

But perhaps Quine failed to appreciate this point when he wrote "On What There Is." The insight on which the argument of the penultimate paragraph is based was not available to contemporary philosophers until the work of Donald Davidson. For this, see Davidson, 1965, who criticizes Quine for a similar failure to appreciate the projectible semantic structure of sentences attributing beliefs in *Word and Object* (1960).

It may be, then, that Quine did not perceive at least the full urgency of the need to give an account of types. But however it was with Quine, (or is with Devitt), the distinction between tokens and types cannot be ignored. Hence a philosophical account of a general sort is required of what it is for different tokens to be of the same type. To refuse to give such an account is to be a metaphysical ostrich.

II.   Quine's Criterion of Ontological Commitment

d→ But there is, of course, something else which insulates Quine from the full impact of the problem of types, from the problem of the One over Many. The insulating material is his extraordinary doctrine that predicates involve no ontological commitment. In a statement of the form '*Fa*,' he holds, the predicate '*F*' need not be taken with ontological seriousness. Quine gives the predicate what has been said to be the privilege of the harlot: power without responsibility. The predicate is informative, it makes a vital contribution to telling us what is the case, the world is different if it is different, yet ontologically it is supposed not to commit us. Nice work: if you can get it.

e →   It is at this very point, however, that Quine may protest, as Devitt does on his behalf, that his Nominalism is at least not an *Ostrich* Nominalism. For although Quine is perfectly cavalier about predicates, he is deadly serious about referring expressions. Suppose that a statement meets three conditions. (1) It makes ostensible *reference* to universals. (2) We account it true. (3) It is impossible to find a satisfactory paraphrase of the statement in which this reference to universals is eliminated. Under these conditions, Quine allows, indeed insists, we ought to admit universals into our ontology. Perhaps the three conditions cannot be met, but if they can be met, why then Quine will turn Realist.

I grant freely that to put forward such a set of conditions is not the behaviour of a philosophical ostrich. On the other hand, I do think that Quine is an ostrich *with respect to the One over Many argument*. Furthermore I think that Quine (and his followers) have been distinctly perfunctory in considering the many statements which answer to conditions (1) and (2) and which *appear* to answer to condition (3).

In chapter 6 of my book[2] I consider the statements:

(1)   Red resembles orange more than it resembles blue
(2)   Red is a colour
(3)   He has the same virtues as his father.

Basing myself upon work by Pap (1959) and Jackson (1977), I argue that these statements cannot be analyzed in a way which removes their ostensible reference to universals, or at least to property-instances. (I try to show the incoherence of the doctrine of property-instances, that is, particularized properties, in chapter 8.)

It would in fact have been desirable also to have made reference to Hilary Putnam's "On Properties" (1970) which considers the statement:

(4)   There are undiscovered fundamental physical properties.

To this might be added an example suggested by David Stove:

(5)   Acquired characteristics are never inherited.

and many others.

Now we might expect reasonably extended discussions of examples of this sort in Quine. Our expectation, however, is disappointed. In "On What There Is" he does mention:

---

[2]   Devitt correctly noted that it was misleading to call the chapter "Arguments for Realism" in spite of the fact that what I take to be the main argument for Realism, the One over Many, is deployed in earlier chapters and is not deployed in chapter 6. As Frank Jackson has pointed out, the title should really be "Arguments for Realism that work even if Quine is right about ontological commitment."

(6)   Some zoological species are cross-fertile

and says that, unless we can paraphrase it in some way, it commits us to "abstract"[3] objects, viz. species. But he does not say what account he would give of (6).

As Devitt points out, in *Word and Object* (1960, §25), Quine does give brief consideration to:

(7)   Humility is a virtue

along with:

(8)   Redness is a sign of ripeness.

For (8) he suggests

(8′)   Red fruits are ripe

which perhaps may be allowed to pass. But (7), which resembles (2), cannot be rendered, as he seems to suggest, by:

(7′)   Humble persons are virtuous.

First, the truth of (7) is compatible with there being humble persons who are not virtuous. Indeed, it is compatible with *no* humble persons being virtuous. For it may be that every humble person is so full of glaring faults that, although they have the virtue of humility, they are not virtuous persons.

Second, and more seriously, the truth of (7′) is compatible with humility not being a virtue. Consider an example suggested by Graham Nerlich. Suppose it was true, and well known to be true, that tall people are always virtuous.

---

[3]   Quine appears to mean by an "abstract" entity one that is outside space and time. This is a misuse of the term, on a par with using "disinterested" to mean the same as "uninterested." An abstract object is one which can be *considered* apart from something else, but cannot *exist* apart from that thing. Being outside space and time has no special connection with abstraction. He holds that both classes, if they exist, and universals, if they exist, are abstract in his sense. He also says that classes *are* universals (1953, pp. 115–23), probably because he takes "universal" to be a convenient synonym for "abstract." In fact classes are particulars, even if, as Quine claims, non-spatio-temporal particulars. This is because, unlike universals, they are not ones which may run through many. There can be many instances of redness, but not many instances of the class of men or the class of colours. A "Nominalist," for Quine, is simply one who does not recognize abstract objects in his sense, a "Platonist" is one who does recognize them. So when he reluctantly admitted classes Quine became a "Platonist." The misuse of all these terms has contributed to muddling a whole philosophical generation about the Problem of Universals.

(7″)   Tall persons are virtuous

is exactly parallel to:

(7′)   Humble persons are virtuous.

But nobody would wish to suggest that it would then be a truth that:

(7‴)   Tallness is a virtue.[4]

So not only does (7) fail to entail (7′) which was the first objection, but (7′) fails to entail (7).

As Devitt says, Quine then postpones general discussion of the problem of "abstract objects" until chapter 7. In that chapter, Quine, without discussing examples, suggests that all apparent reference to attributes and relations should be dispensed with in favour of talk of "eternal" open sentences (or general terms) and/or talk of "classes".

Here, I agree, he has moved beyond his original position to some form of Predicate and/or Class Nominalism. But he does not discuss the rather well-known difficulties for these varieties of Nominalism. (Devitt, it may be noticed, appears to think that the difficulties are insoluble.)

It seems, then, that Quine is in trouble, even under his own rules. But the more important question, I think, is why we should grant him his rules. Devitt can only say that:

> . . . we need a criterion of ontological commitment. Perhaps Quine's criterion has difficulties, but something along that line is mandatory.

After this less than full-blooded defence, one can only ask 'Why not a criterion which allows predicates a role in ontological commitment?'

⟦f⟧→ At this point, appeal may be made to semantics. Devitt makes such an appeal. He says that one can give the truth-conditions of 'Fa' by saying that it is true if and only if 'a' denotes some particular which 'F' applies to. He says that this shows that 'Fa' can be true even though the 'F' carries no ontological commitment. But two points may be made in reply. First, there may be alternative, and perhaps more satisfying, ways of giving the semantics for 'Fa.' Devitt offers no argument against this possibility. Second, and more important, the semantics of 'applies' has been left totally obscure. The Realist may well argue, correctly I believe, that a convincing account of

---

[4]   Equally, supposing it to be true that:

(7⁗) Humble persons are amphibious

it does not follow that:

(7″″″) Humility is an amphibian.

the semantics of 'applies' cannot be given without appeal to the properties and/or relations of the object *a*. (I owe this point to John Bishop.)

III.   Problems for Realism

Besides supporting Quine in his rejection of the One over Many argument, Devitt also argues directly against Realism. He confines himself to the problem, familiar to all Realists, of how particulars stand to universals. I agree with Devitt that this is the central difficulty in the Realist position. So I will finish what I have to say by making some remarks about it. But Devitt's own remarks are brief, and I think it best to expound the problem anew.

The problem is a sub-problem of the problem about the nature of particulars. For one who denies the existence of properties *in re* (whether these properties be universals or particulars), particulars are a sort of structureless blob. They can have parts. Predicates can be hung on them, concepts applied to them, they can be herded into classes, they may even have resemblances to other particulars if a Resemblance Nominalism is adopted, but they lack real internal structure. For those who accept properties *in re*, however, particulars are sort of layer-cake. The *one* particular somehow unites within itself *many* different properties (another One over Many). The question is: how is this possible?

The problem divides at this point because a defender of properties *in re* may develop the theory of particulars in different ways. According to one view, a particular is nothing but its properties. It is not, of course, a mere class of properties, but is a certain *bundling* of properties. A certain relation holds between all and only the properties of a particular, and the holding of this relation is what makes it a particular. This "Bundle" view in turn divides into two, because the properties in the bundle may be conceived either as universals or as property-instances. Russell held the Bundle view in its first form, Donald Williams in its second.

However, the more orthodox view among those who accept properties *in re* is that, besides their properties, particulars involve a factor of particularity, an individuating component. This view in turn divides into two in the same way as before. There are those who make the properties into particulars. Locke is a probable example. However, the more orthodox version of this more orthodox view takes the properties to be universals.

Since our special concern here is with the problems of *Realism*, we may ignore the views which give an account of particulars by appealing to property-instances. The view that a particular is nothing but a bundle of universals is exposed to many grave difficulties (some of which I try to spell out in chapter 9 of my book), but I do not think that the difficulty raised by Devitt is among them. The problem proposed by Devitt only arises, I think, if one holds (as I do hold) that a particular involves a factor of particularity (*haeccitas*, thisness) together with properties which are universals. The question is then this: how are the two components of a particular to be put together?

There are, broadly, two sorts of answer to the question which Realists have given. According to the first, the factor of particularity stands in a certain *relation* to the properties. It really is correct to speak of the *related components* of a full-blooded particular. For this line of thought it is quite natural to reify the factor of particularity and to think of it as a "bare particular." This line of thought, it seems further, ought to be reasonably sympathetic to the idea that bare particulars might exist without any properties, and properties might exist which are not properties of any particular. For why should not the relation fail to hold? A synthetic necessity could be postulated to ensure that the factors only exist in relation, but it is hard to see the necessity for this necessity.

But whether or not bare particulars can exist apart from properties, or properties from bare particulars, difficulties arise for this conception of a particular. Let the relation be I, a bare particular be B, and wholly distinct properties of the particular be P', P''.... An ordinary particular containing B will then be constituted by a conjunction of states of affairs $I(B,P)$, $I(B,P')$...etc. The difficulty then is that I is a *relation* and so, on this view, is a universal. As a result, a *new* relation of instantiation will be required to hold between I, on the one hand, and the elements which it relates, on the other. The new relation will then be involved in the same difficulty. The difficulty has been appreciated at least since the work of F. H. Bradley.

Various shifts may be attempted in the face of this regress, for instance, it may be suggested that the regress exists, but is not vicious. Without arguing the matter here, I will just say that I do not think that this way out, or any other, succeeds.

$\boxed{g}\mapsto$ In common with many other Realists, I therefore favour the view that, while we can *distinguish* the particularity of a particular from its properties, nevertheless the two "factors" are too intimately together to speak of a *relation* between them. The thisness and the nature are incapable of existing apart from each other. Bare particulars and uninstantiated universals are vicious abstractions (in the non-Quinean sense of "abstraction," of course!) from what may be called states of affairs: this-of-a-certain-nature. The thisness and the nature are therefore not related.

$\boxed{h}\mapsto$ Frege says of his concepts that they are "unsaturated." Fregean concepts are not something mental. They are close to being the Realist's properties and relations. His idea, I think, was that the concepts have, as it were, a gap in their being, a gap which must be filled by particulars. If we think of the particularity of particulars as *also* "unsaturated," then I think Frege's metaphor is helpful.

All this is profoundly puzzling. As a result, Devitt is able to claim, not implausibly, that all I have done is to substitute inexplicable mystery for the relational view. Realism requires a relation between particularity and universality. Yet to postulate such a relation appears to lead to insoluble problems. So, he says, I simply "unite" the two factors in an incomprehensible manner.

I accept some of the force of this. But I have three things to say which I think ought to make Devitt look upon this "Non-Relational Immanent Realism" with a little more sympathy.

First, as was made clear already, the problem arises not simply where a particular has a property, but where two or more particulars are related. Suppose *a* has *R* to *b*. If *R* is a universal, and *a* and *b* are particulars, and if we think that a relation is needed to link a universal to its particulars, then we shall require a further relation or relations to link *R* to *a* and *b*. This seems intolerable. It seems much better, therefore, to say that, while we can distinguish the relation from the particulars, yet the three "entities" are together in a way which does not require any further relation to *get* them together. Now, if we think this way about the polyadic case, it seems to me that when we go back to the monadic case we ought in consistency take the same line, and deny that the particularity of a particular is related to the properties of the particular. Contrariwise, if we admit a relation in the monadic case, should we not admit an extra relation in the polyadic case?

I hope that this generalization of the problem will at least show Devitt how strong an intellectual pressure there is for a Realist to adopt a non-relational view. It may be crooked, but it looks to be the best (Realist) game in town.

Second, I appeal to what Devitt says himself. He says:

> Talk of "particulars" and "universals" clutters the landscape without adding to our understanding. We should rest with the basic fact that *a* is *F*.

Now, of course, I accept the *second* sentence just as much as Devitt. (There is, as it were, *f. a.* in my philosophy as much as there is in Devitt's.) Let us consider the sentence. Devitt will surely admit that '*a*' is a token-word, picking out just this thing *a*, while '*F*' is a type-word, applicable, potentially at least, to many things. Now why should we need two words of just this semantic sort to record the basic fact? Does not some explanation seem called for? Is it so very extreme an hypothesis that, while '*a*' names a particular, '*F*' captures something repeatable, something universal, about the situation?

I might add that I think that the dispute between Devitt and myself here is an instance of a very deep dispute indeed. There are those who, apparently like Devitt, think of reality as made up of *things*. There are others who, like me, think of it as made up of *facts* or *states of affairs*. We cannot expect any easy resolution of such an argument. (All the more reason to try to argue it of course.)

Third, I offer a second *ad hominem* criticism of Devitt's position. Devitt rejects the "One over Many." But he agrees that the problems posed for Quine by the arguments of Arthur Pap and Frank Jackson, retailed by me in the chapter "Arguments for Realism," are hard to solve. He makes no attempt to improve upon the unsatisfactory paraphrases suggested by Quine of statements ostensibly referring to universals. So it seems that he thinks that it may be necessary to postulate universals. If he does have to postulate them, how will *he* solve the problem of how universals stand to their particulars? I think he will end up saying something similar to what I (and indefinitely many other Realists) have had to say.

Commentary on Armstrong

To recap, many realists argue for their position by claiming that positing universals is the best way of explaining the phenomenon of the one over the many: sameness of type. If *a* and *b* are both *F*, such realists argue, then they must both be *F in virtue of something*, and this something can only be that both *a* and *b* instantiate the same universal. To this argument, Devitt makes the following objection: the problem of the one over the many is unreal. For *a* and *b* to be of the same type (e.g. *F*) is just for it to be the case that

(2)   *a* and *b* are both *F*;

and this obtains in virtue of the obtaining of the following:

(3)   *a* is *F*
(4)   *b* is *F*.

Does the fact that *a* is *F* require further explanation of a kind that might commit us to the existence of a universal, *F*-ness? No, says Devitt. If 'is *F*' is a fundamental predicate, there is nothing to say about what makes *a* *F*; it just *is*.

Armstrong's reply to Devitt does not see him merely attempt to rehabilitate the problem of the one over the many. He also presents additional, distinct arguments for realism, as well as defending his own version of 'non-relational Immanent Realism' against the charge of obscurity. Roughly speaking, the structure of the article is as follows. In section 1 Armstrong defends the thesis that the problem of the one over the many is a genuine problem. In section 2 he argues both that predicates express universals, and that there are sentences that are ontologically committed to universals, which do not admit of nominalist paraphrase. Finally, in section 3 Armstrong tries to explain and defend what he means by the claim that the tie of instantiation between a particular and a universal is non-relational.

Section 1

Armstrong starts section 1 (at $\boxed{a} \!\!\mapsto$) by acknowledging that he takes the problem of the one over the many to be the main argument for universals. Despite Devitt's objections, he regards the problem as genuine and best solved by adopting realism.

> 1. Armstrong denies that the argument from the one over the many 'proves straight off that there are universals'. What, precisely, does Armstrong mean by this? Do you think Armstrong believes there to be *any* arguments that demonstrate realism to be true 'straight off'?

The main argument in section 1 (from $\boxed{b} \!\!\mapsto$ until the end of the section) against the position taken by Quine and Devitt seems to take the form of a dilemma. The first horn is this: if the Quinean is happy to talk of *a* and *b* being *of the same type* (e.g. red), then he must explain what this sameness of type consists in, which just goes to show that the phenomenon of sameness of type stands in need of philosophical explanation. As Armstrong himself puts it, the Quinean 'keeps on saying that he does not deny that many different objects are all of them red, but what this ostensible sameness is he refuses to explain (except to say that it is ultimate and irreducible)'.

The second horn, at $\boxed{c} \!\!\mapsto$, is this: if the Quinean abjures all talk of 'sameness of type', his position is unsustainable. For even to understand the claim that *a* and *b* are both red, one must understand that 'is red' is a predicate-*type*. And what this means is that the Quinean cannot eliminate 'type'-talk and, hence, by the dilemma's first horn, that he owes us an account of what sameness of type consists in. Either way, sameness of type – the one over the many – is a phenomenon that requires explanation.

> 2. Explain in your own words why Armstrong believes that even a nominalist must take the predicate 'is red' to be a type.
> 3. On Armstrong's dilemma: (i) Would Devitt be happy to occupy the dilemma's second horn? *Does he* seek to eliminate all 'type'-talk? Take another look at Devitt's $\boxed{a} \!\!\mapsto$. (ii) On the first horn, has Armstrong demonstrated that Devitt's refusal to explain sameness of type is the behaviour of an ostrich rather than that of someone who sees through a mirage? (Take another look at Devitt's $\boxed{c} \!\!\mapsto$, where Devitt distinguishes the substantial questions concerning *a*'s being *F* from the (to him, bogus) problem of the one over the many.)

Section 2

This section sees Armstrong change tack somewhat, to focus on the issue of the ontological commitments of our discourse. Indeed, at $\boxed{d} \!\!\mapsto$ and $\boxed{f} \!\!\mapsto$ Armstrong claims that we should favour an account of predication according to which predicates express properties. In particular, at $\boxed{f} \!\!\mapsto$, Armstrong objects to Devitt's suggestion that an adequate semantics for '*a* is *F*' can be provided without taking 'is *F*' to express a property.

4. Remind yourself of Devitt's suggestion of how '*a* is *F*' can be true without our being committed to the existence of universals (Devitt, $\boxed{b}\mapsto$). What, exactly, are Armstrong's objections to it (at $\boxed{f}\mapsto$ in his paper)? Are Armstrong's objections compelling? Why or why not?

Besides including a critique of Devitt's account of predication, section 2 also sees Armstrong return to the question – briefly mentioned by Devitt at $\boxed{h}\mapsto$ and discussed in the Introduction to this chapter – of how sentences containing ostensible reference to universals should be analysed. The problem, remember, is that sentences such as

(F)   Red is a colour,
(G)   Humility is a virtue,

and

(H)   He has the same virtues as his father,

are true and yet seem to contain reference to universals. Armstrong, in the discussion from $\boxed{e}\mapsto$, concludes that nominalistic paraphrases of these sentences cannot be found, and, hence, that realism is the best game in town: universals exist.

5. Even if it turned out that the likes of (F), (G) and (H) committed us to the existence of universals, would the main thrust of Devitt's paper have been undermined? (Take a look at the final paragraph of Armstrong's paper, but remember that Devitt's main objective is to demonstrate the bogus nature of the 'one over the many' problem.)

Section 3

The final section of Armstrong's paper sees him tackle the (infamous) objection to realism raised by Devitt at $\boxed{e}\mapsto$. This objection, to recap, is that the realist owes us an account of the nature of *instantiation*: of how a particular can *have* a universal. As Devitt explains, instantiation cannot be a relation on pain of setting off an infinite and vicious regress. But equally, argues Devitt (from $\boxed{g}\mapsto$), Armstrong's claim that the particular and the universal are not related, but *bonded together*, is hopelessly obscure. What is the nature of this *bonding* supposed to be?

It is this question that Armstrong seeks to answer at the end of his paper. In the passage from $\boxed{g}\mapsto$ to $\boxed{i}\mapsto$, Armstrong says that it is a mistake to think of instantiation as a relation: if *a* is *F*, *a* and *F* are 'too intimately together to speak of a relation between them'. So how *does a* come to have *F*? We think that Armstrong's response to this question is best viewed as an attempt to explain why the question is based on a mistake. A philosopher asking this question presumes particulars and universals to be the basic atoms of the universe, and *then* asks how a particular can instantiate a universal. Armstrong, by contrast, thinks that someone who takes this approach has dug too deep. For according to Armstrong, the universe's basic constituents are not particulars and universals, but *states of affairs*: *particulars-having-universals*. As he himself puts it, '[b]are particulars and universals are vicious abstractions' from states of affairs: 'the thisness and the nature are incapable of existing apart from each other'. So there *is no* problem concerning instantiation: '[t]he instantiation of universals by particulars is just the state of affairs itself' (Armstrong 1997: 119). There only *appears* to be a problem of characterizing a *relation* of instantiation, if we fail to see that states of affairs are ontologically basic.

> 6. (i) What, exactly, do you think it means to say that particulars and universals are abstractions from states of affairs? (ii) Explain in your own words why Armstrong believes that thinking of particulars and universals as abstractions from states of affairs enables us to avoid the conception of instantiation as a relation.

To help his cause in explaining the nature of instantiation, Armstrong appeals to Frege (1891), the celebrated logician and one of the founding fathers of analytical philosophy (along with Russell and G. E. Moore). Famously, Frege took properties (he called them 'concepts') to be 'unsaturated' or *gappy* entities: essentially incomplete items that may have their gap 'filled' by an object. On this view, for example, the property *is wise*, when filled by Socrates, yields something that, when expressed in language, is true ('Socrates is wise'). This, Armstrong suggests ($\boxed{\text{h}} \mapsto$), goes some way towards explaining what he means by claiming instantiation to be non-relational, given the proviso that we treat particulars, as well as universals, as gappy. Both particulars and universals require completion by an item from the corresponding ontological category. Since neither a particular nor a universal is a complete entity in itself, they are not sufficiently distinct to require a relation to bind them together.

> 7. Does the appeal to the metaphor of unsaturatedness provide additional support for Armstrong's position on the nature of instantiation?
> 8. Explain in your own words Armstrong's three reasons, from $\boxed{\text{i}} \mapsto$, why he thinks Devitt should look on 'non-relational Immanent realism' with more sympathy. Should Devitt be convinced by any of them?

Further Reading

A good introduction to the issues discussed here is to be found in Loux 1998, chs. 1 and 2. Armstrong engagingly discusses the varieties of nominalism in his aptly titled 1989, chs. 1–3. Armstrong's ontology of states of affairs is elucidated and defended in his 1997, chs. 1 and 8, and in his 2004, ch. 4. Mellor and Oliver 1997 is an excellent collection of papers on the nature of properties, which includes both the paper by Devitt and that by Armstrong.

Essay Questions

1. What is 'the problem of the one over the many' supposed to be? Is it a genuine problem?
2. Are there any convincing reasons for adopting realism concerning universals?
3. What are the most pressing objections facing the realist about universals? Can she adequately reply to them?
4. Does the 'vicious regress' problem provide us with a convincing reason for admitting states of affairs into our ontology?

5

Possible Worlds

Introduction

What are possible worlds for?

In this chapter, we consider another ontological question (that is, a question concerning what there is): do other possible worlds exist – worlds in which, perhaps, there are talking donkeys, or Time Lords, or where the human race was completely destroyed in the 1960s?

Why should the question of whether there are other possible worlds (whatever they are) be of interest to philosophers? Before we answer that question, recall the starting-point for another ontological question: the question, Do universals exist? As we saw in chapter 4, Armstrong holds that we *need* to believe in universals in order to be able to explain how it can be that, for example, two sofas are both red, or have the same weight. Manifestly, plenty of things *are* the same colour or the same weight – or at least, this is something we seem to take for granted in our ordinary thought and talk about the world; but what kinds of entity do there need to be, in order for this to be so? Armstrong argues that we should take our ordinary talk at face value: when we say that two sofas are the same colour, we mean that there is something – a colour – that they literally share.

Now consider a range of other things we seem to take for granted in our ordinary talk and thought about the world. We say things like, 'I might have been a millionaire by now', 'Real Madrid would have scored just now if Beckham had passed the ball to Ronaldo', 'emus can't fly', and 'I just couldn't help myself – I *had* to have the last biscuit'. What all these claims have in common is that they are *modal* claims: claims about what must, or might be, or might have been the case, or claims about what *would* have been the case if things had gone differently. We take it for granted in our ordinary talk and thought that modal claims are at least sometimes true. (It's an interesting question what counts as a good reason to *believe* a given modal claim – how, for example, would you go about trying to persuade someone that you might have been a millionaire by now? – but it is not a question we'll have much to say about. The fact that you could coherently have an argument with someone about whether or not you might have been a millionaire by now seems to show that there are modal facts, even if in some cases we do not know how to decide *which* modal facts there are.)

A natural philosophical question now emerges: in virtue of *what* are modal claims true? Modality is a rather mysterious phenomenon. For example, we might suppose that the claim that emus can't fly is true in virtue of a property of emus: they have the property of *being unable to fly*. Or perhaps it's true in virtue of their *lacking* a different property: the property of *being able to fly*. But either way, it seems that we are countenancing a very peculiar property. If someone asked you to list the properties of a particular emu, you might list its size, weight, colour, how many feathers, legs and eyes it has, and so on. It probably wouldn't occur to you to list amongst its properties what it is and is not able to do. It seems just as odd to think that, say, the ability or inability to fly is a genuine universal as it does to think that, say, being shorter than 14 feet or not-being-blue are genuine universals.

And there is worse to come. It seems that 'the winner of the election won the election' is a necessary truth: trivially, nobody could be the winner of the election without having won the election. Suppose we do think of things as having 'modal properties'. Then it seems that we should understand the necessary truth of that sentence as being a matter of a particular person (the winner of the election) having the property of *having necessarily won the election*. On the other hand, 'Blair won the election' is *not* a necessary truth: he *might* have lost, even though he in fact won. So it seems we should understand the contingent (that is, non-necessary) truth of *that* sentence as being a matter of a particular person (Blair) *lacking* the property of *having necessarily won the election*. But of course Blair *is* the winner of the election. And so we appear to have got ourselves into the unfortunate situation of holding that that person – Blair, the winner of the election – both has and lacks the very same property. And that, of course, is impossible.

What's gone wrong here? Well, W. V. Quine (1953b) famously concluded from this kind of problem that all modality is '*de dicto*' modality, and that there is no such thing as '*de re*' modality. What does this mean? Well, roughly, to hold that all modality is *de dicto* modality is to hold that modal properties can only attach to *sentences* (or propositions). It makes sense to say of a particular sentence – 'all mathematicians are clever', say, or 'the winner of the election won the election', or 'Blair won the election' – that it is necessarily true, or necessarily false, or possibly true, or possibly false. According to believers in *de re* modality, by contrast, modal properties can also attach to *things*: things can have properties such as being essentially or necessarily human, being only contingently the winner of the election, and so on. It was the assumption that modal properties can attach to Blair himself that led us into trouble in the above example; Quine's solution is to deny this assumption. There is no conflict between holding that 'the winner of the election won the election' is necessarily true while 'Blair won the election' is not. The conflict only arises if we also think that the person who won the election – Blair himself – has modal properties.

Few philosophers since Quine, however, have been willing to simply shun *de re* modality. And in any case, shunning *de re* modality does not constitute an answer to the question we started with, namely: in virtue of *what* are modal claims true? To say that necessity and possibility attach to sentences rather than anything else (e.g. objects) does not, in itself, tell us what it *is* to ascribe necessity or possibility to a sentence. So we are no closer to an answer to our original question: in virtue of what are modal claims true? Part of the problem here is that there seem to be lots of *different* senses of modal terms. For example, the meaning of 'couldn't' in the sentence 'Gavin couldn't help himself – he *had* to have the last biscuit' seems to be different to its meaning in the sentence '2 + 2 *couldn't* equal anything other than 4'. What we might call mathematical necessity – the kind of necessity involved in the claim that, necessarily, 2 + 2 = 4 – seems to be a different *kind* of necessity to that involved in the claim that, necessarily, Gavin had the last biscuit.

Talk of possible worlds began as a response to the demand to give precise meanings to 'necessarily' and 'possibly'. Roughly, the idea is that we understand claims involving necessity as claims about *every possible world*. To say that, necessarily, 2 + 2 = 4, is to say that 2 + 2 = 4 *in (or at) every possible world*. And to say that it is possible for Chelsea to win the Cup is to say that *there is a possible world* in which Chelsea win the Cup. Modal claims can thus be interpreted as claims *about possible worlds*. A modal claim implicitly 'quantifies over' possible worlds: it says something about whether *there is* a possible world in which a given proposition is true, whether a given proposition is true in *all* possible worlds, and so on.

Interpreting modal claims as claims about possible worlds also allows us to make sense of the idea that there are different 'kinds' of necessity and possibility, for we can think of a given modal claim as implicitly quantifying over either absolutely all possible worlds, or alternatively over just some subset of them. For example, consider the debate about 'could have done otherwise' discussed in chapter 2. Van Inwagen's claim that determinism is incompatible with the judge's being such that he couldn't have done otherwise than raise his hand turns into this claim: that *there is no possible world with the same laws of physics and exactly the same distant past* in which the judge fails to raise his hand. Part of Dennett's response to van Inwagen amounts to the claim that there are different senses of 'could have done otherwise', and in at least some sense of 'could have done otherwise' (a sense, moreover, that is relevant to whether or not the judge acted freely) the judge *could* have done otherwise. In possible-worlds-speak, the claim is that in order to capture the sense of 'could have done otherwise' that is relevant to free will, we must cast our net rather wider than just the set of possible worlds with the same laws of physics and *exactly* the same distant past. With the set of relevant possible worlds made larger in this way, we will find that it includes some possible worlds at which the judge *does* fail to raise his hand, thus making it true that he *could* have done so, in a different sense of 'could' to van Inwagen's.

Similarly, we might, for certain philosophical purposes, be interested in the set of *nomologically possible worlds* – that is, the set of possible worlds which have exactly the same laws of nature as our own – or the set of *epistemically possible worlds*, the set of worlds at which whatever is the case is consistent with what someone takes themselves to know about the actual world. For example, suppose that Eleanor knows, but Susan does not, that Julian is currently watching the television. Then possible worlds in which Julian is now *not* watching the television are epistemically possible worlds for Susan, but not for Eleanor. (Susan might reasonably say, but Eleanor would not, that for all she knows, Julian *might* be practising the saxophone at the moment.)

Of course, in our ordinary modal talk, we typically do not explicitly say which possible worlds we are to be understood to be quantifying over when we make a modal claim. But one might reasonably argue that this is something we can normally tell from the context within which the claim is made. For example, if Eleanor were to say, 'Julian *can't* be practising the saxophone – he's right here, in front of the television', we would not attribute to her the view that there is no possible world whatsoever in which Julian is practising the saxophone (since clearly there are such possible worlds). We would instead take her to be talking about *epistemically* possible worlds. Similarly, if a biologist were to say that a cat cannot breed with an elephant, we might reasonably take them to be making a claim about what is *nomologically* impossible, rather than what is *logically* impossible.

The idea here, then, is that talk of different kinds of possibility or impossibility is, in effect, talk that implicitly quantifies over different sets of possible worlds. And such implicit quantifier restriction is a familiar feature of our ordinary talk in any case. When someone says, while standing in front of the fridge with the door open, 'there isn't any milk', we know not to interpret them as meaning that there is no milk anywhere in the whole universe; we would reasonably take them instead to be talking only about (that is, quantifying over) the contents of the fridge.

The development of what is sometimes known as 'possible world semantics', that is, an analysis of the meanings of modal claims in terms of possible worlds, has been responsible for a huge resurgence of interest in questions about what must or might be or could have been the case – questions that were thought by many twentieth-century analytical philosophers (Quine included), until around the 1970s, to be at best rather mysterious, and at worst utterly unintelligible unless restricted to relatively well-understood modal notions such as provability and definition. Possible worlds have not just been put to use in analysing straightforwardly modal talk involving claims about necessity, possibility, contingency, essences, and counterfactual conditionals ('if I hadn't struck the match, it wouldn't have lit'). Much of contemporary analytical philosophical discourse is up to its neck in possible-world talk; for example, discussions of the nature of laws and causation, the relationship between the mental and the physical, and the nature of knowledge. Some philosophers – the leading example being David Lewis – have deployed possible-world talk to provide accounts of the nature of properties, events, propositions, and so on. Possible worlds seem to be very useful things.

Possible worlds may be useful – but do they really exist, and if so, what on earth *are* they? Talk of possible worlds may seem to have reaped enormous rewards, but unless we have a plausible account of what exactly such talk is talk *about*, it seems that we are not really entitled to claim that any such rewards have really been gained. It is at this point – finally – that we enter into the familiar territory of ontological dispute. When we say that *there is* a possible world containing purple cows, we seem to be expressing belief in the existence of something, namely, a possible world containing a purple cow. But what is it that we thereby apparently ontologically commit ourselves to? Is it to the existence of other, real universes, containing real, flesh-and-blood purple cows? Or is it merely to the existence of something rather less exotic? Or should we regard possible-world talk with a pinch of salt, as no more than a convenient way of talking, just as Devitt thinks that talk of two things sharing a property is merely a convenience that does not commit us to the existence of an entity that is literally present in both objects? (See chapter 3.)

What are Possible Worlds?

Lewis's modal realism

The most well-known view about the nature of possible worlds is David Lewis's view, which he calls 'modal realism'. Lewis's basic view is really very simple: he thinks that other possible worlds are real, 'concrete' entities that are of just the same kind as the actual world – the world we happen to inhabit. A merely possible cat – that is, a cat that inhabits a different possible world to ours – is no different to actual cats. It has real fur, purrs when stroked, hunts real mice for fun, and eats real cat food. Of course, other possible worlds are not *exactly* the same as the actual world – some contain purple cows, some contain no life forms whatsoever, some contain planets inhabited by super-intelligent aliens, and so on – but the possible worlds themselves are every bit as real as our own.

The natural question to ask at this point is, given Lewis's view, what exactly is *special* about the *actual* world? It is natural (though not of course unproblematic) to think that what *actually* exists – you and I, the chair you are sitting on, and so on – is somehow more real or more tangible than the shadowy entities that exist in the realm of the merely possible.

Lewis's response is to insist that the only thing 'special' about the actual world is that it happens to be the world *we* inhabit. 'Actual', for Lewis, is an *indexical* – just like 'I' or 'you' or 'here' or 'now'. Consider 'I'. The meaning of 'I' depends on who is thinking or uttering or writing the sentence containing the word 'I': when Bill Clinton says 'I used to be President of the USA', he means something different to what Tony Blair would mean if he were to say 'I used to be President of the USA' – that's why what one of them says is true, and what the other says is false. Similarly, when we say 'there are no purple cows in the actual world', or 'there aren't actually any purple cows', we speak the truth, but when inhabitants of purple-cow-containing worlds say 'there aren't actually any purple cows', they say something false: the world that is actual for *them* is *their* world, and not ours. Lewis thus denies outright that there is anything 'shadowy' about the merely possible, or that the actual world is 'more real' than other possible worlds; indeed, he denies that it makes any sense to assert such things. Existence is existence – something either exists or it doesn't. And something's being 'real' is just a matter of its existing. There just aren't different ways of existing or degrees of existing, and so there is no way for the actual world to be more 'real' than other possible worlds.

Ersatzism

The 'ersatzist' view of possible worlds goes something like this. Imagine someone writing an enormous book which describes, in minutest detail, all the (non-modal) truths there are to be had about the world. The description contained in the book will necessarily be *consistent* – that is, nothing the book says will contradict anything else the book says – since by hypothesis the book contains all and only the truths about the world, and so cannot contain any contradictions. It cannot, for example, say both that Helen went shopping at 3 pm on 5 April 2005 and also that she did not go shopping then, because one of those claims must be false.

Now imagine an enormous book that is similarly internally consistent but which does *not* contain all and only the (non-modal) truths about the world. Instead, at least some of the sentences in the book are false. For example, imagine that we start out with *The Hound of the Baskervilles* – a book that contains many descriptions of the world that are, in fact, false, since (amongst other things) there was no such person as Sherlock Holmes and no murderous beast roaming Dartmoor during the Victorian era. And now imagine that we extend the book, in a consistent way, so that it details everything else Sherlock Holmes and all the other characters in the book ever did, who their parents were, where their grandparents met, when and where their children and grandchildren and great-grandchildren were born, where they went to school – and so on, and on, until we have a *complete* description of, as it were, what happens at some entirely fictional version of the world.

According to Lewis's conception of possible worlds, such a book, if internally consistent, exactly describes what really happens at some possible world (not the actual world, of course, but some other possible world). According to 'ersatzism', by contrast, we should think of the 'possible world' that the book 'describes' as just *being* the set of sentences contained in the book. In other words, the book does not genuinely *describe* some independently-existing entity, in the way that a description of you genuinely describes *you* – an entity that exists independently of that description. Instead, the description contained in the book *is* a 'possible world'. So, for example, 'the Hound of the Baskervilles exists' is *possibly* true just in virtue of the fact that there is *some* complete and internally consistent set of sentences which contains the sentence 'the Hound of the Baskervilles exists'. We might express this fact, according to the ersatzist, by saying that there is a possible world at which the Hound of the Baskervilles exists; but when we do so, we do not mean that there really is a description-independent entity – a possible world in Lewis's sense – in which the Hound genuinely roams Dartmoor. There is just, if you like, the story, but not what the story purports to represent or describe.

The problem of transworld identity

One of Quine's original objections to modal talk was that 'possibilia' do not have clear 'criteria of individuation' (Quine 1948). If we understand 'it is possible that there is a fat man in the doorway' and 'it is possible that there is a man in the doorway' as saying, respectively, that *there is* a possible fat man in the doorway and that *there is* a possible man in the doorway, is there just one possible (fat) man in the doorway, or is the possible fat man a different entity from the possible man? How many possible men *are* there lurking in the doorway? It seems that we can give no principled answer to this question – which is to say, we have no way of 'individuating' the possible men in the doorway.

Once we deploy possible-world talk, the first two sentences above get analysed slightly differently. It is no longer a matter of there being one or more possible men in *this*, actual, doorway; instead, the first sentence says that there is a possible world in which there is a fat man in the doorway (a doorway that is located in that other possible world, and not in the actual world), and the second says that there is a possible world in which there is a man in the doorway. This seems to get us out of Quine's original problem, since at any given possible world we might think of, there is a perfectly determinate number of men in the doorway. But it raises a further problem, often known as the problem of 'transworld identity'. It seems true to say that Julian might not have been a philosopher. (After all, he could have decided to be a teacher or a banker or a long-distance runner.) Given a possible-worlds understanding of the truth conditions for modal claims, this seems to commit us to thinking that there are other possible worlds in which Julian is a teacher (or a banker, or . . .). But this is extremely peculiar. How can *Julian* – that very person – exist in other possible worlds, when he appears to be so firmly located right here at the actual world?

It's easy to see how different conceptions of the nature of possible worlds might affect the nature of the problem of 'transworld' identity (identity across possible worlds). Consider ersatzism. The problem here is not going to be that of making any sense at all of the idea of Julian being somehow located both at the actual world and also at other possible worlds, since 'other possible worlds' are merely consistent stories. And it's not hard to make sense of the thought that there are consistent stories according to which Julian becomes a banker. On the other hand, what conditions does such a story need to fulfil in order to be a story *about Julian* – this particular individual – as opposed to a story about some completely different person who happens to bear the name 'Julian Dodd'? For presumably the mere fact that there is some consistent story containing the sentence 'Julian Dodd is a banker' does not suffice to make it true that *this very person*, who in fact has that name, might have been a banker. (Consider: there is a consistent story about the world according to which there is a cat called 'Socrates'. This does not suffice to make it true that Socrates might have been a cat rather than a Greek philosopher.)

If, on the other hand, we take a realist position on possible worlds, so that we think of other possible worlds as genuine entities of the same kind as the actual world, the problem seems to be one of basic intelligibility: how can one and the same concrete entity, Julian, exist simultaneously in more than one possible world, if we conceive of possible worlds as Lewis does? Lewis's answer is that this is, indeed, completely unintelligible. According to Lewis, no entity, whether it is a person, a rock, a chair or a hydrogen molecule, literally exists at more than one possible world. We are all, as it is sometimes put, 'worldbound individuals'. How, then, on Lewis's view, can we make modal claims about Julian? Doesn't 'Julian might have been a banker' just *mean*, on Lewis's view, 'There is some possible world at which Julian is a banker'? And if that claim cannot be true, since Julian exists only at the actual world, doesn't it follow that on Lewis's view, Julian couldn't have been a banker after all?

The answer, according to Lewis, lies in what has become known as 'counterpart theory'. The basic idea goes like this. While no other possible world contains *Julian* himself, there are plenty of other possible worlds that contain people sufficiently similar to Julian to count as 'counterparts' of Julian, and it is the properties of these counterparts that serve to ground modal claims about Julian himself. For example, some counterparts of Julian are bankers, and this is what makes it true that Julian might have been a banker. So what makes 'Julian might have been a banker' true is not that there are possible worlds at which *Julian* is a banker, but rather that there are possible worlds at which a *counterpart* of Julian is a banker. Thus, for Lewis, there is, strictly speaking, no transworld *identity* at all; there are merely 'counterpart relations' between entities at different possible worlds, which is to say, other possible worlds contain counterparts of Julian, George Bush, the chair you are currently sitting on, and so on.

This is not to say that Lewis's theory is completely unproblematic. For one thing, counterpart theory still faces a problem similar to the problem raised above for ersatzism, namely: what determines whether or not a given entity at some other possible world is a counterpart of, say, Julian? Presumably their being *called* 'Julian Dodd' is neither necessary nor sufficient for their being a counterpart of Julian. Must they have exactly the same genetic make-up, have all or most or some of the same personality traits, be the same nationality, the same sex?

The texts

The passage from chapter 4 of David Lewis's *Counterfactuals* (1973) reproduced below sees Lewis arguing for modal realism – and in particular for the claim that belief in possible worlds is perfectly justified. The second text, from Saul Kripke's *Naming and Necessity* (1980), defends *de re* modality both against the kind of objection raised towards the beginning of this Introduction and against the problem of transworld identity. Kripke argues that this problem can be avoided, so long as we do not follow Lewis in thinking that a possible world is, as Kripke puts it at $\boxed{g} \mapsto$, 'like a foreign country'.

David Lewis, extract from
Counterfactuals

4.1   Possible Worlds

It is time to face the fact that my analysis rests on suspect foundations. Doubly so: possible worlds are widely regarded with suspicion, and so is similarity even among entities not themselves suspect. If the common suspicion of possible worlds and of similarity were justified, then my analysis could have little interest: only the interest of connecting mysteries to other mysteries. I shall argue, however, that the suspicions are not well justified.

I believe that there are possible worlds other than the one we happen to inhabit. If an argument is wanted, it is this. It is uncontroversially true that things might be otherwise than they are. I believe, and so do you, that things could have been different in countless ways. But what does this mean? Ordinary language permits the paraphrase: there are many ways things could have been besides the way they actually are. On the face of it, this sentence is an existential quantification. It says that there exist many entities of a certain description, to wit 'ways things could have been'. I believe that things could have been different in countless ways; I believe permissible paraphrases of what I believe; taking the paraphrase at its face value, I therefore believe in the existence of entities that might be called 'ways things could have been'. I prefer to call them 'possible worlds'.

I do not make it an inviolable principle to take seeming existential quantifications in ordinary language at their face value. But I do recognize a presumption in favor of taking sentences at their face value, unless (1) taking them at face value is known to lead to trouble, and (2) taking them some other way is known not to. In this case, neither condition is met. I do not know any successful argument that my realism about possible worlds leads to trouble, unless you beg the question by saying that it already *is* trouble. (I shall shortly consider some unsuccessful arguments.) All the alternatives I know, on the other hand, do lead to trouble.

If our modal idioms are not quantifiers over possible worlds, then what else are they? (1) We might take them as unanalyzed primitives; this is not an alternative theory at all, but an abstinence from theorizing. (2) We might take them as metalinguistic predicates analyzable in terms of consistency: '*Possibly φ*' means that ϕ is a consistent sentence. But what is consistency? If a consistent sentence is one that could be true, or one that is not necessarily false, then the theory is circular; of course, one can be more artful than I have been in hiding the circularity. If a consistent sentence is one whose denial is not a theorem of some specified deductive system, then the theory is incorrect rather than circular: no falsehood of arithmetic is possibly true, but for any deductive system you care to specify either there are falsehoods among its theorems or there is some falsehood of arithmetic whose denial is not among its theorems. If a consistent sentence is one that comes out true under some assignment of extensions to the non-logical vocabulary, then the theory is incorrect: some assignments of extensions are impossible, for instance one that assigns overlapping extensions to the English terms 'pig' and 'sheep'. If a consistent sentence is one that comes out true under some possible assignment of extensions, then the theory is again circular. (3) We might take them as quantifiers over so-called 'possible worlds' that are really some sort of respectable linguistic entities: say, maximal consistent sets of sentences of some language. (Or maximal consistent sets of atomic sentences, that is *state-descriptions*; or maximal consistent sets of atomic sentences in the language as enriched by the addition of names for all the things there are, that is *diagrammed models*.) We might call these things 'possible worlds', but hasten to reassure anyone who was worried that secretly we were talking about something else that he likes better. But again the theory would be either circular or incorrect, according as we explain consistency in modal terms or in deductive (or purely model-theoretic) terms.

I emphatically do not identify possible worlds in any way with respectable linguistic entities; I take them to be respectable entities in their own right. When I profess realism about possible worlds, I mean to be taken literally. Possible worlds are what they are, and not some other thing. If asked what sort of thing they are, I cannot give the kind of reply my questioner probably expects: that is, a proposal to reduce possible worlds to something else.

I can only ask him to admit that he knows what sort of thing our actual world is, and then explain that other worlds are more things of *that* sort, differing not in kind but only in what goes on at them. Our actual world is only one world among others. We call it alone actual not because it differs in kind from all the rest but because it is the world we inhabit. The inhabitants of other worlds may truly call their own worlds actual, if they mean by 'actual' what we do; for the meaning we give to 'actual' is such that it refers at any world *i* to that world *i* itself. 'Actual' is indexical, like 'I' or 'here', or 'now': it depends for its reference on the circumstances of utterance, to wit the world where the utterance is located.[1]

My indexical theory of actuality exactly mirrors a less controversial doctrine about time. Our present time is only one time among others. We call it alone present not because it differs in kind from all the rest, but because it is the time we inhabit. The inhabitants of other times may truly call their own times 'present', if they mean by 'present' what we do; for the

---

[1] For more on this theme, see my 'Anselm and Actuality', *Noûs* 4 (1970): 175–88.

meaning we give to 'present' is such that it is indexical, and refers at any time t to that time t itself.

[g]→   I have already said that it would gain us nothing to identify possible worlds with sets of sentences (or the like), since we would need the notion of possibility otherwise understood to specify correctly which sets of sentences were to be identified with worlds. Not only would it gain nothing: given that the actual world does not differ in kind from the rest, it would lead to the conclusion that our actual world is a set of sentences. Since I cannot believe that I and all my surroundings are a set of sentences (though I have no argument that they are not), I cannot believe that other worlds are sets of sentences either.

    What arguments can be given against realism about possible worlds?
[h]→ I have met with few arguments – incredulous stares are more common. But I shall try to answer those that I have heard.

[i]→   It is said that realism about possible worlds is false because only our own world, and its contents, actually exist. But of course unactualized possible worlds and their unactualized inhabitants do not *actually* exist. To actually exist is to exist and to be located here at our actual world – at this world that we inhabit. Other worlds than ours are not our world, or inhabitants thereof. It does not follow that realism about possible worlds is false. Realism about unactualized possibles is exactly the thesis that there are more things than actually exist. Either the argument tacitly assumes what it purports to prove, that realism about possibles is false, or it proceeds by equivocation. Our idioms of existential quantification may be used to range over everything without exception, or they may be tacitly restricted in various ways. In particular, they may be restricted to our own world and things in it. Taking them as thus restricted, we can truly say that there exist nothing but our own world and its inhabitants; by removing the restriction we pass illegitimately from that truth to the conclusion that realism about possibles is false. It would be convenient if there were one idiom of quantification, say *'there are ... '*, that was firmly reserved for unrestricted use and another, say *'there actually exist ... '*, that was firmly reserved for the restricted use. Unfortunately, even these two idioms of quantification can be used either way; and thus one can pass indecisively from equivocating on one to equivocating on another. All the same, there are the two uses (unless realism about possibles is false, as has yet to be shown) and we need only keep track of them to see that the argument is fallacious.

[j]→   Realism about possible worlds might be thought implausible on grounds of parsimony, though this could not be a decisive argument against it. Distinguish two kinds of parsimony, however: qualitative and quantitative. A doctrine is qualitatively parsimonious if it keeps down the number of fundamentally different *kinds* of entity: if it posits sets alone rather than sets and unreduced numbers, or particles alone rather than particles and fields, or bodies alone or spirits alone rather than both bodies and spirits. A doctrine

is quantitatively parsimonious if it keeps down the number of instances of the kinds it posits; if it posits 10^{29} electrons rather than 10^{37}, or spirits only for people rather than spirits for all animals. I subscribe to the general view that qualitative parsimony is good in a philosophical or empirical hypothesis; but I recognize no presumption whatever in favor of quantitative parsimony. My realism about possible worlds is merely quantitatively, not qualitatively, unparsimonious. You believe in our actual world already. I ask you to believe in more things of that kind, not in things of some new kind.

k⊢→   Quine has complained that unactualized possibles are disorderly elements, well-nigh incorrigibly involved in mysteries of individuation.[2] That well may be true of any unactualized possibles who lead double lives, lounging in the doorways of two worlds at once. But I do not believe in any of those. The unactualized possibles I do believe in, confined each to his own world and united only by ties of resemblance to their counterparts elsewhere (see Section 1.9 [in *Counterfactuals*]) do not pose any special problems of individuation. At least, they pose only such problems of individuation as might arise within a single world.

l⊢→   Perhaps some who dislike the use of possible worlds in philosophical analysis are bothered not because they think they have reason to doubt the existence of other worlds, but only because they wish to be told more about these supposed entities before they know what to think. How many are there? In what respects do they vary, and what is common to them all? Do they obey a non-trivial law of identity of indiscernibles? Here I am at a disadvantage compared to someone who pretends as a figure of speech to believe in possible worlds, but really does not. If worlds were creatures of my imagination, I could imagine them to be any way I liked, and I could tell you all you wish to hear simply by carrying on my imaginative creation. But as I believe that there really are other worlds, I am entitled to confess that there is much about them that I do not know, and that I do not know how to find out.

One comes to philosophy already endowed with a stock of opinions. It is not the business of philosophy either to undermine or to justify these preexisting opinions, to any great extent, but only to try to discover ways of expanding them into an orderly system. A metaphysician's analysis of mind is an attempt at systematizing our opinions about mind. It succeeds to the extent that (1) it is systematic, and (2) it respects those of our pre-philosophical opinions to which we are firmly attached. Insofar as it does both better than any alternative we have thought of, we give it credence. There is some give-and-take, but not too much: some of us sometimes change our minds on some points of common opinion, if they conflict irremediably with a doctrine that commands our belief by its systematic beauty and its agreement with more important common opinions.

[2]   Willard V. Quine, 'On What There Is', in *From a Logical Point of View* (Harvard University Press: Cambridge, MA, 1953): 4.

So it is throughout metaphysics; and so it is with my doctrine of realism about possible worlds. Among my common opinions that philosophy must respect (if it is to deserve credence) are not only my naive belief in tables and chairs, but also my naive belief that these tables and chairs might have been otherwise arranged. Realism about possible worlds is an attempt, the only successful attempt I know of, to systematize these preexisting modal opinions. To the extent that I am modally opinionated, independently of my philosophizing, I can distinguish between alternative versions of realism about possible worlds that conform to my opinions and versions that do not. Because I believe my opinions, I believe that the true version is one of the former. For instance, I believe that there are worlds where physics is different from the physics of our world, but none where logic and arithmetic are different from the logic and arithmetic of our world. This is nothing but the systematic expression of my naive, pre-philosophical opinion that physics could be different, but not logic or arithmetic. I do not know of any non-circular argument that I could give in favor of that opinion; but so long as that *is* my firm opinion nevertheless, I must make a place for it when I do metaphysics. I have no more use for a philosophical doctrine that denies my firm, unjustified modal opinions than I have for one that denies my firm, unjustified belief in chairs and tables.

Commentary on Lewis

The interest of this extract from Lewis 1973 lies not just in what Lewis has to say about possible worlds in particular, but in the fact that the kinds of argument for and against the existence of possible worlds which he considers are kinds of argument that one might bring to bear on any ontological debate – the debate about the existence of universals, say, or numbers, or God, or any other kind of entity whose existence someone might take themselves to have philosophical reasons to be sceptical about.

That this is so should be obvious to you within the first two paragraphs. (If not, go back and look at chapter 4 again.) Lewis starts with the observation that 'things might have been otherwise than they are' can be paraphrased as 'there are many ways things could have been besides the way they actually are'. He then, at $\boxed{a}\!\!\rightarrow$, claims that there is 'a presumption in favor of taking sentences at their face value, unless (1) taking them at face value is known to lead to trouble, and (2) taking them some other way is known not to'.

This should remind you of the debate between Armstrong and Devitt (chapter 4) about the existence of universals, where the question of whether a sentence should be taken at 'face value' played a prominent role. In the case of universals, we were concerned with sentences such as 'the sofa and the pillar box are both red', which one might naturally paraphrase as 'there is a property – redness – that is shared by the pillar box and the sofa'. A realist about universals might make the same claim about

universals at this point as Lewis makes about possible worlds: we should take the
second sentence at face value – that is, as expressing an ontological commitment to
universals – unless conditions (1) and (2) are met.

1. (i) Explain in your own words what Lewis means by taking the claim that there
are many ways things might have been 'at face value'. (ii) Describe how someone
who had a view about possible worlds that is analogous to Devitt's view about
universals might respond to Lewis's claim that we should take such claims at face
value.

2. At $\boxed{b}\mapsto$, Lewis says that to claim that realism about possible worlds 'already *is*
trouble' is to 'beg the question'. Why do you think someone might hold that
realism about possible worlds 'already *is* trouble', and what do you think Lewis
means by saying that to say this begs the question? Do you agree with him? If not,
why not? And if so, can you articulate what the distinction between the claim that
realism about possible worlds 'is trouble' and the claim that it 'leads to trouble' – a
distinction which Lewis here appeals to – amounts to?

Lewis then proceeds, more or less, to take conditions (1) and (2) in reverse order:
he first argues that doing anything other than taking claims about 'ways the world
might have been' at face value leads to trouble, and then argues that taking them at
face value does *not* lead to trouble.

In the paragraph from $\boxed{c}\mapsto$, then, Lewis very briefly surveys three alternative
views according to which 'our modal idioms are not quantifiers over possible worlds'.
He starts with the view that they are instead 'unanalyzed primitives', and complains
that 'this is not an alternative theory at all, but an abstinence from theorizing'.

3. Do you think this is a good objection? If not, why not? If so, is this kind of
objection *always* good? That is, should we *always* prefer a 'theory' of a given concept
over the claim that the concept is just primitive, i.e. is not susceptible to analysis?

The next proposal that Lewis considers is the view that modal idioms are 'metalinguistic predicates analyzable in terms of consistency'. In other words, to say, for
example, 'possibly snow is yellow' is to say, *of the sentence* 'snow is yellow', that that
sentence is consistent (that is, non-contradictory). ('Possibly' here is conceived as a
metalinguistic predicate because it is used to talk about linguistic items, namely,
sentences.) And he argues that such a view is either circular or false. He does this by
considering in turn four different candidate meanings of 'consistent' (each one
starting with 'If a consistent sentence is . . . '). He argues that according to the first
and fourth, the proposed analysis of modal idioms is circular, and according to the
second and third, it is false.

4. Describe in your own words Lewis's circularity objection to the first and fourth
proposed analyses of 'consistent'.

The problems with the second and third candidate meanings of 'consistent' are a bit more technical – though if you don't understand the content of the proposed analyses, it should at least be clear to you that Lewis thinks they are both false and that he argues for this by giving a counter-example in each case.

5. The second candidate analysis of 'consistent', stated at $\boxed{d}\mapsto$, is this: 'a consistent sentence is one whose denial is not a theorem of some specified deductive system'. Lewis' argument that this analysis is inadequate turns on Gödel's Incompleteness Theorem. Find out what this theorem is and explain in your own words how it refutes the proposed analysis. (Searching Google for 'Gödel's Incompleteness Theorem' should deliver several fairly simple, non-technical explanations of what the theorem says.)

The third and final proposal according to which 'our modal idioms are not quantifiers over possible worlds', which Lewis discusses at $\boxed{e}\mapsto$, is that modal idioms do quantify, but what they quantify over are not *really* possible worlds in Lewis's sense at all, but 'some sort of respectable linguistic entities'. This view is the 'ersatzist' view described in the Introduction.

6. (i) Why might someone think that the ersatzist position on possible worlds is (at least *prima facie*) more 'respectable' than Lewis's? (Bear in mind that the talk of 'books' in the Introduction was just to get the general idea across; the 'sets of sentences' that the ersatzist identifies with possible worlds are not literally inscriptions on pieces of paper.) (ii) Describe Lewis's objection to ersatzism in your own words.

In the next two paragraphs, from $\boxed{f}\mapsto$, Lewis rehearses two of the central tenets of his modal realism: that other possible worlds are the same sorts of thing as the actual world (contrary to what the ersatzist claims), and that 'actual' here is an indexical, like 'I' or 'here' or 'now'.

7. In the paragraph starting at $\boxed{g}\mapsto$, Lewis provides an additional argument against ersatzism. Describe the argument in your own words. Are you convinced by it? How do you think the ersatzist would respond?

Lewis spends the next couple of pages, from $\boxed{i}\mapsto$, responding to some typical objections to modal realism – although he starts, at $\boxed{h}\mapsto$, by noting that 'incredulous stares' are the most common response.

8. Lewis is here implicitly claiming that an 'incredulous stare' does not count as an objection in its own right. Give the most plausible reason you can think of why he might hold this. Do you agree?

The first objection Lewis addresses, at $\boxed{i}\mapsto$, is the objection that 'realism about possible worlds is false because only our world, and its contents, actually exist'. Lewis complains that this argument either 'tacitly assumes what it purports to prove', or else it 'proceeds by equivocation'.

9. Explain both of Lewis's objections to the argument in your own words.

The next objection, at $\boxed{j}\mapsto$, is that realism about possible worlds 'might be thought objectionable on grounds of parsimony'.

10. (i) Explain Lewis's response to this objection in your own words, giving your own examples to explain the distinction between quantitative and qualitative parsimony. (ii) Can you think of any good reasons to deny that there is 'no presumption whatever in favor of quantitative parsimony'? (iii) Lewis says at the outset that the objection cannot in any case be a 'decisive argument' against modal realism. Give the best reason you can think of for agreeing with Lewis here. Do *you* agree with Lewis?

The third objection, at $\boxed{k}\mapsto$, is that 'unactualized possibles are disorderly elements, well-nigh incorrigibly involved in mysteries of individuation' – an objection discussed briefly in the Introduction to this chapter.

11. Why do you think Lewis says that, on his account, unactualized possibles 'do not pose any special problems of individuation'? Do you agree?

In the paragraph at $\boxed{l}\mapsto$, Lewis addresses those who 'wish to be told more about these supposed entities, before they know what to think' – though it is rather unclear whether he is attempting to raise and counter a distinctive *objection* to modal realism. None the less, there are certainly some possible objections in the offing on this issue. Here is one. Facts about what might or might not have existed – the fact that blue kangaroos might have existed, for example – are, for Lewis, facts about real, mind-independent, concrete objects; but they are objects to which we cannot have the sort of epistemic access that we have to ordinary, actual-world objects (actual kangaroos, for example). Roughly speaking, our knowledge of mind-independent, concrete, actual-world objects arises from causal interactions between us, or our senses, and the objects themselves (perhaps mediated by testimony from other people who have interacted with such objects in cases where we have not done so ourselves). Our knowledge of possible blue kangaroos, by contrast, does not arise through any such causal contact: other possible worlds are not in any sense causally connected with the actual world.

By contrast, by and large, or at least in a wide range of cases, our method for 'finding out' which modal claims are true is that of imagining certain sorts of situation. For example, in order to satisfy ourselves that blue kangaroos might have existed, we simply imagine a possible world in which blue kangaroos *do* exist. And this is, to say the least, rather curious: it is curious to say that we can come by

knowledge of the existence of mind-independent, concrete objects simply by employing our imagination, given that when it comes to *actual* concrete objects – actual
kangaroos, for example – our imagination doesn't deliver any knowledge at all. We
cannot establish that kangaroos exist just by imagining them. So how can it be that
we *can* establish that *possible* blue kangaroos exist just by imagining them? How – to
put the matter crudely – can the epistemic standards for claims about what exists be
so low in the case of possible but non-actual objects, when the standards are much
higher in the case of actual objects?

Someone who thinks that 'possible worlds' (and hence possible blue kangaroos)
are entirely different kinds of things to the actual world (and actual kangaroos) seems
to have the better of the matter here: different kinds of entity require different
methods for ascertaining whether or not they exist. For example, on an ersatzist
conception of possible worlds, to believe that blue kangaroos are possible is to believe
that there is a complete and consistent set of sentences that contains the sentence
'there are blue kangaroos'. And there is no mystery as to why our methods for
establishing that such a set of sentences exists are very different to our methods
for establishing that kangaroos exist.

12. How convinced are you by this epistemic objection to modal realism? Can you
think of a response that might be made on Lewis's behalf?

The extract ends with Lewis attempting to fit modal realism into a general
conception of what philosophy is *for*: what it is that philosophers ought to be aiming
to do, and how we are to judge the extent to which they succeed in realizing those
aims. In particular, he claims that it is not the business of philosophy to 'undermine'
our 'preexisting opinions', but only to expand them into 'an orderly system'. And so a
philosophical theory should be judged according to how well it succeeds in providing
an orderly system, and to what extent it 'respects those pre-philosophical opinions to
which we are firmly attached'. 'There is some give-and-take,' he says, 'but not too
much'.

13. Do you agree with this conception of the 'business of philosophy'? Do you
think, for example, that it is not the business of philosophy to undermine our pre-
existing opinions? What if pre-existing opinions differ widely, or if we disagree
about which ones are 'important'? Can you think of any philosophical theories
whose plausibility has caused you to reject a view you had before you started
thinking philosophically about it? If so, why did you change your mind?
14. Lewis says that realism about possible worlds is 'an attempt…to systematize…preexisting modal opinions', such as the belief 'that these tables and chairs
might have been otherwise arranged'. (i) Given Lewis's commitment to counterpart theory, do you think that his realism about possible worlds really accommo-
dates the belief that *these* tables and chairs might have been otherwise arranged?
Explain your answer. (ii) If you don't, what reply do you think Lewis might give?

Saul Kripke, extract from
Naming and Necessity

There is one more question I want to go into in a preliminary way. Some philosophers have distinguished between essentialism, the belief in modality *de re*, and a mere advocacy of necessity, the belief in modality *de dicto*. Now, some people say: Let's *give* you the concept of necessity.[1] A much worse thing, something creating great additional problems, is whether we can say of any particular that it has necessary or contingent properties, even make the distinction between necessary and contingent properties. Look, it's only a *statement* or a *state of affairs* that can be either necessary or contingent! Whether a *particular* necessarily or contingently has a certain property depends on the way it's described. This is perhaps closely related to the view that the way we refer to particular things is by a description. What is Quine's famous example? If we consider the number 9, does it have the property of necessary oddness? Has that number got to be odd in all possible worlds? Certainly it's true in all possible worlds, let's say, it couldn't have been otherwise, that *nine* is odd. Of course, 9 could also be equally well picked out as *the number of planets*. It is *not* necessary, not true in all possible worlds, that the number of planets is odd. For example if there had been eight planets, the number of planets would not have been odd. And so it's thought: Was it necessary or contingent that Nixon won the election? (It might seem contingent, unless one has some view of some inexorable process. . . .) But this is a contingent property of Nixon only relative to our referring to him as 'Nixon' (assuming 'Nixon' doesn't mean 'the man who won the election at such and such a time'). But if we designate Nixon as 'the man who won the election in 1968', then it will be a necessary truth, of course, that the man who won the election in 1968, won the election in 1968. Similarly, whether an object has the same property in all possible worlds depends not just on the object itself, but on how it is described. So it's argued.

---

[1] By the way, it's a common attitude in philosophy to think that one shouldn't introduce a notion until it's been rigorously defined (according to some popular notion of rigor). Here I am just dealing with an intuitive notion and will keep on the level of an intuitive notion. That is, we think that some things, though they are in fact the case, might have been otherwise. I might not have given these lectures today. If that's right, then it is *possible* that I wouldn't have given these lectures today. Quite a different question is the epistemological question, how any particular person knows that I gave these lectures today. I suppose in that case he does know this is *a posteriori*. But, if someone were born with an innate belief that I was going to give these lectures today, who knows? Right now, anyway, let's suppose that people know this *a posteriori*. At any rate, the two questions being asked are different.

It is even suggested in the literature, that though a notion of necessity may have some sort of intuition behind it (we do think some things could have been otherwise; other things we don't think could have been otherwise), this notion [of a distinction between necessary and contingent properties] is just a doctrine made up by some bad philosopher, who (I guess) didn't realize that there are several ways of referring to the same thing.

b→ I don't know if some philosophers have not realized this; but at any rate it is very far from being true that this idea [that a property can meaningfully be held to be essential or accidental to an object independently of its description] is a notion which has no intuitive content, which means nothing to

c→ the ordinary man. Suppose that someone said, pointing to Nixon, 'That's the guy who might have lost'. Someone else says 'Oh no, if you describe him as "Nixon", then he might have lost; but, of course, describing him as the winner, then it is not true that he might have lost'. Now which one is being the philosopher, here, the unintuitive man? It seems to me obviously to be

d→ the second. The second man has a philosophical theory. The first man would say, and with great conviction, 'Well, of course, the winner of the election *might have been someone else*. The actual winner, had the course of the campaign been different, might have been the loser, and someone else the winner; or there might have been no election at all. So, such terms as "the winner" and "the loser" don't designate the same objects in all possible worlds. On the other hand, the term "Nixon" is just a *name* of *this man*'. When you ask whether it is necessary or contingent the *Nixon* won the election, you are asking the intuitive question whether in some counterfactual situation, *this man* would in fact have lost the election. If someone thinks that the notion of a necessary or contingent property (forget whether there *are* any nontrivial necessary properties [and consider] just the *meaningfulness* of the notion[2]) is a philosopher's notion with no intuitive content, he is wrong. Of course, some philosophers think that something's having intuitive content is very inconclusive evidence in favor of it. I think it is very heavy evidence in favor of anything, myself. I really don't know, in a way, what more conclusive evidence one can have about anything, ultimately speaking. But, in any event, people who think the notion of accidental property unintuitive have intuition reversed, I think.

e→ Why have they thought this? While there are many motivations for people thinking this, one is this: The question of essential properties so-called is supposed to be equivalent (and it is equivalent) to the question

---

[2] The example I gave asserts a certain property – electoral victory – to be *accidental* to Nixon, independently of how he is described. Of course, if the notion of accidental property is meaningful, the notion of essential property must be meaningful also. This is not to say that there *are* any essential properties – though, in fact, I think there are. The usual argument questions the *meaningfulness* of essentialism, and says that whether a property is accidental or essential to an object depends on how it is described. It is thus *not* the view that all properties are accidental. Of course, it is also not the view, held by some idealists, that all properties are essential, all relations internal.

of 'identity across possible worlds'. Suppose we have someone, Nixon, and there's another possible world where there is no one with all the properties Nixon has in the actual world. Which one of these other people, if any, is Nixon? Surely you must give some criterion of identity here! If you have a criterion of identity, then you just look in the other possible worlds at the man who is Nixon; and the question whether, in that other possible world, Nixon has certain properties, is well defined. It is also supposed to be well defined, in terms of such notions, whether it's true in all possible worlds, or there are some possible worlds in which Nixon didn't win the election. But, it's said, the problems of giving such criteria of identity are very difficult. Sometimes in the case of numbers it might seem easier (but even here it's argued that it's quite arbitrary). For example, one might say, and this is surely the truth, that if position in the series of numbers is what makes the number 9 what it is, then if (in another world) the number of planets had been 8, the number of planets would be a different number from the one it actually is. You wouldn't say that that number then is to be identified with our number 9 in this world. In the case of other types of objects, say people, material objects, things like that, has anyone given a set of necessary and sufficient conditions for identity across possible worlds?

Really, adequate necessary and sufficient conditions for identity which do not beg the question are very rare in any case. Mathematics is the only case I really know of where they are given even *within* a possible world, to tell the truth. I don't know of such conditions for identity of material objects over time, or for people. Everyone knows what a problem this is. But, let's forget about that. What seems to be more objectionable is that this depends on the wrong way of looking at what a possible world is. One thinks, in this picture, of a possible world as if it were like a foreign country. One looks upon it as an observer. Maybe Nixon has moved to the other country and maybe he hasn't, but one is given only qualities. One can observe all his qualities, but, of course, one doesn't observe that someone is Nixon. One observes that something has red hair (or green or yellow) but not whether something is Nixon. So we had better have a way of telling in terms of properties when we run into the same thing as we saw before; we had better have a way of telling, when we come across one of these other possible worlds, who was Nixon.

Some logicians in their formal treatment of modal logic may encourage this picture. A prominent example, perhaps, is myself. Nevertheless, intuitively speaking, it seems to me not to be the right way of thinking about the possible worlds. A possible world isn't a distant country that we are coming across, or viewing through a telescope. Generally speaking, another possible world is too far away. Even if we travel faster than light, we won't get to it. A possible world is *given by the descriptive conditions we associate with it*. What do we mean when we say 'In some other possible world I would not have given this lecture today?' We just imagine the situation where I didn't decide to give this lecture or decided to give it on some other day. Of course, we don't imagine everything that is true or false, but only those things relevant to my giving the lecture; but, in theory, everything needs to be decided to make a total description of the world. We can't really imagine that except in part; that, then, is a 'possible world'. Why can't it be part of the *description* of a possible world that it contains *Nixon* and that in that world *Nixon* didn't win the election? It might be a question, of course, whether such a world *is* possible. (Here it would seem, *prima facie*, to be clearly possible.) But, once we see that such a situation is possible, then we are given that the man who might have lost the election or did lose the election in this possible world is Nixon, because that's part of the description of the world. 'Possible worlds' are *stipulated*, not *discovered* by powerful telescopes. There is no reason why we cannot *stipulate* that, in talking about what would have happened to Nixon in a certain counterfactual situation, we are talking about what would have happened to *him*.

 Of course, if someone makes the demand that every possible world has to be described in a purely qualitative way, we can't say, 'Suppose Nixon had lost the election', we must say, instead, something like, 'Suppose a man with a dog named Checkers, who looks like a certain David Frye impersonation, is in a certain possible world and loses the election.' Well, does he resemble Nixon enough to be identified with Nixon? A very explicit and blatant example of this way of looking at things is David Lewis's counterpart theory,[3] but the literature on quantified modality is replete

---

[3] David K. Lewis, 'Counterpart Theory and Quantified Modal Logic', *Journal of Philosophy* 65 (1968), 113–26. Lewis's elegant paper also suffers from a purely formal difficulty: on his interpretation of quantified modality, the familiar law $(y)((x)A(x) \supset A(y))$ fails, if $A(x)$ is allowed to contain modal operators. (For example, $(\exists y)((x)\Diamond(x \neq y))$ is satisfiable but $(\exists y)\Diamond(y \neq y)$ is not.) Since Lewis's formal model follows rather naturally from his philosophical views on counterparts, and since the failure of universal instantiation for modal properties is intuitively bizarre, it seems to me that this failure constitutes an additional argument against the plausibility of his philosophical views. There are other, lesser, formal difficulties as well. I cannot elaborate here.

 Strictly speaking, Lewis's view is not a view of 'transworld identification'. Rather, he thinks that similarities across possible worlds determine a counterpart relation which need be neither symmetric nor transitive. The counterpart of something in another possible world is *never* identical with the thing itself. Thus if we say 'Humphrey might have won the election (if only he had done such-and-such), we are not talking about something that might have happened to *Humphrey* but to someone else, a "counterpart".' Probably, however, Humphrey could not care less whether someone *else*, no matter how much resembling him, would have been victorious in another possible world. Thus, Lewis's view seems to me even more bizarre than the usual notions of transworld identification that it replaces. The important issues, however, are common to the two views: the supposition that other possible worlds are like other dimensions of a more inclusive universe, that they can be given only by purely qualitative descriptions, and that therefore either the identity relation or the counterpart relation must be established in terms of qualitative resemblance.

Many have pointed out to me that the father of counterpart theory is probably Leibnitz. I will not go into such a historical question here. It would also be interesting to compare Lewis's views with the Wheeler–Everett interpretation of quantum mechanics. I suspect that this view of physics may suffer from philosophical problems analogous to Lewis's counterpart theory; it is certainly very similar in spirit.

with it.[4] Why need we make this demand? That is not the way we ordinarily think of counterfactual situations. We just say 'suppose this man had lost'. It is *given* that the possible world contains *this man*, and that in that world, he had lost. There may be a problem about what intuitions about possibility come to. But, if we have such an intuition about the possibility of *that* (*this man's* electoral loss), then it is about the possibility of *that*. It need not be identified with the possibility of a man looking like such and such, or holding such and such political views, or otherwise qualitatively described, having lost. We can point to the *man*, and ask what might have happened to *him*, had events been different.

⬚ 1 ⟶   It might be said 'Let's suppose that this is true. It comes down to the same thing, because whether Nixon could have had certain properties, different from the ones he actually has, is equivalent to the question whether the criteria of identity across possible worlds include that Nixon does not

⬚ m ⟶ have these properties'. But it doesn't really come to the same thing, because the usual notion of a criterion of transworld identity demands that we give purely qualitative necessary and sufficient conditions for someone being Nixon. If we can't imagine a possible world in which Nixon doesn't have a certain property, then it's a necessary condition of someone being Nixon. Or a necessary property of Nixon that he [has] that property. For example, supposing Nixon is in fact a human being, it would seem that we cannot think of a possible counterfactual situation in which he was, say, an inanimate object; perhaps it is not even possible for him not to have been a human being. Then it will be a necessary fact about Nixon that in all possible worlds where he exists at all, he is human or anyway he is not an inanimate object. This has nothing to do with any requirement that there be purely qualitative *sufficient* conditions for Nixonhood which we can spell out. And should there be? Maybe there is some argument that there should be, but we can consider these questions about *necessary* conditions without going into any question about *sufficient* conditions. Further, even if there were a purely qualitative set of necessary and sufficient conditions for being Nixon, the view I advocate would not demand that we find these conditions *before* we can ask whether Nixon might have won the election, nor does it demand that we restate the question in terms of such conditions. We can simply consider *Nixon* and ask what might have happened to *him* had various circumstances been different. So the two views, the two ways of looking at things, do seem to me to make a difference.

[4]   Another *locus classicus* of the views I am criticizing, with more philosophical exposition than Lewis's paper, is a paper by David Kaplan on transworld identification. Unfortunately, this paper has never been published. It does not represent Kaplan's present position.

Commentary on Kripke

The text reprinted above is a section of Lecture I of the three lectures contained in Kripke's famous and hugely influential *Naming and Necessity* (1980). The lectures as they appear in the book are transcribed from the lectures Kripke gave at Princeton University in 1970, without notes, at the age of 29.

Being just a part of one of the lectures, the text is not self-contained but rather plunges you in at the deep end, and does not end with a nice summary or conclusion. But (as you should by now have noticed) it certainly contains some arguments; and Lewis's 'counterpart theory', which you have already come across, is one of Kripke's targets.

The text begins with Kripke laying out something close to Quine's view, as described in the Introduction to this chapter: that necessity and contingency attach only to 'statements' or 'states of affairs' (though it's unclear what Kripke means by 'states of affairs' here), and that whether a particular has a property necessarily or contingently depends on how the particular is described.

Kripke says, at $\boxed{a} \mapsto$, that this view 'is perhaps closely related to the view that the way we refer to particular things is by a description'. We need to give a bit of background before sense can be made of what he says here. Proper names – 'Nixon', 'Socrates', and so on – have been a source of philosophical puzzlement. Consider the following two sentences:

(1)   Hesperus is Hesperus.
(2)   Hesperus is Phosphorus.

We can know *a priori* that (1) is true: you don't need to know anything about the world at all (what object 'Hesperus' refers to, for example) to be able to tell that it is true. But we cannot know *a priori* whether or not (2) is true. For all we know *a priori*, 'Hesperus' might be the name of Frege's pet dog, for example; and 'Phosphorus' might be the name of a Roman emperor – in which case, of course, (2) would be false. Or it might be that 'Hesperus' and 'Phosphorus' are two names for the very same object, in which case (2) would be true. But we have no way of knowing which of these situations obtains. In fact, (2) is true: 'Hesperus' and 'Phosphorus' are both names for the planet Venus. But the name 'Hesperus' was originally given to a celestial body visible at a certain location in the evenings, and the name 'Phosphorus' was given to a celestial body visible in the mornings. It was a significant astronomical discovery that the names in fact referred to one and the same object: Venus.

A puzzle arises if we suppose that the *meaning* of a proper name is simply the object it refers to. For in that case, 'Hesperus' and 'Phosphorus' would mean exactly the same, and we would not be able to explain why, given their sameness of meaning, the truth of (2) cannot be known *a priori*.

Frege famously distinguished between 'sense' (or 'meaning') and 'reference' in order to resolve the puzzle, which is often called 'Frege's Puzzle'. (See Frege 1980, part of which is reprinted with commentary in Hornsby and Longworth 2006.) On Frege's view, the reference of 'Hesperus' – the object to which that proper name refers – is the planet Venus, while (at least on one interpretation of Frege) the sense or meaning of 'Hesperus' is 'the celestial body visible in the night sky...' (where we fill in the '...' with some description that uniquely identifies Venus amongst all the other celestial bodies visible in the night sky – position relative to other stars and planets, say). And the reference of 'Phosphorus' is also Venus, but the *meaning* of 'Phosphorus' is 'the celestial body visible in the early morning sky...'. The distinction between sense and reference resolves the puzzle, since on Frege's view the *meanings* of 'Hesperus' and 'Phosphorus' are not the same. And so we can explain why we cannot know (2) *a priori*.

Kripke has already spent some time, earlier on in the lecture, arguing against theories which hold we can identify the meaning of a proper name with some description (such as 'the celestial body visible in the night sky...'). One standard problem with such views is that if we say that the meaning of some proper name N is something of the form 'the object that satisfies such-and-such description', it turns out to be analytically true that the bearer of the name N does, in fact, satisfy that description. And that in itself creates a new puzzle. For example, if we say that the meaning of 'Socrates' is 'the snub-nosed Greek philosopher who taught Plato', then it turns out to be analytically or necessarily true that Socrates had a snub-nose and taught Plato. But it follows from this that Socrates *could not have failed* to have a snub-nose or be the teacher of Plato. And that seems wrong. Surely we it *could* have been the case that Socrates never met Plato – which is to say that it is merely a contingent fact about Socrates that he taught Plato. In possible-worlds-speak, surely there is a possible world in which Socrates dies in infancy, or Plato's family move far away from Athens before Plato is born and he never gets to meet Socrates, or whatever.

Kripke will eventually argue that something like the view that generates Frege's Puzzle is in fact correct: the meaning of a proper name is simply the object to which the name refers. But the important point for present purposes is that Kripke claims a connection between (a) the view that 'the way we refer to things' (that is, our use of proper names) is 'by a description' (since the meaning of proper names is given by some description of the object referred to), and (b) the view that whether an object has a particular property necessarily or contingently 'depends on the way it's described'.

1. Kripke gives a couple of examples, in the same paragraph as $\boxed{a}\mapsto$, of cases where one might argue that something's having a particular property necessarily or contingently depends on how it is described. Think of your own example.

Kripke argues next (around $\boxed{b}\mapsto$) that the idea that a property can meaningfully be held to be an accidental or an essential property of an object is 'a notion' which has 'intuitive content'. And at $\boxed{c}\mapsto$ he imagines an exchange between two people arguing about whether Nixon might have lost the election.

2. Kripke says that it is the second person in the exchange who is being 'the philosopher, the unintuitive man'. Explain in your own words what his point is here and why the imaginary exchange is supposed to demonstrate it.

At $\boxed{d}\mapsto$, Kripke describes how the first person in the exchange might respond to the second person's claim, and in so doing he gives us a glimpse of his own positive view. Descriptions, Kripke thinks, can in principle apply to different objects in different possible worlds. To take a more recent example, the description 'the winner of the 2005 UK General Election' might refer to Tony Blair in the actual world, but to Michael Howard in some other possible world, and to Charles Kennedy in some other possible world again, and to Michael Portillo in still another possible world, and so on. A name, on the other hand – 'Tony Blair' or 'Michael Howard' – refers to *the same object in every possible world*. To use an expression Kripke will later introduce, names are 'rigid designators'.

3. (i) If the first person's response, at $\boxed{d}\mapsto$, is correct, what implications does it have for the claim that proper names have meanings that can be characterised as descriptions of the object named? (ii) Given that Kripke's own positive view accords with the view expressed by the first person in the exchange, what virtue is he implicitly claiming for his own view?

Kripke next, from $\boxed{e}\mapsto$, describes one reason why one might think 'the notion of accidental property unintuitive' – that is, why one might want to hold that whether a property of an object is 'accidental' or 'essential' is relative to how the object is described; which is to say, in effect, that there is not really any such thing as *de re* modality.

The reason he gives is that in order to make sense of the question, 'which properties does Nixon have essentially, and which accidentally?', we have to be able to 'look' at some other possible world and work out which person (if any) in that world is Nixon. For example we might find someone born on the same day at the same time but who goes on to be a school teacher rather than the President of the USA. And, in the same possible world, we might find someone who becomes President at the same time as the actual Nixon, but who is a bit shorter and went to a different school. In order to be able to say whether or not a given property is an essential or an accidental property of Nixon, it looks like we *first* have to be able to work out which of these two people in the possible world just described *is Nixon*. For only then will we be able to work out which properties Nixon has in all possible worlds (in which he exists), and which properties he has in some possible worlds but lacks in others.

Kripke points out at $\boxed{f}\mapsto$ that identity criteria which do not 'beg the question' are very rare – even if we only restrict ourselves to the actual world. Personal identity, the topic of chapter 1 above, is a good example: there is very little agreement amongst philosophers about what the criteria are for personal identity across time. Even if we solved *that* problem, for example by defining personal identity in terms of psychological continuity, we would still be a long way off having criteria for personal identity across possible worlds. Knowing that what makes Nixon-at-time-1 the same person as Nixon-at-time-2 is the fact that the second is psychologically continuous with the first doesn't seem to help us at all with the question whether Nixon-in-world-1 is the same person as Nixon-in-world-2, given that manifestly Nixon-in-world-2 cannot be psychologically continuous with Nixon-in-world-1 (because, for one thing, there can be no causal relations between the two). In view of all this, one might be inclined to abandon the view that essential and accidental properties are genuine *properties* of things at all, as opposed to merely artefacts of the way an object is described. For the legitimacy of that belief apparently depends upon the prior belief that there are transworld identity criteria to be had – and that prior belief is now looking decidedly fishy.

However, according to Kripke, this kind of worry about identity across possible worlds – the kind of worry which, he thinks, might lead one to reject *de re* modality – 'depends on the wrong way of looking at what a possible world is. One thinks, in this picture, of a possible world as if it were like a foreign country' ($\boxed{g} \mapsto$). He spends the next couple of pages (up to $\boxed{1} \mapsto$) explaining what exactly is wrong with it, and how we *should* think of 'what a possible world is'. His own position is summed up in the sentence: ' "Possible worlds" are *stipulated*, not *discovered* by powerful telescopes' ($\boxed{h} \mapsto$); and the view he is attacking – a view of which he says Lewis's counterpart theory is a 'very explicit and blatant example' ($\boxed{j} \mapsto$) – is summed up at $\boxed{i} \mapsto$ as: 'every possible world has to be described in a purely qualitative way'.

What exactly does Kripke's positive position – the claim that possible worlds are stipulated rather than discovered – amount to, and how does it differ from the view he denies? Well, the idea is something like this. Suppose we specify the nature of a given possible world by listing all the sentences that are true at that world. The list might include a lot of sentences about someone with such-and-such characteristics who is called 'Richard Nixon', who won the US presidential election in 1968 but lost the 1972 election. Or it might include a lot of sentences about someone with slightly (or very) different characteristics who was re-elected in 1972 and resigned in 1974; or about someone with different characteristics again who was re-elected in 1972 and did not resign.

Now, if we specify the characteristics of other possible worlds in something like this way, it seems that it is an open question – a question we have to figure out the answer to – whether any or all of the people just described *are* Nixon – that is, are the person who, in fact, we call 'Nixon'. This is the kind of position Kripke is opposed to.

Kripke's own positive view is that we do not (and should not) *start* with this kind of 'purely qualitative' description of some possible world, and then try to 'discover' which person (if any) in that possible world is Nixon. Rather, when we say something like 'Nixon might have lost the 1968 election', we *stipulate* that there is a possible world in which Nixon himself – the very man who in fact won that election – loses the 1968 election. As Kripke puts it, it is 'part of the *description* of a possible world that it contains *Nixon* and . . . in that world *Nixon* didn't win the election'.

4. Why, on Kripke's view, would the fact that some possible world is accurately described by the sentence 'Someone called "Richard Nixon" lost the 1968 presidential election', or 'Someone with such-and-such properties lost the 1968 presidential election', *not* amount to its being the case that *Nixon* might have lost the election?

5. In this part of the text, between $\boxed{g}\mapsto$ and $\boxed{l}\mapsto$, is Kripke merely stating his view, and how it differs from the alternative view, or is he attempting to provide us with reasons to think that his view is correct and alternative views (e.g. Lewis's) false? If the latter, exactly what reasons is he purporting to provide?

You may have noticed that the view Kripke has been attacking does not – despite the fact that Kripke attributes it to Lewis – actually resemble Lewis's view very closely, since Lewis denies that Nixon himself exists in any possible world apart from the actual world. What exist in other possible worlds are *counterparts* of Nixon. Kripke notes this in a footnote, at $\boxed{k}\mapsto$. But, he says, the basic issue is still more or less the same, since Lewis stills supposes that 'other possible worlds . . . can be given only by purely qualitative descriptions'. The only real difference is that for someone who makes this supposition but believes in genuine identity across possible worlds, *identity* across worlds must be established 'in terms of qualitative resemblance', while for Lewis it is the counterpart relation that must be so established.

In this footnote, Kripke also raises a different objection to Lewis's counterpart theory, sometimes called the 'objection from concern', from which he concludes that Lewis's view is 'even more bizarre than the usual notions of transworld identification that it replaces'.

6. Describe this objection in your own words, giving your own example instead of the Humphrey example. How persuasive do you think it is? Can you think of any responses that are available to Lewis?

Next, from $\boxed{l}\mapsto$, Kripke considers a possible objection – an objection according to which there is not in fact any real difference between the view Kripke is advancing and the view he is denying. The gist of the objection is this. Suppose we ask whether Nixon could have lacked property *P.* Then we are asking whether *P* is an essential property of Nixon or not. (If Nixon could have lacked *P,* then *P* is an accidental property of Nixon, and if Nixon could not have lacked *P,* then *P* is an essential property of him.) But that question is really equivalent to the question of whether or not the identity criteria across possible worlds for Nixon include property *P.* (If they do include *P,* then Nixon could not have lacked the property, since anything lacking *P* would fail to meet the criteria for being Nixon. If they don't include *P,* then Nixon could have lacked the property, since *P* is not one of the criteria for being Nixon.)

Kripke's response, at $\boxed{m}\mapsto$, is to point out that when we ask whether Nixon might have lacked a certain property *P,* we are only asking about the *necessary* conditions for something's being Nixon; we are not asking anything about the *sufficient* conditions for something's being Nixon.

We need to get clear about the difference between necessary and sufficient conditions, and their connection with identity criteria, before we can understand this response. Suppose, for example, we claim that it is a *necessary* condition for some object *o* being Nixon that *o* is a human being. In that case, we are claiming that nothing non-human could possibly be *Nixon*. But being human is clearly not a sufficient condition for being Nixon – otherwise we, and all human inhabitants of all possible worlds, would all be Nixon, which we are not. A set of *sufficient* conditions for being Nixon would have to be a set of conditions such that, if an object *o* meets those conditions, it is guaranteed to be Nixon.

When we provide identity criteria for an object, we give a set of necessary *and* sufficient conditions. If we say that conditions *A*, *B*, *C* and *D* are necessary and sufficient conditions for Nixon (that is, *A*, *B*, *C* and *D* constitute the identity criteria for Nixon), then we are saying that *if* something meets all four conditions, then that thing is Nixon; and if it *lacks* any of the four conditions, then it is *not* Nixon.

Kripke's point, then, is this. Suppose we ask whether some person at another possible world who lacks property *P* is Nixon – and hence whether Nixon might have lacked *P*. Then we are asking whether *P* is a *necessary* condition of being Nixon. We can answer that question without having any idea how to spell out what the ('purely qualitative') *sufficient* conditions of being Nixon are, or even without there *being* any set of such sufficient conditions. Hence what we need in order to answer the question, of whether or not Nixon might have lacked *P*, falls a long way short of what we would need in order to provide identity criteria for Nixon. So the two questions – the question about whether Nixon might have lacked *P* and the question about Nixon's identity criteria – are not equivalent, contrary to what is claimed by the objection.

It's worth stepping back for a moment to see what, exactly, has been going on overall in the text. Recall that Kripke starts out by considering the Quinean view that all modality is *de dicto* modality – that whether or not an object has a property essentially or accidentally depends on how that object is described. He then cites the problem of transworld identity as one reason why one might be inclined to adopt this Quinean position, and in effect says that the problem is the result of having a mistaken conception of what possible worlds are and how we 'find out' about them. But by this stage he no longer seems to be addressing the Quinean, but rather the kind of philosopher (Lewis, for example) who *does* believe in *de re* modality.

What, then, is Kripke up to? We take it that it's something like this. There are three broad ways in which one might respond to the problem of transworld identity. One is to accept that it is a genuine problem, to think that there is no sensible way of solving it, and thus to repudiate *de re* modality. This would be the Quinean position. The second is to accept that it is a genuine problem, but to think that it can be solved, and thus to retain belief in *de re* modality. Lewis would be one philosopher who falls into this category. The third response is Kripke's – to think that the 'problem' is an artefact of a mistaken conception of the nature of possible worlds. Thus, since there is no problem of transworld identity, there is no need to repudiate *de re* modality.

7. State, as succinctly as you can, Kripke's reasons for holding that the third response is preferable to either of the other responses.

8. Thinking about why Lewis introduced counterpart theory in the first place, do you think Kripke is right to think that there is no genuine problem of transworld identity? What sort of view of the metaphysics of possible worlds do you think it is possible to attribute to Kripke, given what he says in the text? (For example, might he be a realist in Lewis's sense about possible worlds? Might he be an ersatzist?)

Further Reading

An excellent introductory textbook on modality is Melia 2003; you might also try Nolan 2005, ch. 3, for a discussion of Lewis. Divers 2002 provides a much more extensive discussion of possible worlds.

Loux 1979 contains many of the central texts, together with a long and very helpful Introduction. Some of the early moves in the debate are to be found in the articles reproduced in Linsky 1971, though they tend to be rather technical. Lewis 1986 is the definitive statement of modal realism, and much of it is quite accessible, especially the early stages of chapter 1 and also chapter 2 (which responds to some standard objections to Lewis's view). Kripke, of course, also has much more to say than is reproduced above; his 1980 is well worth reading from cover to cover. An influential, and again accessible, article is Rosen 1990. Rosen argues that we can salvage what is important and useful in Lewis's modal realism without actually believing in possible worlds, by adopting a position he calls 'modal fictionalism'.

Essay Questions

1. Should we take the claim that there are many ways the world might have been at face value? If not, how *should* we take it? And if so, is the claim true or false?

2. Does Lewis satisfactorily solve the problem of transworld identity?

3. Is the problem of transworld identity a genuine problem?

4. To what extent is Lewis's modal realism a systematization of our pre-existing modal opinions?

5. Is there such a thing as *de re* modality, or is there only modality *de dicto*?

6

Persistence over Time

Introduction

Endurance and perdurance: two accounts of persistence

In this, the final chapter of this book, we shall be considering the following question: what is it for everyday objects – the entities we unreflectively class as *things* – to persist over time? People, planets and pillar boxes come into existence at a time, go out of existence at a later time, and exist at all the times between. Eleanor, for example, came in to being in 1994 and has enjoyed unbroken existence ever since. What we want to know is what such persistence consists in. Here we have a complementary question to that which we considered in chapter 1. When thinking about the nature of personal identity, we asked what it was for X (at a time) to be the same person as Y (at a later time). In putting the question in this way, we presupposed that persons can genuinely persist over time: our interest was solely in coming up with a defensible account of the differences between X and Y that can be tolerated before we have to say that Y is not the same person as X. Now is the time to ask about the very nature of persistence.

At this point, however, one might be tempted to protest at the prospect of spending a whole chapter on such a question: not because the issue seems abstruse or recondite (as, perhaps, did philosophers' concern with the existence and nature of possible worlds), but because the answer might seem to be blindingly obvious. One is tempted to insist that Eleanor persists by virtue of existing at every moment from the moment she is born until the exact time at which she dies. But what exactly is it for Eleanor to *exist at* each moment of her life? It is now that the 'blindingly obvious' answer to our question becomes explicitly philosophical. For the thought lurking behind this answer is surely this: Eleanor persists over time by persisting *through* it. In other words, for Eleanor to exist at each moment of her life is for her to be *wholly* present at each moment of her life. Time, on this view, is not something that Eleanor is *spread out* in; she is not *extended* in time as she is in space. This is why we can be said to see Eleanor *in her entirety*, and not merely a part of her, at any moment at which we see her.

With a view to shedding further light on this natural account of how Eleanor persists, we may contrast the persistence of things with the persistence of events and processes. Events are things that happen: things such as the 1975 FA Cup Final and the resignation of Margaret Thatcher. Processes are sequences of successive events: things such as the Industrial Revolution or a particular caterpillar's metamorphosis into a butterfly. Now, when it comes to both events and processes, it is (near enough) undeniable that they persist over time in a very different way from the way in which we have presumed Eleanor to. For events such as the 1975 FA Cup Final precisely *are extended* in time. The 1975 Cup Final was not *wholly* present at each moment from its start to its finish. It was not the case, for example, that at the kick-off *the whole match* was then present to our senses. Witnessing the whole match required one to be present for (at least) 90 minutes. The match was spread out in time in an analogous way to the way in which Eleanor is spread out in space.

To put the point in another way, events and processes have *temporal parts*: the playing of the 1975 Cup Final had a first and a second half and can be divided further in time; likewise, the Industrial Revolution can be similarly broken down into early and late stages. When it comes to the nature of persistence, the key point would seem to be this: that the way in which an item persists is determined by whether it has temporal parts or not. Events and processes – items with temporal parts – persist by *perduring*, that is, by having different temporal parts at the times at which they – the perduring entities – exist. Events and processes are rather like *parades*: parts successively show up, one after another. (Lewis introduces this comparison at $\boxed{b} \mapsto$ in second Lewis text featuring in this chapter, 'Tensing the Copula'.). According to our intuitive view of the persistence of *things*, however, such things do not persist in this way. Such things are not spread out in time – they do not have temporal parts – and so they can only persist by *enduring*: that is, by being wholly present – and not merely present in part – at each time at which they exist.

The crucial point, then, is that our natural – one might say 'pre-philosophical' – account of the nature of persistence is disjunctive in nature. According to this folk theory, while events and processes have temporal parts, the items we tend to call 'things' – but which we will now term 'continuants' – do not. Events and processes persist by being *spread out in time*; continuants persist by being *wholly present through time*.

Perdurantism about continuants

So much for our pre-philosophical theory of persistence. But you know by now that philosophers delight in exploring regions of conceptual space that are off the beaten track. The philosopher's aim is not simply to describe how we commonly think about the phenomena under study, but to consider whether there are alternative ways of thinking that might, in fact, turn out to make better sense. (Just think about David Lewis's position on possible worlds.) Given that this is so, the discussion of the previous section should have made it apparent that there is available a position according to which the persistence of continuants is of the same kind as that of events and processes: a view that takes people, planets and pillar boxes to be *perduring* entities. Indeed, this is precisely the position that Lewis defends in the two extracts from his work that we shall be looking at presently.

What does perdurantism about continuants look like? The key idea is that a continuant's occupancy of time is analogous to its occupancy of space. Continuants, it is argued, are extended in time as well as in space: they have temporal parts in addition to spatial parts. While our disjunctive, pre-philosophical view of persistence takes only events and processes to be spread out in time, the perdurantist in this respect assimilates continuants to events and processes. Indeed, the perdurantist has it that Eleanor is much like the process that is *her life*. Eleanor's life comprises the totality of its temporal parts (which include her whole life as an 'improper part' of itself). In just the same way, the perdurantist claims, Eleanor herself is divisible in time so that it is literally true that she – the person – has a distinct part at every instant at which she exists. These parts themselves are parts of larger parts (such as her first two years of existence), but the crucial claim is that Eleanor does not merely have spatial parts; she has temporal parts too. She is extended in time as well as in space. Her persistence over time is a matter of her having distinct temporal parts at a succession of times. While Eleanor's temporal parts go out of existence as the times by which they are individuated pass, Eleanor continues to exist by virtue of these temporal parts being parts of *her*.

A further analogy, together with one of the view's consequences, should help you to get a firmer grip on the theory. First, the analogy. According to the card-carrying perdurantist, a person's journey through time is like a road's journey through space (Sider 2001: 2–3). Think of the dimension along which the road travels as time; think of a perpendicular axis across the road as space. Slices cut the long way – from one end of the road to the other – are akin to a continuant's spatial parts; slices cut across the road – from one side of the road to the other – are akin to a continuant's temporal parts. So, for example, rather like the way in which the part of the Fulham Palace Road beside Bishop's Park is just one part of the road, the part of Eleanor existent in 2006 is a mere part of her. And what this means for the perdurantist, to press the analogy further, is that a change in a continuant will be akin to a change in a road. As the Fulham Palace Road changes from being straight to being curved by virtue of having successive straight and curved stretches, so Eleanor changes over time from being in bed to eating her breakfast by virtue of having a temporal part that is in bed and having a later temporal part that is at the breakfast table. (In fact, as we shall see, one of Lewis's arguments for perdurantism about continuants is that this account of change is markedly superior to what the endurantist has to say on this subject.)

Now for the consequence. If, as the perdurantist supposes, continuants have temporal parts as well as spatial parts, then there are *two* reasons why, if you were to shake Eleanor's hand, you would only directly touch a part of her. One reason we are familiar with: the item directly touched – her hand – is just one of her spatial parts; in touching Eleanor's hand, one touches the whole person only in an indirect, derivative sense. But if perdurantism is correct, and if a continuant's occupancy of time is analogous to its occupancy of space, there is an additional reason why shaking Eleanor's hand would only be to touch directly a part of her. For Eleanor, according to the perdurantist, is an aggregate of *temporal* parts, and hence it is not the case that the whole person is present at that time to be touched. As Theodore Sider puts it, '[t]o touch all of a person you must hold him in an interpenetrating embrace from his birth until his death; only thus would you have access to all his past and future temporal parts' (Sider 2001: 3).

Pointing out this consequence presents you with a vivid picture of the perdurantist's thesis. You might think such a consequence, and the picture it illuminates, strange. But as you will have noted already in our discussion of possible worlds, an incredulous stare is by no means a reason for rejecting a philosophical thesis. Indeed, as we shall see in the remainder of this introduction, perdurantists take themselves to have sound motivation for their position.

Why be a perdurantist about continuants?

So what is to be said for the thesis that continuants have temporal parts? At this point, an endurantist might go on the offensive, supplementing her incredulous stare with an appeal to ordinary language. She might argue, for example, that our ordinary thought and talk merely reinforces the disjunctive pre-philosophical account of persistence that we met with in the first section of this introduction. For the way in which we describe events and processes on the one hand, and continuants on the other, would seem to suggest that they fall into disparate ontological categories. Compare, for example, Eleanor (the continuant) with Eleanor's life (the process). Eleanor's life *began* and will *end*, but Eleanor herself *came into* and will *go out of* existence. Eleanor's life will *last* from one time to another, but Eleanor herself does not *last*: she *exists at* various times. Eleanor's life has a *length*, but Eleanor herself has an *age*. Furthermore – and here is the most forceful linguistic evidence that we regard processes as perdurants but continuants as endurants – we straightforwardly ascribe temporal parts to processes but not to continuants. We quite happily divide Eleanor's life into temporal parts: we might say, for example, that the *first half* of her life was blissful but that its second half consisted of long periods of gloom punctuated by brief moments of ecstasy. We say no such thing about the person whose life this is: we do not describe Eleanor as having a first half or of consisting of periods of time. Our language, then, seems to enshrine the thesis that continuants, unlike events and processes, persist by genuinely enduring.

At this point, however, the perdurantist may reply by sharply distinguishing between common-or-garden talk about persistence and metaphysical enquiry into what persistence consists in (Sider 2001: 211–12). Perdurantism, it will be claimed, is not a thesis concerning how we tend to think and speak about continuants; it is a metaphysical doctrine concerning their nature. Consequently, the fact that perdurantism conflicts with our pre-philosophical talk about continuants should not count against it, so long as it offers the best available solutions to the philosophical problems that an account of persistence should solve. And this it does, according to the perdurantist. Perhaps the chief motivation for adopting perdurantism about continuants is that it elegantly enables us to solve puzzles concerning identity over time. One such puzzle – the puzzle of how an object can persist through change – is the focus of this chapter, and it is Lewis's contention (in both extracts from his hugely influential work in this area) that the most satisfying solution to this puzzle requires us to accept perdurantism.

So what is the puzzle, and what is the nature of the perdurantist's solution to it? The puzzle itself is easily stated and has become known as *the problem of temporary intrinsics*. (It is also known sometimes as *the problem of change*.) Objects persist through changes in their intrinsic properties: that is, in properties – such as *having a bent shape* and *having a straight shape* – that objects have purely in virtue of how *they* are, independently of any other object. So, for example, if Eleanor at time t is sitting down and then at $t + 1$ stands up, she persists through the change from having a bent shape to having a straight shape. Now for the puzzle. For Eleanor to persist through this change, she would seem to have to somehow instantiate *incompatible* properties: that is, be both bent and straight. But nothing can be both bent and straight, so it is mysterious how such an intrinsic change can occur. To put the problem another way, Leibniz's Law – *the indiscernibility of identicals* – states that if a and b are identical, then a and b have all the same properties. And this law would seem to be correct. If, for instance, Eleanor has brown hair and Holly has blonde hair, then we may justifiably conclude that Eleanor and Holly are not one and the same: any difference in properties had by Eleanor and Holly entails that Eleanor and Holly are not identical. The problem, of course, is that analogous reasoning would seem to apply to our case of everyday persistence through time: Eleanor cannot be said to survive getting up because Eleanor-sitting and Eleanor-standing have different properties, and hence must be different entities. It would seem to be impossible for a single thing to survive this change.

Such a consequence – that no object can persist through change in its intrinsic properties – is extremely counter-intuitive. And it is at this point that perdurantism can come to the rescue. According to the perdurantist, the correctness of Leibniz's Law does, indeed, entail that the thing that has a bent shape is a distinct thing from the thing that has a straight shape; but the twist is that this is said to be compatible with taking Eleanor to survive the change her getting up brings about. Let us see how the trick is pulled off.

The perdurantist's main claim, of course, is that Eleanor is the sum of her temporal parts. So, as we have mentioned already, it is *Eleanor-at-t* – a temporal part of Eleanor – that has a bent shape, while it is *Eleanor-at-t* $+$ 1 – another temporal part of Eleanor – that has the property of being straight. True enough, this entails that Eleanor-at-t does not survive Eleanor's getting up, but the crucial point is that *Eleanor herself does*; for Eleanor is neither *Eleanor-at-t* nor *Eleanor-at-t* $+$ 1, but the sum of her temporal parts, *Eleanor-at-t* and *Eleanor-at-t* $+$ 1 included. Given that this is so, Eleanor survives her getting up – that is, persists though an intrinsic change – by virtue of having intrinsically different temporal parts. In short, then, the puzzle evaporates for two reasons: because the incompatible properties are possessed by different temporal parts of Eleanor, thereby avoiding contradiction and upholding Leibniz's Law; and because, as a result, such an account allows for the fact that Eleanor genuinely persists through change in her intrinsic properties.

Temporary intrinsics and nominalism

As we have just explained, Lewis claims that a continuant's intrinsically changing over time consists in its having successive temporal parts that differ in their intrinsic properties. But at this point, if you have read chapter 4, you might wonder whether the issue in question – namely, how it can be possible for an object to change with respect to its intrinsic properties – presupposes the truth of realism concerning properties. Surely, one might ask, a nominalist such as Devitt – someone who denies that there are such things as properties – will simply declare the topic of the present chapter to be non-issue? There *are* no properties, so there is no problem about how something can come to lack, or gain, properties over time.

In fact, to take this line would be a mistake. Indeed, Lewis himself is a nominalist, as he hints in his discussion of Bradley's regress (from $\boxed{\text{i}}\!\!\mapsto$ in the extract from 'Tensing the Copula'). The crucial point is this: even a nominalist must accept that something may at first have a straight shape and at a later time become bent in shape; so even a philosopher such as Devitt, while he denies that our property-talk is ontologically committal, must acknowledge that Leibniz's Law and the phenomenon of intrinsic change have to be reconciled. The problem does not somehow evaporate if nominalism is assumed.

The extracts

The three extracts you will now read nicely set out the problem of temporary intrinsics and the various ways in which philosophers have tried to solve it. The first extract, a few pages from David Lewis's *On The Plurality of Worlds*, concisely explains the problem, sets out what he takes to be the available solutions, and then swiftly explains why he takes the perdurantist option. Sally Haslanger's brief article is largely a response to Lewis, arguing that there is a variety of endurantism that evades his objections. Finally, in his 'Tensing the Copula', Lewis replies to Haslanger.

David Lewis, extract from
On the Plurality of Worlds

Our question of overlap of worlds parallels the this-worldly problem of identity through time; and our problem of accidental intrinsics parallels a problem of temporary intrinsics, which is the traditional problem of change.[1] Let us say that something *persists* iff, somehow or other, it exists at various times; this is the neutral word. Something *perdures* iff it persists by having different temporal parts, or stages, at different times, though no one part of it is wholly present at more than one time; whereas it *endures* iff it persists by being wholly present at more than one time. Perdurance corresponds to the way a road persists through space; part of it is here and part of it is there, and no part is wholly present at two different places. Endurance corresponds to the way a universal, if there are such things, would be wholly present wherever and whenever it is instantiated. Endurance involves overlap: the content of two different times has the enduring thing as a common part. Perdurance does not.

(There might be mixed cases: entities that persist by having an enduring part and a perduring part. An example might be a person who consisted of an enduring entelechy ruling a perduring body; or an electron that had a universal of unit negative charge as a permanent part, but did not consist entirely of universals. But here I ignore the mixed cases. And when I speak of ordinary things as perduring, I shall ignore their enduring universals, if such there be.)

Discussions of endurance versus perdurance tend to be endarkened by people who say such things as this: 'Of course you are wholly present at every moment of your life, except in case of amputation. For at every moment all your parts are there: your legs, your lips, your liver. . . .' These endarkeners may think themselves partisans of endurance, but they are not. They are perforce neutral, because they lack the conceptual resources to understand what is at issue. Their speech betrays – and they may acknowledge it willingly – that they have no concept of a temporal part. (Or at any rate none that applies to a person, say, as opposed to a process or a stretch of time.) Therefore they are on neither side of a dispute about whether or not persisting things are divisible into temporal parts. They understand neither the affirmation nor the denial. They are like the people – fictional, I hope – who say that the whole of the long road is in their little village, for not one single lane of it is missing. Meaning less than others do by 'part', since they omit parts cut crosswise, they also mean less than others do by 'whole'. They say the 'whole' road is in the village; by which they mean that every 'part' is; but by that, they only mean that every part cut lengthwise is. Divide the road into its least lengthwise parts; they cannot even raise the question whether those are in the village wholly or only partly. For that is a question about crosswise parts, and the concept of a crosswise part is what they lack. Perhaps 'crosswise part' really does sound to them like a blatant contradiction. Or perhaps it seems to them that they understand it, but the village philosophers have persuaded them that really they couldn't, so their

---

[1] My discussion of this parallel problem is much indebted to Armstrong, 'Identity Through Time' (1980), and to Johnston (see e.g. 1984). I follow Johnston in terminology.

impression to the contrary must be an illusion. At any rate, *I* have the concept of a temporal part; and for some while I shall be addressing only those of you who share it.[5]

Endurance through time is analogous to the alleged trans-world identity of common parts of overlapping worlds; perdurance through time is analogous to the 'trans-world identity', if we may call it that, of a trans-world individual composed of distinct parts in non-overlapping worlds. Perdurance, which I favour for the temporal case, is closer to the counterpart theory which I favour for the modal case; the difference is that counterpart theory concentrates on the parts and ignores the trans-world individual composed of them.

 The principal and decisive objection against endurance, as an account of the persistence of ordinary things such as people or puddles, is the problem of temporary intrinsics. Persisting things change their intrinsic properties. For instance shape: when I sit, I have a bent shape; when I stand, I have a straightened shape. Both shapes are temporary intrinsic properties; I have them only some of the time. How is such change possible? I know of only three solutions.

(It is *not* a solution just to say how very commonplace and indubitable it is that we have different shapes at different times. To say that is only to insist – rightly – that it must be possible somehow. Still less is it a solution to say it in jargon – as it might be, that bent-on-Monday and straight-on-Tuesday are compatible because they are 'time-indexed properties' – if that just means that, somehow, you can be bent on Monday and straight on Tuesday.)

First solution: contrary to what we might think, shapes are not genuine intrinsic properties. They are disguised relations, which an enduring thing may bear to times. One and the same enduring thing may bear the bent-shape relation to some times, and the straight-shape relation to others. In itself, considered apart from its relations to other things, it has no shape at all. And likewise for all other seeming temporary intrinsics; all of them must be reinterpreted as relations that something with an absolutely unchanging intrinsic nature bears to different times. The solution to the problem of temporary intrinsics is that there aren't any temporary intrinsics. This is simply incredible, if we are speaking of the persistence of ordinary things. (It might do for the endurance of entelechies or universals.) If we know what shape is, we know that it is a property, not a relation.

Second solution: the only intrinsic properties of a thing are those it has at the present moment. Other times are like false stories; they are abstract representations, composed out of the materials of the present, which represent or misrepresent the way things are. When something has different intrinsic properties according to one of these ersatz other times, that does

---

[5]   I attempt to explain it to others in *Philosophical Papers*, volume I, pages 76–7. But I have no great hopes, since any competent philosopher who does not understand something will take care not to understand anything else whereby it might be explained.

not mean that it, or any part of it, or anything else, just *has* them – no more so than when a man is crooked according to the *Times*, or honest according to the *News*. This is a solution that rejects endurance; because it rejects persistence altogether. And it is even less credible than the first solution. In saying that there are no other times, as opposed to false representations thereof, it goes against what we all believe. No man, unless it be at the moment of his execution, believes that he has no future; still less does anyone believe that he has no past.

Third solution: the different shapes, and the different temporary intrinsics generally, belong to different things. Endurance is to be rejected in favour of perdurance. We perdure; we are made up of temporal parts, and our temporary intrinsics are properties of these parts, wherein they differ one from another. There is no problem at all about how different things can differ in their intrinsic properties.

Commentary on Lewis

In this short passage from a book in which he argues for the robust variety of modal realism we encountered in chapter 5, David Lewis neatly introduces the problem of temporary intrinsics and then sets out three possible solutions to it. In a delightfully insouciant move, he claims that the third solution – the adoption of the apparently counter-intuitive perdurantist picture set out in the final section of the Introduction to this chapter – turns out be the view *least* disruptive of our intuitions.

The extract begins, at $\boxed{a} \mapsto$, with Lewis introducing the distinction between endurance and perdurance: something *perdures* just in case it persists by having different temporal parts at different times, while something *endures* just in case it persists by being wholly present – that is, not merely present in part – at more than one time.

Having introduced the two conceptions of persistence, Lewis, at $\boxed{b} \mapsto$, then goes on to tackle those who insist that no sense can be made of the claim that continuants persist by perduring.

> 1. (i) Explain in your own words the analogy Lewis draws (in the paragraph from $\boxed{b} \mapsto$) between philosophers who profess not to understand perdurantism and the people who say that the whole of a long road is in their little village. (ii) Has Lewis succeeded in demonstrating that perdurantism about continuants makes sense?

Having taken himself to have shown that perdurantism at least makes sense, Lewis sets out the problem of temporary intrinsics at $\boxed{c} \mapsto$. But at $\boxed{d} \mapsto$, before going on to outline three possible solutions to the problem, he dismisses the claims of two potential objectors. The first objector aims to demonstrate that the problem is not real, claiming that no problem is presented by Eleanor's being bent at t and yet straight at $t + 1$, since she has these incompatible properties *at different times*. The second objector claims that a simple solution to the problem is available: namely, that we should deny that there are any genuinely incompatible properties by 'indexing' properties to times.

2. (i) Explain Lewis's replies to the two objectors introduced at $\boxed{d}$→. (ii) Is the speed with which he rejects them justified?

This brings us to the three serious possible solutions to the problem, which Lewis pithily lays out in the three paragraphs from $\boxed{e}$→. The first option, Lewis explains, is to stick with our endurantist intuitions but to deny that the apparently incompatible properties are really incompatible. This is achieved by taking the temporary intrinsic properties to be disguised relations to times. On this view, there is no such property as *having a bent shape*; rather, for Eleanor to have a bent shape at *t* is for her to have the relational property of *having-a-bent-shape-at-t*. (To see what Lewis is getting at here, consider the property of *being taller than Julian*: this is a property all right, but it is a relational property, a property that something has just in case it stands in a certain relation to Julian. The endurantist who takes intrinsic properties to be disguised relational properties thinks of all properties as similarly relational, but relational to *times*. Something has the property of *having-a-bent-shape-at-t* just in case it stands in a certain relation to *t*.)

With this move having been made, it becomes clear that Eleanor is no longer presumed to have the incompatible properties of bentness and straightness at *t* and *t* + 1 respectively: a position which, given Leibniz's Law, would force us to conclude that Eleanor-at-*t* and Eleanor-at-*t* + 1 are different entities. Rather, the point is that Eleanor has, unchangingly, two relational (that is, extrinsic) properties that are quite compatible: *having-a-bent-shape-at-t* and *having-a-straight-shape-at-t* + 1. As a result, Eleanor-at-*t* and Eleanor-at-*t* + 1 share exactly the same (relational) properties, and so we are under no pressure to think that there are two distinct objects with different properties involved. And what this means is that Eleanor *can* genuinely persist through the intrinsic change from having a bent shape to having a straight shape.

3. Lewis's objection to this endurantist solution is that it takes shapes to be disguised relations, and thus ends up committed to the implausible thesis that shapes are not intrinsic properties at all. As he himself puts it, '[i]f we know what shape is, we know that it is a property, not a relation [to a time]' ($\boxed{e}$→). Elsewhere, Lewis puts the point like this: the endurantist cannot allow for the obvious fact that objects are just 'plain straight', *i.e.* straight intrinsically, rather than by virtue of being related to a time (Lewis 1988: 66).

Here is an endurantist reply. 'It only *seems* as if we regard objects as 'plain straight' because our talk about them appears to lack temporal qualification. But when we say 'Eleanor is straight' we really mean that she is straight *now*: the temporal qualification, though implicit, is present. Given that this is so, why *should* we accept that things are *ever* "plain straight"?' (i) What do you think of this reply? (ii) How should Lewis respond to it?

The second solution is more radical. According to the position we may call *presentism*, only the present time is real, and hence the only things that exist are things that exist in the present. As a result, if *t* is the present time, then there is no incompatibility between the properties possessed by Eleanor for the simple reason that there is no time other than the present and, hence, no other time at which she differs from how she is now. Eleanor has a bent shape and that is that. No problem.

4. (i) Why does Lewis reject the presentist solution? (ii) Is he right to do so?

Finally, there is the perdurantist position that Lewis favours. As we saw in the Introduction, the idea is that the problem of change dissolves because the incompatible properties involved in Eleanor's change from being bent to being straight are had by different entities (that is, different temporal stages of her). When Eleanor stands up, the intrinsic change she undergoes consists in there being an intrinsic difference between two of her temporal parts. She persists through this intrinsic change by virtue of being an entity that has Eleanor-at-*t* and Eleanor-at-*t* + 1 as parts.

Lewis presents the endurantist solution as winning by default. The endurantist and presentist solutions are, he thinks, *so* counter-intuitive as to rule them out almost at once.

Sally Haslanger, 'Endurance and Temporary Intrinsics'

In a number of places David Lewis has argued that the problem of temporary intrinsics rules out the possibility that objects endure through change.[1] Lewis maintains that to account for temporary intrinsics we should say that objects do not endure through change, but rather perdure.[2] I disagree; Lewis's arguments do not demonstrate that an endurance theory cannot accommodate temporary intrinsics.

The problem of temporary intrinsics is this: ordinary objects persist through changes in their intrinsic properties, i.e. those properties which an object has in virtue of the way *it* is, independently of anything else. To use Lewis's example, 'when I sit I'm bent, when I stand, I'm straight'. But an object cannot have incompatible properties. So how is intrinsic change possible?

---

[1]   Most recently Lewis argues this in his 1988; and in [the Lewis extract immediately above].
[2]   I follow Lewis's terminology here; see [the Lewis extract above].

a⊢→   Lewis initially outlines three solutions to this problem, of which he favours the third. The first is the view that properties are really relations to times; the second is the view that only the present exists; the third is the doctrine of temporal parts. It is important to note that Lewis's solution, like the others he mentions, requires a trade off in our intuitions about intrinsic change. Although on his view it is true that there are persisting objects (the perdurers), and it is also true that properties such as shape are genuinely intrinsic (to the stages), there is nothing such that it persists through a change in *its* intrinsic properties. The intrinsic properties of the stages are not properties of the perdurer. The perdurer itself is not simply bent and then straight; if it were we'd be left with the original problem. The perdurer has properties which are significantly correlated with these, e.g. the property of having a part which is bent (and one which is straight), but these properties involve a relation between the perdurer and one of its momentary parts. Even if one were to hold that a perdurer's relations to its distinct parts are intrinsic (which is not obviously correct), at any rate such properties of the perdurer are not temporary. So what persists is not what has the relevant temporary intrinsic. Like the other 'solutions', Lewis must say that it is not possible for an object to persist through a change in *its* intrinsic properties. So why are we forced to make Lewis's compromise?

I have argued elsewhere for the importance of maintaining endurance in an account of change to accommodate the idea that the past (causally) constrains the present (see 1989b). If one is concerned to preserve endurance, there are at least two options which hold some appeal. The first is to bite the bullet and deny that there are temporary *intrinsics*, i.e. treat all
b⊢→   temporary properties as relational. I will not discuss this option here. The second is to develop what Lewis calls the 'adverbial' variant of the first alternative in such a way that it avoids the problems he indicates (see 1988, p. 65, fn. 1). I prefer this second option, and will sketch some ways to carry it out.

The intuitive idea behind the so-called 'adverbial' option is that objects have properties at times, and that time should modify this 'having', rather than the subject or the property. Lewis interprets this in terms of a commitment to a three-place instantiation relation which takes objects,
c⊢→   properties, and times as arguments. He rightly points out that this interpretation of the view still treats intrinsic properties as relational; and raises the further question, 'what does standing in some relation to straightness have to do with just plain being straight?' (in 1988, p. 66, fn. 1).

I think the right response here is to deny that the intuitions underlying the 'adverbial' account need commit one to the three-place instantiation relation. Along these lines, E. J. Lowe, in his response to Lewis, suggests that we
d⊢→   should take the account to claim that '*a*'s having a bent shape *obtains at t* while *a*'s having a straight shape *obtains at t'* (1988, p. 75). He also remarks that, 'a thing's *being shaped* itself stands in relation to times, not that a thing's

being shaped is partly a matter of *that thing's* standing in relations to times' (1988, p. 75).

In developing the idea that objects have properties at times, we may note that there are a variety of semantical options one might take in spelling out the role of temporal elements in propositions.[3] Reviewing a number of these semantical options facilitates a discussion of the ontological options suggested by the semantics. For the purposes of responding to Lewis, the endurance theorist may remain agnostic about which of the options is semantically superior; and at this point, the endurance theorist may even remain agnostic about the details of the ontology. The goal is simply to show that there are some ways of developing the idea that objects have properties at times without falling prey to Lewis's objections.

Lowe's comments suggest two ways to incorporate temporal elements into one's semantics: the first is to leave temporal elements out of propositions and instead to evaluate propositions with respect to times (just as one evaluates propositions with respect to worlds); the second is to include temporal elements in the proposition without incorporating them into the semantical value of the predicate (or the subject). Treating time as part of the circumstances of evaluation (as in the first suggestion) offers a temporalist view of propositions such that propositions can change truth-value from time to time; treating time as an additional constituent of the proposition (perhaps not explicit in the sentence expressing the proposition but determined via the context of utterance) offers eternalist propositions. On neither view is the property of the object construed as a relation to a time (though, of course, there may be some propositions which do concern a relation between a property and a time); and on neither view have we reified a distinct instantiation relation.[4]

One might complain, however, that none of the options I have indicated avoids commitment to a three-place instantiation relation which holds between an object, a property, and a time; so we have not been given a model which demonstrates how we might construe temporary predications without relying on such a relation. For example, consider the option of accepting temporal propositions which are evaluated with respect to times. On this view, the temporal proposition that Lewis is bent is true at some times and not others. We may note that given that at some time *t*, the proposition that Lewis is bent is true, there is a three-place relation between Lewis, bentness, and a time *t*, such that the proposition that Lewis is bent holds at *t*. In spite of the fact that this temporalist account does not employ a

---

[3] For simplicity, I am considering only simple propositions which contain no explicit temporal operators. The problems become much more complex when we consider sentences embedded within temporal (and other) operators and the function of temporal indexicals. See, e.g., Kaplan 1977, and Richard 1982.

[4] There are other options. See, e.g., Nathan Salmon's treatment of time as a component of the 'information value' of the predicate in an eternalist proposition in 1986, ch. 2.

primitive three-place instantiation relation, nevertheless, we may define an analogous three-place relation within the temporalist framework. Therefore, the commitment to such a relation remains.[5]

f⊢⟶ But does the recognition of this defined three-place instantiation relation demonstrate that we must construe the relation between an object and its properties as problematically relational? I think not. The danger of a three-place instantiation relation is that it invites us to treat objects as related to their properties as individuals are related to other individuals; this would be undesirable. But note that the three-place relation indicated above, viz., the relation between an object a, property F, and time t, such that the proposition that a is F holds at t, is a relation defined partly in terms of a more basic notion of a's being F, i.e., of an object instantiating its properties. Even if we grant that the three-place relation is an instantiation relation, the primary instantiation of the property F by the object a, need not be construed relationally. Lewis is bent by instantiating bentness, and this instantiation holds at some times and not others. The fact that we can further define a three-place relation between the object, the property, and the time, need not commit us to treating the basic notion of an object's instantiating its properties as relational. Thus, at least one of the options offers a genuine alternative that Lewis has not addressed. This response suggests a strategy which we might also employ in defending other options.

The question remains, however, whether any of these options make metaphysical sense. Lewis thinks that they don't; his worry is that a temporary predication (of whatever sort) does not adequately capture the connection between an object and its intrinsic properties. We can find the basis for his concern about the adverbial variants by considering his argument against the original proposal that properties are 'really' relations to times. He writes,

> Imagine trying to draw a picture of two different times t_1 when I sit, and t_2 when I stand. You draw two circles, overlapping because I exist at both times so you want to draw me in the intersection. But then you have to draw me bent and also straight, which you can't do; and if *per impossible* you could, you still wouldn't have done anything to connect the bentness to t_1 and the straightness to t_2 instead of vice versa. What to do? The first solution says to draw the circles overlapping, draw me in the intersection as a mere dot or shapeless blob, draw a line labelled 'bent-at' from me to the t_1 circle and a line labelled 'straight-at' to the t_2 circle. A queer way to draw a shape! (1988, p. 67)

Presumably, to capture the adverbial variant, Lewis would draw two circles overlapping; himself a dot or shapeless blob in the intersection. But this time, bentness and straightness would be abstract entities outside the circles,

---

5 I owe this objection to David Lewis.

and the picture would include two branched lines labelled 'instantiates at', one linking himself, bentness, and the t_1 circle, and the other linking himself, straightness, and the t_2 circle. Like the original picture, this is a 'queer way to draw a shape'.

The argument seems to be this: if the enduring thing has a particular shape, e.g. bent, then to say that *it* (the enduring thing) is straight results in contradiction. Instead, we must say that the shapeless thing has shape by being related to bentness or straightness (at times) – or alternatively is related to times by a 'bent-at' or 'straight at' relation. Given this model, we find ourselves committed to a modified substratum (modified because it may have some permanent intrinsics, and so needn't be a bare substratum), combined with a relational conception of temporary intrinsic predication. Such a relational conception of predication fails to treat the properties in question as genuinely intrinsic; e.g. standing in some relation to shape is not the same as being shaped.

There are three crucial premises in this argument. The first is that the enduring thing has no shape intrinsically; the second is that if the enduring thing has no shape intrinsically, then it has shapes by standing in some relation to them; the third is that a relational conception of having shape is unacceptable. I will focus on the first premiss.

On Lewis's view, there is some way that a temporal part can be shaped, e.g. bent, that is not available to an enduring thing. But why not? Why can't the endurance theorist simply insist that the enduring thing is bent in just the same way that the temporal part is bent, except that the enduring thing is not bent in this way throughout its existence? In other words, why must we represent the enduring object as 'a shapeless blob'?

Lewis suggests that if the enduring thing is bent at one time and straight at another, then it must have these shapes extrinsically and not intrinsically.[6] It is because shape is only extrinsic to the enduring thing that it is properly represented as 'shapeless'. But why must we say that temporary properties are extrinsic? Admittedly, if we say that the enduring thing is intrinsically both bent and straight, this results in contradiction. However, there is no contradiction in saying that it is intrinsically bent at one time and intrinsically straight at another. Moreover, if we take seriously the proposals mentioned above, we are fully entitled to make this claim; as we saw, one need not construe an object's having a property at a time either in terms of its standing in relation to a time, or in terms of its standing in a temporarily relativized instantiation relation to the property in question. To assume that an enduring object's temporary properties must be extrinsic is to assume what is at stake in the debate with the ('adverbial') endurance theorist.

[6] This pattern of inference has a venerable history. Some find it in Aristotle's comments about prime matter (e.g., see *Metaphysics* VII:3), and it is clearly linked to the arguments which some have used to argue for bare substrata.

Let me put this in more positive terms. Consider the idea of an intrinsic property. Lewis suggests that a property is intrinsic iff the object has the property in virtue of the way *it* is independently of anything else. An endurance theorist will demand a temporally sensitive construal of this condition, e.g. that a property is (at a time) intrinsic iff the object has (at that time) the property in virtue of the way *it* is (at that time), independently of anything else. On this revised condition, Lewis is intrinsically bent (at one time) and intrinsically straight (at another).[7] One might deny this interpretation of the condition and insist on a temporally insensitive construal of intrinsic properties, yet in doing so one fails to address the endurance theorist's position.

Lewis might complain, however, that the ontology of the endurance picture remains mysterious. Suppose we want to describe the enduring subject of predication in a way which captures how it is throughout its existence. The endurance theorist is likely to claim that such a description will involve a characterization of it as having different properties at different times. But there is still a question about how it is, abstracted from its changing history, i.e. abstracted from its variation from time to time. We cannot describe the enduring object in these terms as simply bent or straight; so it could only be shapeless. But how can this shapeless thing be the subject of the relevant shape predications?

The endurance theorist's response is to point out that although a description of the enduring object which abstracts from its changing history does not include a particular shape as part of that description (though it may include 'being shaped' since this description applies throughout its changes), such a description is incomplete; most importantly, it doesn't include all of the intrinsic properties of the object because some of the intrinsic properties of the object are had at some times and not at others. Returning to Lewis's diagram, we might say that it is not surprising that the 'shapeless blob' in the intersection of the circles seems incomplete, for to take the exercise as adequately characterizing the enduring object is to assume that we can draw how the enduring thing intrinsically is, once and for all. But if some of its properties, e.g. shape, are temporary intrinsics, this is not possible. The endurance theorist denies that the description which characterizes the object 'timelessly' is the description which captures all of the intrinsic properties of the object. The enduring object is bent and then straight; it is not a shapeless blob.

There is a sense in which these responses to Lewis's concerns are simply a stubborn resistance to his intuitions about what it is to predicate an intrinsic

---

[7] Further, on the endurance theory, a duplicate of an enduring object will also be an enduring object. If the original undergoes change, its duplicate undergoes changes as well. Thus, if an enduring object undergoes a change from being bent to being straight, its duplicate will undergo a change from being bent to being straight, though the change may occur at a different time.

property of an object. Admittedly, predication is a murky issue, and more work needs to be done in working out a theory of endurance through change. However, the temporal parts theory does not offer a sufficiently compelling account of predication to rule out an account which is consistent with a commitment to endurance. Although Lewis's concerns are rightly placed on the issue of predication, his argument rests on assumptions which the endurance theorist need not grant. Although the endurance theorist's resistance does not demonstrate that endurance is preferable to perdurance overall, it does offer a response to the charge that the endurist position is metaphysically untenable. That the position is tenable is significant, for it is the endurance theory which allows us to preserve the intuition that there are some objects which persist through a change in their intrinsic properties.[8]

Commentary on Haslanger

Sally Haslanger's brief article sees her take issue with Lewis's contention that the problem of temporary intrinsics can only be satisfactorily solved by embracing perdurantism. To this end, she argues for two claims. First, she denies that perdurantism can give us a convincing account of intrinsic change. Second, she claims that Lewis's three alternative solutions do not exhaust the available options. In her view, there is a variety of endurantism that can allow for intrinsic change and yet deny that intrinsic properties are really relations to times.

Having crisply introduced the problem of temporary intrinsics, at $\boxed{a} \mapsto$ Haslanger sets about seeking to make good her first claim. To recap, Lewis's objection to the first, endurantist, solution he considers is that, in treating shapes (and other temporary intrinsics) as relations to times, it is thereby committed to denying that objects are 'plain straight' (that is, straight intrinsically). According to Lewis, an object is straight *simpliciter*: it is not straight by virtue of bearing a relation to something else (namely, a time). But Haslanger argues that perdurantism itself faces a strikingly similar objection. For the perdurantist must deny that objects are 'plain straight' in the following sense: while a perduring object's *temporal parts* may be simply bent or straight, this is *not* true of the perduring object itself. (Indeed, if the perduring object *did* have a bent shape and then a straight shape, the original problem would resurface, as Haslanger remarks at $\boxed{a} \mapsto$). The perduring object, then, can only be straight in a *derivative* sense: by virtue of having a temporal part that is straight. Consequently, the thing that persists – the perduring object – turns out *not* to be the thing that changes its intrinsic properties: a most paradoxical result.

[8]   I am grateful to John Broome, Mark Johnston, David Lewis, George Myro, Scott Soames, and Stephen Yablo, for helpful discussions on the issues addressed in this paper.

1. (i) Explain in your own words both Lewis's objection to the first, endurantist solution (in his $\boxed{e}\mapsto$) and Haslanger's objection to Lewis's position (in her $\boxed{a}\mapsto$). (ii) Is Haslanger right to claim that Lewis's position fares no better than the endurantism he rejects?

Having sought to undermine Lewis's preferred solution to the problem of temporary intrinsics, Haslanger then introduces, at $\boxed{b}\mapsto$, her neglected endurantist alternative. Agreeing with Lewis that a continuant's temporary properties are not relations to times, she argues that the endurantist can regard the time at which an object has a property as modifying, not the property itself, but the *having* of the intrinsic property by the object. This, she thinks, is reflected in a proper account of the semantics of ascriptions of properties at times. In an ascription of a property to an object at a time, it is the *verb* (the 'has') that is temporally modified, and so, when we say that Eleanor has a bent shape at t, 'at t' functions as an adverb (like 'quickly' in 'Helen cycled to work quickly'). Indeed, to make the adverbial status of 'at t' more obvious, we could paraphrase 'Eleanor has a bent shape at t' as 'Eleanor has-at-t a bent shape', or even 'Eleanor has at-t-ly a bent shape'. The fact that Eleanor changes from having a bent shape at t to having a straight shape at $t+1$ consists in her having-at-t straightness and having-at-$t+1$ bentness.

To see how Haslanger's suggestion differs from both the first posited solution Lewis rejects and Lewis' own perdurantist view, we can distinguish them according to which thing they take to be temporally qualified when an object has a property at a time. Lewis, as we have seen, takes the *object* to be temporally qualified: for Eleanor to be straight at t is for a *temporal part* of her to have this property. The upholder of the first solution, by contrast, takes t to enter at the level of the *property*: Eleanor's being straight at t is a matter of her having the relational property *being straight-at-t*. Haslanger, by contrast, takes neither of these options: Eleanor is an endurant who has-at-t the non-relational property of being straight; the thing that is temporally qualified is Eleanor's *having* the property.

2. Following Lewis's own lead – quoted by Haslanger in the paragraph before $\boxed{g}\mapsto$ – try to represent the differences between Lewis's theory, the first endurantist solution, and Haslanger's theory diagrammatically.

At present, Haslanger's proposal is looking rather schematic. What exactly does this amount to? In order to shed light upon the details of Haslanger's account, we can see how she deals with an objection to her position that has been raised by Lewis (in another work). As Haslanger points out at $\boxed{c}\mapsto$, it looks like her solution amounts to simply construing instantiation – the way in which an object and a property come to be unified – as, in reality, a three-place relation that obtains between an object, a property and a time. And the problem here is that, if this were true, Lewis's objection to his endurantist would also apply to Haslanger: intrinsic properties would come out as relational; to be straight would be to stand in some relation to a time (just as *being taller than Julian* is to stand in a certain relation to Julian).

Haslanger denies that she need view instantiation as a three-place relation. According to the spelling out of the adverbial approach that Haslanger favours, Eleanor's having a bent shape is *itself* an entity – something Haslanger calls a 'proposition' (⟨d⊢→⟩) – in which Eleanor and straightness come together to form something that obtains. (To see what Haslanger is getting at here, take another look at Armstrong ⟨e⊢→⟩ in chapter 4: what Haslanger calls a 'proposition' is the same kind of thing that Kripke calls a 'state of affairs', that is, the coming together of an object and a property.) Now, according to Haslanger (⟨d⊢→⟩), if Eleanor has a bent shape at *t*, this is not a matter of a three-place relation holding between Eleanor, bentness and *t*; it consists in a *two-place relation* (the relation of *obtaining* or *being the case*) holding between the *proposition* – Eleanor's having a bent shape – and *t*. Instantiation – the tie between Eleanor and bentness in the proposition – is left exactly where it was.

3. In your view, what, if anything, *is* wrong with treating instantiation as a three-place relation? (Take a look at Haslanger's remark, at ⟨f⊢→⟩, that its danger is that 'it invites us to treat objects as related to their properties as individuals are related to other individuals'). Is treating instantiation as a three-place relation any worse than treating it as a two-place relation? (Think about the discussion of instantiation in chapter 4.)
4. At ⟨e⊢→⟩, Haslanger addresses the worry that she might, after all, end up committed to a three-place instantiation relation. How convincing is her reply at ⟨f⊢→⟩?

The remainder of Haslanger's paper is devoted to defending the claim that her variety of endurantism makes 'metaphysical sense'. At ⟨g⊢→⟩, she sets out an objection that, once more, has its origin in the work of Lewis, its key claim being that an enduring thing can have no shape intrinsically (⟨h⊢→⟩). The argument for this conclusion would seem to go as follows. Suppose Eleanor – an enduring thing – has a bent shape at *t* and a straight shape at *t* + 1. In order to avoid ascribing incompatible properties to Eleanor, an endurantist must hold that Eleanor has a shape only in a derivative sense: by being related to bentness or straightness (at times). But if this is right – if, that is, Eleanor *stands in some relation* to shape rather than simply *being* a certain shape – then she is shapeless *in herself*: she has no shape intrinsically. Since standing in some relation to shape is not to *be* shaped, Eleanor does not have a shape *simpliciter*. Rather, she is, intrinsically, a mere 'shapeless blob': an item whose shape is extrinsic to her.

Haslanger's reply to this argument, from ⟨h⊢→⟩ through ⟨i⊢→⟩, is highly compressed, but would seem to amount to this. Lewis is wrong in thinking that an enduring thing can have no shape intrinsically, for the adverbial construal of endurantism avoids ascribing incompatible properties to Eleanor, and yet does so *without* taking her to bear a *relation* of instantiation to bentness and straightness (at different times). Indeed, once the adverbial proposal is properly understood, such a way of thinking about instantiation can be seen as clearly uncompulsory: in taking Eleanor's having a bent shape at t to consist in the obtaining of a proposition (that is, the unity of Eleanor and bentness) obtaining at t, Haslanger, no less than the perdurantist, can resist construing the unification of Eleanor and bentness relationally, and so insist that Eleanor has the property intrinsically.

As Haslanger explains at ⌐i⌐→, once the endurantist has made the adverbial move just suggested – and thereby side-stepped a relational construal of instantiation – she is free to allow that an object may be intrinsically bent at t but intrinsically straight at $t + 1$. Unable to see the availability of this position – and convinced that an endurantist must treat an object as *related* to its properties – Lewis comes to the false conclusion that the bearers of intrinsic properties (which, for him, are the temporal parts of objects) have their intrinsic properties throughout their existence. So, while Lewis takes a temporal part's intrinsic properties to be had by that part throughout its existence, and hence equates temporary properties with extrinsic ones, Haslanger denies this. Temporary properties may yet be intrinsic.

According to Haslanger, once the tie between the temporary and the extrinsic has been cut, the adverbial endurantist need not regard Eleanor as a shapeless blob. On the contrary, Eleanor first of all has a bent shape intrinsically, and then becomes intrinsically straight in shape: a claim which makes play with an understanding of 'intrinsic' that, unlike Lewis's, is temporally sensitive (⌐j⌐→). As Haslanger herself puts it, at ⌐k⌐→, '[t]he endurance theorist denies that the description which characterizes the object "timelessly" is the description which captures all of the intrinsic properties of the object'.

> 5. (i) Sum up, in your own words, what you take to be the crux of the dispute between Lewis and Haslanger. (ii) Do you think Haslanger has succeeded in avoiding Lewis's objections to the version of endurantism he discusses in *On the Plurality of Worlds?*

David Lewis, 'Tensing the Copula'

A solution to the problem of intrinsic change for enduring things should meet three conditions. It should not replace monadic intrinsic properties by relations. It should not replace the having *simpliciter* of properties by standing in some relation to them (unless having them *simpliciter* always means standing in some relation to them, which is refuted by Bradley's regress). It should not rely on an unexplained notion of having an intrinsic property at a time. Johnston's solution satisfies the first condition at the expenses of the second. Haslanger's solution satisfies the first and second at the expense of the third.

1.   The Problem about Persistence

[a] ⊢→   The problem about persistence is the problem of change, insofar as it pertains to intrinsic properties.[1] Things somehow persist through time. When they do, they have some of their intrinsic properties temporarily. For instance shape: sometimes you sit, and then you are bent; sometimes you stand or lie, and then you are straight. How can one and the same thing have two contrary intrinsic properties? How does it help that it has them at different times? Three solutions are on offer.

[b] ⊢→   I favour the hypothesis of *perdurance*. It says that persisting things are sums of temporal parts; their temporary intrinsic properties belong in the first instance to their temporal parts; and it is no problem that two different temporal parts can differ in their intrinsic properties. A persisting thing is like a parade: first one part of it shows up, and then another. (Except that most persisting things are much more continuous than most parades.) The only trouble with this hypothesis is that very many philosophers reject it as counterintuitive, or revisionist, or down-right crazy (except in the case of events or processes).[2] It is a mystery why. Unfortunately, those who try to explain why they reject the hypothesis merely restate it. They say, perhaps, that it likens a persisting thing to a parade (apart from the extent of the discontinuities). Or they say that 'its full craziness comes out' because it implies that 'if I have had exactly one bit of chalk in my hand for the last hour, then there is something in my hand . . . which is chalk, which was not in my hand three minutes ago' – namely, a temporal part of the chalk beginning less than three minutes ago (Thomson 1983, p. 213). All we learn is that they reject the hypothesis because it says what it does. We are none the wiser.

The hypothesis of *presentism* treats the modifiers 'in the past' and 'in the future' like the 'counterfeit' in 'counterfeit money'. These modifiers often attach to falsehoods to make truths. What exists (only) in the past or in the future is not something that exists and is located in the past or in the future; it is something that does not exist at all. Likewise, what has an intrinsic property (only) in the past or in the future does not have that property. These modifiers cannot be explained in terms of a domain including (wholly) past or future things, because there is no such domain. A so-called persisting thing, if it really exists, is located entirely in the present. When the

---

[1]   It is the problem elsewhere called the problem of temporary intrinsics (Lewis 1986, pp. 202ff). Extrinsic change poses no further problem. It is derivative: something undergoes extrinsic change when either it or some part of its surroundings undergoes intrinsic change, or when its intrinsic relations to parts of its surroundings change. (See Humberstone 1996, p. 208.)

[2]   Others claim not to understand perdurance because they lack the concept of a temporal part. I reply to them in Lewis 1983, pp. 76f.

presentist obligingly agrees that it exists in the past and in the future, he is not saying that it or any part of it is located elsewhere in time; he is attaching his modifiers to alleged falsehoods to make truths. Thus he denies what others mean when they say that things persist and undergo intrinsic change. Of course the presentist has no problem of intrinsic change, but he escapes it at far too high a cost.[3]

The hypothesis of *endurance* is far and away the most popular. It deserves a run for its money at least on that account. Things have no temporal parts. Rather, a persisting thing is multiply located in time: the whole of it is at one time and also at another. Yet the same identical thing may have different intrinsic properties at different times at which it is located. You are bent at time t_1, straight at time t_2, but it is the whole of you, not one or another of your alleged temporal parts, that is bent and that is straight. How can that be?[4]

c ▷ Endurance calls to mind two things. One is the power of spatial bilocation traditionally ascribed to saints. If a bilocated saint is wholly in Rome and wholly in Byzantium, and if in Rome he is bent and in Byzantium he is straight, then we have a problem of local intrinsics that exactly parallels the problem of temporary intrinsics for an enduring thing – except that philosophers have been much less eager to solve it. The other is the multiple location in both space and time that is ascribed to immanent universals, if such there be. But unless we can come up with an example of an intrinsic property that a universal has at one of its locations and not at another – and I know of none – we have no problem of temporary or local intrinsics for universals.

2. Intrinsic 'Properties' as Relations to Times

d ▷ There is an obvious solution to the problem of temporary intrinsics for an enduring thing: its so-called temporary intrinsic properties are not really monadic properties, but rather dyadic relations to times. If you are bent at t_1 and straight at t_2, you bear the *bent-at* relation to t_1 and the *straight-at*

---

[3] See Zimmerman 1998 for a defence of the presentist solution to the problem of temporary intrinsics.
[4] Johnston (1984, chs 3 and 5; 1987, pp. 121ff) has discussed a halfway house: *partial endurance*. It allows for at least some persistence by endurance. Consider the non-temporal parts of a persisting thing: spatial parts, and perhaps also abstract parts, tropes. Suppose the parts endure as long as they can endure without undergoing intrinsic change; but when threatened with intrinsic change, they instead go out of existence and are replaced. Thus the persisting thing consists of different parts at different times. Since the enduring parts never undergo intrinsic change, the problem of temporary intrinsics for enduring things is avoided. However, I note that if the persisting thing undergoes constant intrinsic change that affects every spatial or abstract part of it, be this change ever so imperceptible, there is no endurance left. Partial endurance then collapses into perdurance, and will doubtless be rejected no less forcefully.

relation to t_2. There is no problem about how the same thing can bear contrary relations to two different relata.

If we insist on genuine monadic properties of the enduring thing, we can have those as well. They will be relational properties: *bearing-bent- at-to-t_1, bearing-straight-at-to-t_2*.

'Relational' is a classification that applies to *structured* properties: properties taken to have a quasi-syntactic structure whereby they are constructed from their constituents. The relational property just considered has a dyadic relation as one of its constituents, and a suitable relatum as another. Note that structured properties are hyperintensionally individuated: two of them constructed from different constitutents, or from the same constituents in a different way, are different even if they are necessarily coextensive. Note also that a relational property is not the same thing as an extrinsic property: 'extrinsic' is an intensional classification that applies to structured and unstructured properties alike. Suppose Platonism is true, and the forms are necessary beings which cannot be said to accompany things in the world. Then *bearing-imitation-to-the-form-of-Squareness* is a relational property, but it is also intrinsic. It cannot differ between duplicates; and whether something has it or lacks it is independent of whether that thing is accompanied or unaccompanied, and it is neither a disjunctive property nor the negation of one. (See Humberstone 1996, pp. 224ff and 253ff; Langton and Lewis 1998.)

I cannot object to these relations and relational properties. (Not, at least, if they are not alleged to be fundamental properties of the sort that might figure in a minimal basis on which all else supervenes.) I accept similar relations and relational properties myself. You bear *bent-at* to times at which you have bent temporal parts; and if t_1 is one of those times, you have *bearing-bent-at-to-t_1*.

e⊢→ But I do object to leaving the monadic intrinsic properties out of the picture. Some intrinsic properties really are monadic: for instance the property of living three score years and ten. Even the properties *bent* and *straight* could at least sometimes be monadic: for instance when they are properties of momentary things. There is no reason in that case to take them as relations to times. So I want to know: where have the monadic properties *bent* and *straight* gone? What have they to do with our new-found *bent-at* and *straight-at* relations, and our new-found relational properties constructed from these relations? Under the endurance hypothesis, there is nothing left in a case of temporary bentness and straightness to have *bent* or *straight*. Or anyway nothing is left to have them *simpliciter*, without benefit of some sort of modifier that attaches to falsehoods to make truths. Not the temporal parts – they do not exist. Not the enduring thing: it does not have them, it only modifiedly-has them by having them *at t_1* or *at t_2*.

Some will still insist that certain relations to times are just what we *call* 'intrinsic properties', so it is senseless to hanker after *really* intrinsic properties in addition. (See Jackson 1994; but note that he is not arguing for endurance but only for its tenability.) If they are willing to accept the consequence that the so-called intrinsic properties are a divided category, we have reached stalemate.

But there are others, among them Mark Johnston (1987, pp. 127ff), who agree that it will not do to leave the monadic intrinsic properties *bent* and *straight* out of the picture. We need a way to bring them back in without giving up the endurance hypothesis.

3.   Bringing Back the Intrinsic Properties

f→ Johnston's solution is to tense the copula: 'Instantiating a property, it turns out, is instantiating at some time the property' (1987, p. 129). It is not the intrinsic property *bent* or *straight*, but rather the copula that relates this property to a thing that has it, that turns into a relation to times. *Having* was originally thought to be a dyadic relation of things to properties; now it will instead be a triadic relation of things to properties and times. If you have at t_1 the property *bent*, the property *bent* is unscathed: it is still the same old monadic intrinsic property we always thought it was. It is not replaced either by a relation or by a relational property.

I protest that there is still nothing in the picture that has *bent* or *straight simpliciter*. Not you; not your nonexistent temporal parts. Instead of having *bent simpliciter*, you bear the *having-at* relation to it and t_1. But it is one thing to
g→ have a property, it is something else to bear some relation to it. If a relation stands between you and your properties, you are alienated from them.

All you have *simpliciter* is a relational property: *bearing-having-at-to-bent-and-t_1*. The property *bent* must enter into this relational property as a constituent, else there is no connection left between *bent* and the property you have *simpliciter*. In order to say so, we must again assume that we are dealing here with a structured property.
h→ *Tu quoque*? [See Haslanger, this volume.] Don't I also deny that your perduring self has *simpliciter* the property *bent*? Don't I also say that it bears to this property the *having-at-t_1* relation, where this is the relation that a perduring thing bears to a property just in case it contains a temporal part that is located at t_1 and has that property? If bearing a relation to a property rather than having it *simpliciter* alienates you from that property, isn't this equally a problem for perdurance? I think not. There is more to say. To be sure, your perduring self does not have *bent simpliciter*. But as much of you as exists at t_1 does. In talking about what is true at a certain time, we can, and we very often do, restrict our domain of discourse so as to ignore everything located elsewhere in time. Restricting the domain in this way, your temporal part at t_1 is deemed to be the whole of you. So there is a good sense in which you do, after all, have *bent simpliciter*. The protagonist of endurance cannot say the same.

$\boxed{i} \mapsto$ An effective rejoinder to my protest, if it were true, would be to claim
that *all* having of properties is relational. Whenever a thing has a property *P*
simpliciter, that is to be explained by saying that the thing bears a relation of
having to *P*; or, equivalently, that it has the relational property *bearing-having-
to-P*. If that is enough to alienate us from our properties, we are *always*
alienated from our properties. My protest proves too much to deserve belief.
If all having is relational, but not on that account alienating, why is relational
having-at-a-time any worse?

4. That Way Lies Bradley's Regress

$\boxed{j} \mapsto$ I would be willing enough to believe in a *having* relation that something
bears to a property; or in a triadic *having* relation that an enduring thing (if
such there be) bears to a property and a time; or in a relational property of,
say, *bearing-having-to-bent-at-t_1*. (Assuming, once again, that these are not
alleged to be fundamental relations and properties.)

But I do not think these relations can explain having *simpliciter*. Having
simpliciter is not a relation, whatever grammar may suggest. What is it, then? I
don't know what more can be said. It is all very well to say that the copula is a
'non-relational tie' or that properties are 'unsaturated' and await completion
by their bearers. These remarks at least have the merit of pointing away from
the idea that having is relational. But they don't point toward much of anything.

$\boxed{k} \mapsto$ Bradley's regress shows that if we insist on trying to explain having
simpliciter in terms of relational having, the explanation we seek will never
be finished. (See Bradley 1897, ch. 3; Armstrong 1978, pp. 106f.) Run
through it first in terms of relational properties. Keep it simple by ignoring
time: let *P* be a permanent property of *X*.

X has *P* by having *bearing-having-to-P*
. . . by having *bearing-having-to-(bearing-having-to-P)*
. . . by having *bearing-having-to-(bearing-having-to-(bearing-having-to-P))*
. . . by. . . .

And so *ad infinitum*. No sooner have we explained one having relationally
than another one appears, needing its own relational explanation in turn.

If we would rather bypass the relational properties, we can instead resort
to a sequence of having relations of ever greater polyadicity. (Signify an
n-adic relation by a superscript '*n*'.)

X has^1 P by having^2 ($having^1$, P)
. . . by having^3 ($having^2$, $having^1$, P)
. . . by having^4 ($having^3$, $having^2$, $having^1$, P)
. . . by. . . .

And so *ad infinitum*. Again, our explanation can never be finished.

No harm is done, so long as we say that these havings-by-havings are not meant to be explanations, only equivalences. In that case we can stop the regress anywhere we like, and claim that our most recently mentioned having is not a relational having but rather a having *simpliciter*. But then we have given up on explaining having *simpliciter* in terms of relational having; so we have given up on showing that all having is relational; so we've given up on showing that relational having-at-t_1 is no more alienating than any other having.

At this point it is tempting to say that having a property at a time is a sort of hybrid. So far as the property goes, it is a non-relational tie; so far as the time goes, it is a relation. But this is whistling in the dark. We have no developed idea what sort of thing a 'non-relational tie' might be. Still less have we any idea what a hybrid of a non-relational tie and a relation might be.

I said earlier that calling having *simpliciter* a 'non-relational tie' pointed away from error but not toward much of anything; and I have just said that we have no developed idea what a non-relational tie might be. Should we remedy that? We might reify non-relational ties, and say something about them. As follows: a dyadic tie is an entity that ties a thing to a property, and for the most part it is contingent which things are tied to which properties. A triadic tie ties two relata to a dyadic relation, and again it is for the most part contingent what is tied to what. A tetradic tie . . . By now it is all too obvious that 'ties' are relations in all but name. Relations in all but name will serve us no better than relations openly so-called. We can repeat Bradley's regress (in both its versions) to show that we can never finish an attempted explanation of having *simpliciter* in terms of ties; and ties will alienate us from our properties no less than relations do. I conclude that reifying non-relational ties and giving an account of them is a thoroughly misguided thing to do. [. . .]

7.   Another Way to Bring Back the Intrinsic Properties

[1]→ Sally Haslanger [this volume] wants to defend the endurance hypothesis against the problem of temporary intrinsics. She agrees that it will not do to replace the monadic intrinsic properties by relations to times. We need to put the monadic intrinsic properties themselves back into the picture. But she also agrees that it will not do to put them in just as relata of some relation. Rather, they need to be the objects of having *simpliciter*. To explain how you can be bent at t_1, not only do we need to mention the monadic intrinsic property *bent*; we also need to mention the proposition that you have this property *simpliciter*, and we need to say of this proposition that it obtains at t_1. By 'proposition' Haslanger here means something that can

obtain at some times and not at others, rather than something that is true or false once and for all.[6]

What is a proposition that obtains at some times and not others? It seems to behave exactly like a property of times, so let us take it to be just that. It 'obtains' at just those times that have it. If so, the proposition Haslanger mentions is the relational property *being-a-time-t-such-that-you-have-bent-at-t*.

What is this property? It must be a structured property with *bent* as a constituent. If it were an unstructured property, or if it had the *bent-at* relation as a constituent in place of the monadic intrinsic property *bent*, we would not have succeeded in bringing *bent* back into the picture. Further, it must not have the *having-at* relation as a constituent, since it is supposed to be identical to the tensed proposition that you have *bent simpliciter*, not to the tensed proposition that you stand in some sort of relation to *bent*. But now something unfortunate has happened. Within the anatomy of the tensed proposition that obtains at just those times when you are bent, in other words the relational property just considered, we find that we have reintroduced without explanation the very thing we were trying to explain: the notion of an enduring thing having a monadic intrinsic property at a time. I conclude that the proposal fails.

Commentary on Lewis

Lewis returns to the problem of temporary intrinsics in his 2002 paper, 'Tensing the Copula'. Here he revisits his initial typology of possible solutions, defends his original conclusions, and responds to Haslanger.

The article starts, at $\boxed{a}\mapsto$, with what is, by now, a familiar setting up of the problem. We need an account of intrinsic change that avoids committing us to a thing's having incompatible properties. Lewis then goes on to set out his favoured perdurantist solution. According to Lewis, continuants are aggregates of temporal parts, and intrinsic change in such a perduring object consists in the object's having successive temporal parts that differ with respect to their intrinsic properties. Contradiction is avoided because the incompatible properties involved are possessed by different things (that is, by different temporal parts).

---

[6] Haslanger speaks of adverbial modification of the proposition that you have the property. She is to some extent noncommittal about how adverbial modification works; to that extent, we have no definite proposal on the table. But one good way to understand the working of an adverbial phrase 'at so-and-so time', and one that she conspicuously mentions, is as expressing a relation between the proposition and a time, and that is indeed a definite enough proposal to discuss. Haslanger notes that it appears also in Lowe (1988, p. 75).

1. At b $\mapsto$ Lewis says that perduring entities' intrinsic properties 'belong *in the first instance* to their temporal parts' (our italics). This implies that perduring entities *do* possess these very properties in a secondary sense. Is he right about this? Compare this remark with what Haslanger has to say at her a $\mapsto$.

At c $\mapsto$, Lewis contrasts his perdurantist account of change with that suggested by the endurantist, suggesting that the endurantist's idea that one and the same entity may be wholly present at two different times is rather like 'the power of spatial bilocation traditionally ascribed to saints'.

2. How fair is Lewis's analogy between endurantism and spatial bilocation?

Having introduced his own solution, rejected (once more) the presentist alternative, and revealed (what is to his mind) the outlandishness of endurantist thinking, Lewis returns, at d $\mapsto$, to the details of the specific endurantist solution that he discussed in *On the Plurality of Worlds*: the thesis that the seemingly incompatible properties involved in a continuant's undergoing intrinsic change are really relations to times, and hence compatible after all. This move is swiftly rejected at e $\mapsto$, and for a familiar reason: that at least some properties are properly monadic: that is, not relational. Lewis considers the objection that certain intrinsic properties *just are* relations to times – in effect, that his understanding of 'intrinsic' is too restrictive – but he dismisses this option since such a position would have it that properties can be intrinsic to an object in two distinct ways: by being genuinely monadic and by bearing a certain relation to a time.

3. Re-read question 3 in the commentary on Lewis, *On the Plurality of Worlds*. Has your position altered in any way when it comes to the question of the cogency of taking properties to be relations to times? If so, why?

At f $\mapsto$ Lewis considers another endurantist response to the problem of temporary intrinsics: a solution related to, but (as will be obvious at once) significantly distinct from, that offered by Haslanger. According to Mark Johnston (1987), the endurantist should preserve the idea that intrinsic properties are genuinely monadic by taking the *copula* – the 'is' in 'is bent' – to be the thing that is relativized to a time. Here, then, we have precisely that doctrine from which Haslanger was keen to distinguish her own view at her c $\mapsto$. Johnston and Haslanger agree that the endurantist should resist treating the properties involved in intrinsic change as relations to times; but whereas Haslanger takes *Eleanor's being shaped* – a 'proposition' – to be the thing that enters into a two-place relation with a time, Johnston endorses the idea that *instantiation* is a three-place relation, one of whose relata is a time.

In the light of the material covered in this chapter up to now, Lewis's objection to Johnston's view is predictable (though no less pressing for that). To recap, the worry with taking instantiation to be a three-place relation is that it seems to rule out an object's being 'plain straight'. If an object merely bears some kind of relation to straightness, then it is not straight *simpliciter*. To bear some relation to straightness is not to be straight. 'If a relation stands between you and your properties, you are alienated from them' ($\boxed{\text{g}}\!\mapsto$).

> 4. In what sense is an object 'alienated' from its properties, if instantiation is taken to be a relation? (Revisit question 3 from the commentary on Lewis, *The Plurality of Worlds*, and question 3 from the commentary on Haslanger.)

Having charged Johnston with having failed to do justice to the fact that objects can have properties *simpliciter*, Lewis now, at $\boxed{\text{h}}\!\mapsto$, addresses Haslanger's claim (at $\boxed{\text{a}}\!\mapsto$ in Haslanger) that he himself is guilty of the same crime. To recall, the problem facing Lewis is that it seems that he, no less than his endurantist opponent, cannot allow for Eleanor's having, *simpliciter*, a straight shape at $t + 1$. For in order to avoid ascribing incompatible properties to one and the same thing, the perdurantist holds that is a *temporal part* of Eleanor – *Eleanor-at-t* $+ 1$ – that is 'plain straight'. Eleanor herself – *qua* the sum of her temporal parts – merely bears the *having-at-t* $+ 1$ relation to straightness: the relation Eleanor holds to the property just in case she has an existent temporal part at $t + 1$ that has, *simpliciter*, a straight shape. To this, however, Lewis has a reply. While he accepts that Eleanor is not *herself* plain straight at $t + 1$ (or plain bent in shape at t), he none the less argues that the perdurantist comes *closest* to satisfying our intuitions on this matter.

> 5. Put Lewis's reply to Haslanger in your own words. How convincing is it? How do you think Haslanger would reply to Lewis on this point?

Lewis now returns to Johnston's version of endurantism; and, at $\boxed{\text{i}}\!\mapsto$, he anticipates one final move that this brand of endurantist could make. The move is this. Lewis's objection to the treating instantiation as a three-place relation between an object, a property and a time – namely, that to construe an object as related to its properties is to alienate the object from them – proves too much to be plausible. For instantiation *has* to be a relation of *some sort* between an object and its properties, so there can be nothing *especially* wrong with construing instantiation as a *triadic* relation.

Lewis's response to this gambit, at $\boxed{\text{j}}\!\mapsto$, is stark. We must not regard instantiation – the tie that obtains between an object and its properties when it has those properties *simpliciter* – as a relation of *any* sort. And the reason for this is that explaining instantiation relationally launches us upon *Bradley's Regress*: a regress that is infinite and vicious. '[I]f we insist on trying to explain having *simpliciter* in terms of relational having, the explanation we seek will never be finished' ($\boxed{\text{k}}\!\mapsto$).

> 6. At this point, re-read the Introduction to, and section 3 of, Armstrong's paper in chapter 4. Explain Bradley's Regress in your own words. Is it really vicious? If so, why?

At the end of his paper, Lewis explicitly considers Haslanger's adverbial version of perdurantism. And his claim, in the two paragraphs from $\boxed{1}\!\!\mapsto$, is that it ends up being question-begging. The argument is extremely swift but, we think, amounts to this. Saying that the proposition that Eleanor has a bent shape obtains at t can explain what it is for Eleanor to be bent at t, only once the notion of a proposition's obtaining at a time has been explained. However, Haslanger treats the notion of a proposition's obtaining at a time as a primitive. Consequently, Haslanger has not explained *what it is* for Eleanor to have a bent shape at t; she has merely found another form of words for it. We are no further forward.

7. Is Lewis's objection fair?

Further Reading

Sider 2001 gives an excellent and highly readable defence of perdurantism: chapter 1 and chapter 4, section 6, are particularly helpful. Jonathan Lowe offers an account similar to Haslanger's in his 1988. A good discussion of endurantism and perdurantism about continuants is found in Loux 1998, ch. 6.

Essay Questions

1. Outline the problem of temporary intrinsics. Is Lewis's solution to it defensible?
2. Explain the difference between endurantist and perdurantist accounts of persistence through time. Which kind of theory best answers the problem of temporary intrinsics?
3. In order to solve the problem of temporary intrinsics, must an endurantist introduce a three-place relation of instantiation?

Bibliography

Chapter 1

Personal Identity

Bennett, J. (1967). 'The Simplicity of the Soul', *Journal of Philosophy* 64, 648–60.

Butler, J. (1736). 'Of Personal Identity', first appendix to *The Analogy of Religion*; reprinted in Perry 1975.

Care, N. and Grimm, R. (1967). *Perception and Personal Identity: Proceedings of the 1967 Oberlin Colloquium in Philosophy* (Cleveland: Press of Case Western Reserve University).

Casey, E. (1987). *Remembering: A Phenomenological Study* (Bloomington: Indiana University Press).

Chisholm, R. and S. Shoemaker (1967). 'The Loose and Popular and the Strict and Philosophical Senses of Identity', in Care and Grimm 1967.

Duncan Jones, A. (1968). 'Man's Mortality', *Analysis* 28, 65–70.

Eccles, J. (ed.) (1966). *Brain and Conscious Experience.* (Berlin: Springer Verlag).

Fingarette, H. (1969). *Self-Deception* (London: Routledge).

Frankfurt, H. (1975). 'Identification and Externality', in A. Rorty (ed.), *The Identities of Persons* (Los Angeles: University of California Press).

Guttenplan, S., J. Hornsby and C. Janaway (eds.) (2003). *Reading Philosophy* (Oxford: Blackwell).

Hanley, R. (1997). *Is Data Human? The Metaphysics of Star Trek* (New York: Basic Books).

Hume, D. (1985). 'The Sceptic', in his *Essays Moral, Political and Literary*, ed. E. F. Miller (Indianapolis: Liberty Press).

Johnston, M. (1987). 'Human Beings', *Journal of Philosophy* 84, 59–83; reprinted in Kim and Sosa 1999.

Kim, J. and E. Sosa (eds.) (1999). *Metaphysics: An Anthology* (Oxford: Blackwell).

Locke, J. (1690). *An Essay Concerning Human Understanding*, ch. 27; reprinted in Perry 1975.

Nagel, T. (1970). *The Possiblity of Altruism* (Oxford: Oxford University Press).

—— (1986). *The View from Nowhere* (New York: Oxford University Press).

Noonan, H. (2003). *Personal Identity* (2nd ed.) (London: Routledge).

Palma, A. B. (1964). 'Memory and Personal Identity', *Australasian Journal of Philosophy* 42, 53–68.

Parfit, D. (1971). 'Personal Identity', *The Philosophical Review* 80, 3–27

—— (1984). *Reasons and Persons* (Oxford: Clarendon Press).

Penelhum, T. (1967). 'Personal Identity', in P. Edwards (ed.), *The Encyclopedia of Philosophy*, vol. 5 (London: Macmillan), 95–107.

—— (1970). *Survival and Disembodied Existence* (London: Routledge).

Perry, J. (ed.) (1975). *Personal Identity* (Berkeley: University of California Press).

Prior, A. N. (1957). 'Opposite Number', *Review of Metaphysics* 11, 196–201.

—— (1966). 'Time, Existence and Identity', *Proceedings of the Aristotelian Society* LVII, 183–92.

Quinton, A. (1962), 'The Soul', *Journal of Philosophy* 59, 393–409.

Reid, T. (1785). 'Of Memory', in his *Essays on the Intellectual Powers of Man* (essay III, ch. 6); reprinted in Perry 1975.

Schechtman, M. (1990). 'Personhood and Personal Identity', *The Journal of Philosophy* 87 (1990), 71–92

Shoemaker, S. (1963). *Self-Knowledge and Self-Identity* (Oxford: Oxford University Press).

—— (1970a). 'Persons and their Pasts', *American Philosophical Quarterly* 7, 269–85; reprinted in Kim and Sosa 1999.

—— (1970b). 'Wiggins on Identity', *Philosophical Review* 79, 529–44.

Shorter, J. (1962). 'More about Bodily Continuity and Personal Identity', *Analysis* 22, 79–85.

Wiggins, D. (1967). *Identity and Spatio-Temporal Continuity* (Oxford: Blackwell).

Williams, B. (1957). 'Personal Identity and Individuation', *Proceedings of the Aristotelian Society* 57, 229–53.

—— (1961). 'Personal Identity and Bodily Continuity', *Analysis* 21, 43–8.

—— (1966). 'Imagination and the Self', *Proceedings of the British Academy* 52, 105–24.

—— (1970). 'The Self and the Future', *Philosophical Review* 79, 161–80; reprinted in Perry 1975, and Kim and Sosa 1999.

Chapter 2

Free Will

Ayer, A. J. (1954). 'Freedom and Necessity', in his *Philosophical Essays* (London: Macmillan), 271–84.

Beebee, H. and A. R. Mele (2002). 'Humean Compatibilism', *Mind* 111, 201–23.

Brand, M. (ed.) (1970). *The Nature of Human Action* (Glenview, IL: Scott Foresman).

Canfield, J. V. (1962). 'The Compatibility of Free Will and Determinism', *Philosophical Review* 71, 712–36.

Dennett, D. (1984). *Elbow Room* (Cambridge, MA: Bradford Books).

Ekstrom, L. (ed.) (2001). *Agency and Responsibility* (Boulder, CO: Westview Press).

Fischer, J. M. (1982). 'Responsibility and Control', *Journal of Philosophy* 79, 24–40.

—— (1994). *The Metaphysics of Free Will* (Oxford: Blackwell).

Flew, A. (1955). 'Divine Omniscience and Human Freedom', in A. Flew and A. MacIntyre (eds.), *New Essays in Philosophical Theology* (London: Macmillan).

Frankfurt, H. (1969). 'Alternate Possibilities and Moral Responsibility', *Journal of Philosophy* 66, 829–39.

Ginet, C. (1966). 'Might We Have No Choice?', in Lehrer 1966, 87–104.

Hobart, R. E. (1934). 'Free Will as Involving Determination and Inconceivable Without It', *Mind* 43, 1–27.

James, W. (1921). 'The Dilemma of Determinism', in his *The Will to Believe* (New York: Longmans), 145–83.

Kant, I. (1781/1787). *The Critique of Pure Reason*, trans. N. Kemp Smith (London: Macmillan, 1929).

Kane, R. (1999). 'Responsibility, Luck, and Chance', *Journal of Philosophy* 96, 217–40; reprinted in Ekstrom 2001.

Kripke, S. (1971). 'Identity and Necessity', in M. Munitz (ed.), *Identity and Individuation* (New York: New York University Press), 135–64.

Lehrer, K. (ed.) (1966). *Freedom and Determinism* (New York: Random House).

Lewis, D. K. (1981). 'Are We Free to Break the Laws?', *Theoria* 47, 113–21; reprinted in his *Philosophical Papers*, vol. II (Oxford: Oxford University Press, 1986), and in Ekstrom 2001.

Mackie, J. L. (1974). *The Cement of the Universe* (Oxford: Oxford University Press).

Mele, A. R. (1999). 'Ultimate Responsibility and Dumb Luck', *Social Philosophy & Policy* 16, 274–93; reprinted in E. Paul, F. Miller and J. Paul (eds.), *Responsibility* (Cambridge: Cambridge University Press).

Nowell-Smith, P. H. (1948). 'Freewill and Moral Responsibility', *Mind* 57, 45–61.

O'Connor, T. (ed.) (1995). *Agents, Causes and Events: Essays on Indeterminism and Free Will* (Oxford: Oxford University Press).

Quine, W. V. O. (1960). *Word and Object* (Cambridge, MA: MIT Press).

Sellars, W. (1966). 'Fatalism and Determinism', in Lehrer 1966, 141–74.

Smart, J. J. C. (1961). 'Free Will, Praise and Blame', *Mind* 70, 291–306.

Taylor, R. (1965). 'Time, Truth and Ability' (published under the name 'Diodorus Cronus'), *Analysis* 25, 137–41.

van Inwagen, P. (1974). 'A Formal Approach to the Problem of Free Will and Determinism', *Theoria* 24, 9–22.

—— (1975). 'The Incompatibility of Free Will and Determinism', *Philosophical Studies* 27, 189–95.

—— (1978). 'Ability and Responsibility', *Philosophical Review* 87, 201–24.

—— (1983). *An Essay on Free Will* (Oxford: Clarendon).

Watson, G. (ed.) (1983). *Free Will* (Oxford: Oxford University Press).

Wiener, N. (1948). *Cybernetics: or Control and Communication in the Animal and the Machine* (New York: John Wiley and Sons).

Wimsatt, W. (1980). 'Randomness and Perceived-Randomness in Evolutionary Biology', *Synthese* 43, 287–329.

Chapter 3

Realism and Anti-realism

Ayer, A. J. (1936). *Language, Truth and Logic* (London: Victor Gollancz).

Berkeley, G. (1710). *A Treatise Concerning the Principles of Human Knowledge* (Oxford: Oxford University Press, 1998).

Davidson, D. (1969) 'True to the Facts', reprinted in his 1984, 37–54.

—— (1973). 'Radical Interpretation', reprinted in his 1984, 125–40.

—— (1974). 'On the Very Idea of a Conceptual Scheme', *Proceedings and Addresses of the American Philosophical Association* 47, 5–20; reprinted in his 1984, 183–98.

—— (1984). *Inquiries into Truth and Interpretation* (Oxford: Clarendon Press).

Descartes, R. (1641). *Meditations on First Philosophy*, in R. Stoothoff, D. Murdoch and J. Cottingham (eds.), *Descartes: Selected Philosophical Writings* (Cambridge: Cambridge University Press, 1988).

Feyerabend, P. (1962). 'Explanation, Reduction, and Empricism', in *Scientific Explanation, Space, and Time: Minnesota Studies in the Philosophy of Science*, vol. III (Minneapolis: University of Minnesota Press), 28–97.

—— (1965). 'Problems of Empiricism', in R. Colodny (ed.), *Beyond the Edge of Certainty* (Englewood Cliffs, NJ: Prentice-Hall).

Field, H. (1980). *Science without Numbers* (Oxford: Blackwell).

Fodor, J. (1983). *The Modularity of Mind* (Cambridge. MA: MIT Press).

Kant, I. (1781/1787). *The Critique of Pure Reason*, trans. N. Kemp Smith (London: Macmillan, 1929).

Kolakowski, L. (1968). *Towards a Marxist Humanism* (New York: Grove Press).

Kirk, R. (1999). *Relativism and Reality* (London: Routledge).

Kuhn, T. (1962). *The Structure of Scientific Revolutions* (Chicago: University of Chicago Press).

—— (1970). 'Reflection on My Critics', in I. Lakatos and A. Musgrave (eds.), *Criticism and the Growth of Knowledge* (Cambridge: Cambridge University Press), 231–78.

Locke, J. (1690). *An Essay Concerning Human Understanding*, ed. P. Nidditch (Oxford: Clarendon Press, 1975).

Lynch, M. (1998). *Truth in Context* (Cambridge, MA: MIT Press).

Mackie, J. L. (1977). *Ethics: Inventing Right and Wrong* (Harmondsworth: Penguin).

McGinn, C. (1983). *The Subjective View* (Oxford: Oxford University Press).

Nagel, T. (1986). *The View from Nowhere* (Oxford: Oxford University Press).

Putnam, H. (1981). *Reason, Truth and History* (Cambridge: Cambridge University Press).

Quine, W. V. O. (1951). 'Two Dogmas of Empiricism', in his 1953, 20–46.

—— (1953). *From a Logical Point of View* (Cambridge, MA: Harvard University Press).

—— (1969). 'Speaking of Objects', in his *Ontological Relativity and Other Essays* (New York: Columbia University Press), 1–25.

—— (1981). *Theories and Things* (Cambridge, MA: Harvard University Press).

Rorty, R. (1989). *Contingency, Irony, Solidarity* (Cambridge: Cambridge University Press).

Strawson, P. F. (1966). *The Bounds of Sense* (London: Methuen).

—— (1979). 'Perception and its Objects', in G. MacDonald (ed.), *Perception and Identity* (London: Macmillan).

Tarski, A. (1956). 'The Concept of Truth in Formalized Languages', in his *Logic, Semantics, Metamathematics* (Oxford: Clarendon Press).

Whorf. B. (1956). *Language, Thought, and Reality: Selected Writings of Benjamin Lee Whorf*, ed. John B. Carroll (Cambridge, MA: MIT Press).

Williams, B. (1966). 'Imagination and the Self', *Proceedings of the British Academy* 52, 105–24.

—— (1978). *Descartes: The Project of Pure Enquiry* (Harmondsworth: Penguin).

—— (1985). *Ethics and the Limits of Philosophy* (Cambridge, MA: Harvard University Press).

Wright, C. (1992). *Truth and Objectivity* (Cambridge, MA: Harvard University Press).

Chapter 4

Realism and Nominalism

Armstrong, D. M. (1978). *Nominalism and Realism: Universals and Scientific Realism*, vol. 1 (Cambridge: Cambridge University Press).

—— (1989). *Universals: An Opinionated Introduction* (Boulder, CO: Westview Press).

Armstrong, D. M. (1997). *A World of States of Affairs* (Cambridge: Cambridge University Press).

—— (2004). *Truth and Truthmakers* (Cambridge: Cambridge University Press).

Davidson, D. (1965). 'Theories of Meaning and Learnable Languages', reprinted in Davidson 1984, 3–16.

—— (1984). *Inquiries into Truth and Interpretation* (Oxford: Clarendon Press).

Frege, G. (1891). 'Function and Concept', reprinted in Mellor and Oliver 1997, 34–44.

Jackson, F. (1977). 'Statements about Universals', *Mind* 86, 427–9; reprinted in Mellor and Oliver 1997, 89–92.

Locke, J. (1690). *An Essay Concerning Human Understanding*, ed. P. Nidditch (Oxford: Oxford University Press, 1975).

Loux, M. (1998). *Metaphysics: A Contemporary Introduction* (London: Routledge).

Mellor, D. H. and A. Oliver (1997). *Properties* (Oxford: Oxford University Press).

Pap, A. (1959). 'Nominalism, Empiricism and Universals: I', *Philosophical Quarterly* 9, 330–40.

Putnam, H. (1970). 'On Properties', in his *Philosophical Papers*, vol. 1 (Cambridge: Cambridge University Press, 1975), 305–22.

Quine, W. V. O. (1948). 'On What There Is', *Review of Metaphysics* 2, 21–38; reprinted in his 1953, 1–19; and in Mellor and Oliver 1997, 74–88.

—— (1953). *From a Logical Point of View* (Cambridge, MA: Harvard University Press).

—— (1960). *Word and Object* (Cambridge, MA: MIT Press).

Chapter 5

Possible Worlds

Divers, J. (2002). *Possible Worlds* (London: Routledge).

Frege, G. (1980). 'On Sense and Reference', in P. Geach and M. Black, *Translations from the Philosophical Writings of Gottlob Frege*, 3rd ed. (Oxford: Blackwell).

Hornsby, J. and G. Longworth (2006). *Reading Philosophy of Language* (Oxford: Blackwell).

Kripke, S. (1980). *Naming and Necessity.* (Oxford: Blackwell).

Lewis, D. K. (1968). 'Counterpart Theory and Quantified Modal Logic', *Journal of Philosophy* 65, 113–26.

—— (1970). 'Anselm and Actuality', *Nous* 4, 175–88.

—— (1973). *Counterfactuals* (Oxford: Blackwell).

—— (1986). *On the Plurality of Worlds* (Oxford: Blackwell).

Linsky, L. (ed.) (1971). *Reference and Modality* (London: Oxford University Press).

Loux, M. J. (ed.) (1979). *The Possible and the Actual* (Ithaca, NY: Cornell University Press).

Melia, J. (2003). *Modality* (Chesham: Acumen).

Nolan, D. (2005). *David Lewis* (Chesham: Acumen).

Quine, W. V. O. (1948). 'On What There Is', *Review of Metaphysics* 2, 21–38; reprinted in his 1953a, 11–19.

—— (1953a). *From a Logical Point of View* (Cambridge, MA: Harvard University Press).

—— (1953b). 'Reference and Modality', in his 1953a, 139–59.

Rosen, G. (1990). 'Modal Fictionalism', *Mind* 99, 327–54.

Chapter 6

Persistence Over Time

Armstrong, D. M. (1978). *Nominalism and Realism: Universals and Scientific Realism*, vol. 1 (Cambridge: Cambridge University Press).

—— (1980). 'Identity Through Time', in P. van Inwagen (ed.), *Time and Cause: Essays Presented to Richard Taylor* (Dordrecht: Reidel).

Bradley, F. H. (1897). *Appearance and Reality*, 2nd ed. (Oxford: Oxford University Press).

Haslanger, S. (1989a). 'Endurance and Temporary Intrinsics', *Analysis* 49, 119–25.

—— (1989b). 'Persistence, Change and Explanation', *Philosophical Studies* 56, 1–28.

Humberstone, L. (1996). 'Intrinsic/Extrinsic', *Synthese* 108, 205–67.

Jackson, F. (1994). 'Metaphysics by Possible Cases', *Monist* 77, 93–110.

Johnston, M. (1984). *Particulars and Persistence* (Princeton: Princeton University PhD dissertation).

—— (1987). 'Is There a Problem about Persistence?', *Aristotelian Society* supp. vol. 56, 107–35.

Kaplan, D. (1977). 'Demonstratives', unpublished ms.

Langton, R. and D. K. Lewis (1998). 'Defining "Intrinsic"', *Philosophy and Phenomenological Research* 58, 333–45.

Lewis, D. K. (1983). *Philosophical Papers*, vol. 1 (Oxford: Oxford University Press).

—— (1986). *On the Plurality of Worlds* (Oxford: Blackwell).

—— (1988). 'Rearrangement of Particles: A Reply to Lowe', *Analysis* 48, 65–72.

—— (2002). 'Tensing the Copula', *Mind* 111, 1–13.

Loux, M. (1998). *Metaphysics: A Contemporary Introduction* (London: Routledge).

Lowe, E. J. (1988). 'The Problem of Intrinsic Change: Rejoinder to Lewis'. *Analysis* 48, 72–7.

Richard, M. (1982). 'Tenses, Propositions, and Meanings', *Philosophical Studies* 41, 337–51.

Salmon, N. (1986). *Frege's Puzzle* (Cambridge, MA: MIT Press).

Sider, T. (2001). *Four Dimensionalism* (Oxford: Oxford University Press).

van Inwagen, P. and D. Zimmerman (1998). *Metaphysics: The Big Questions* (Oxford: Oxford University Press).

Zimmerman, D. (1998). 'Temporary Intrinsics and Presentism', in van Inwagen and Zimmerman 1998, 206–21.

Index